PRAISE FOR *WHEN HEARTS BECOME FLAME*

This book is arguably one of the best on pastoral counseling to have been published in the past twenty years. Muse follows the ancient ascetical path of Orthodox Christian therapy to teach and disclose a state of personal readiness, which leads to prayerful listening not only to the 'other' or client, but also attention to subtle windows into heaven that appear in sessions. Counseling sessions become holy icons. But this book has an audience far wider than pastoral counselors, because it is not so much a "how-to-do" text as it engages every reader in basic questions. Do I listen well? How do I discern the will of God when helping others? What is important in my encounters with someone? Do I pay attention when others speak to me? What is healing? Make this a text to share among your friends. Give a copy to your favorite priests.

InCommunion Magazine

One of the strengths of Muse's book is the theological frame within which it is written ... He describes several profound mystical experiences that have transformed his life. The simple affirmation that God is a real presence that loves and transforms human beings seems to be at the heart of his message ... I recommend Muse's book to all believers who love God and want personal knowledge and experience of God in Jesus Christ. There is a third presence in pastoral counseling that transforms both pastor and person so that we "become [ourselves] without even knowing how." Pastoral theology is the articulation of this insight, and Muse has shown himself to be a mature pastoral theologian.

Journal of Pastoral Theology

When the book arrived I put it aside for later reading and on impulse picked it up. Two hours later I tore myself away to return to what I was supposed to be doing. I was totally taken with your work. It is the first truly *pastoral* counseling I have ever come across. Thank you. Magnificent Work.

Rev. Eugene H. Peterson.

With painstaking accountability to the great Tradition of the Eastern Church as well as to the discipline of psychology, Dr. Stephen Muse takes an apophatic "leap" of faith, offering through his "altar of the heart" a life-giving synergy of doxology, collaborative wisdom, earthiness and personal encounter while witnessing to the love of the living Lord. This book is a must read for Orthodox Christians and others who are interested in learning *and* experiencing the *"phronema"* and *"synedesis"* of pastoral counseling from a contemporary Eastern Christian perspective. This is a joy to read and read again.

> **Kyriaki Karidoyanes FitzGerald, M.Div., Ph.D., Adjunct Professor in Theology, Holy Cross Greek Orthodox School of Theology, co-author, *Living the Beatitudes: Perspectives from Orthodox Spirituality*, editor, *Encountering Women of Faith: The St. Catherine's Vision Collection, vols. 1 & 2***

This very important and timely offering of an Eastern Orthodox approach to pastoral care and counseling opens the spiritual and psychological depth of the caregivers' vocational world and does not allow the reader to relax or to stay indifferent. The author's experience and ideas make your brain think, your soul pray, your eyes cry, your ears listen to the heart and your heart love God and people. Psychotherapists, clergy and other caregivers whose work is "a way of prayer" needed such a book long ago. It's a precious gift. May God hold in the Palm of His hand all caregivers, one of whom is the author Stephen Muse.

> **Tatiana Filipieva, Ph.D, psychologist, St. Sergius Orthodox Theological School, Moscow, Russia**

Stephen Muse draws from the philosophical, theological, spiritual and mystical treasures of Eastern Orthodoxy as he reflects on his ministry of pastoral counseling. Each chapter is simultaneously thoughtful, inviting, compelling, passionate and intriguing as the reader is drawn into the personal vision of a deeply human teacher who humbly shares his humanity as he offers insight into his experience of the holy in his pastoral counseling ministry. A master teacher, Dr. Muse artfully draws from theologians, philosophers, psychologists and the spiritual masters of Eastern Orthodoxy as he personally encounters clients in their struggle towards wholeness. *When Hearts Become Flame* is a uniquely rich resource for counselors and pastors who seek a holistic understanding of counseling & psychotherapy which includes the spiritual and religious dimension.

> **Barry K. Estadt, Ph.D, psychologist, Professor Emeritus, Loyola University of Maryland, Co-editor of *Pastoral Counseling* and *The Art of Clinical Supervision: A Pastoral Counseling Perspective***

Eastern Orthodoxy as a mere institution can spawn what most religions spawn. Concerns about administrative power and prerogatives, vicious gossip, cultism, religious platitudes, and fundamentalistic theological trivialities. Orthodoxy as the genuine philosophy of life in Christ leads the human person to re-creation, restoration, the healing of sin and its spiritual and psychological consequences, and deification by union with Christ. In this collection of his writings, Dr. Muse adds to our increasing understanding of the psychological dimensions of the Orthodox way of life and the emerging practice of so-called Orthodox psychotherapy among mental health professional and pastors. I commend him for these significant contributions to this new and important field.

    Archbishop Chrysostomos, former Larson Fellow in Health and Spirituality, U.S. Library of Congress and author of *A Guide to Orthodox Psychotherapy*

The humble acknowledgement that healing is not primarily "technical" so much as relational and the "Trialogue" model of Pastoral Counseling, argued for by Dr. Muse, are potent enough to set 'hearts aflame', towards humility and healing. This optimally relevant book is sure to attract wide readership, not just in Orthodox Circles, but in other Churches and religions as well, in our generation where persons are "malnourished by an impoverished civil religion." In India especially, where the individual is acknowledged as a spiritual entity, who is identified with the Transcendent at the height of enlightenment, this innovative work is most welcome.

    Metropolitan Dr. Yakob Mar Irenaios, Malankara Orthodox Church, India

Taking the presence of God in pastoral counseling as seriously as Dr. Wayne Oates did in his book with that title, Dr. Stephen Muse invites pastoral counselors to fully experience God's companionship. He poetically describes the journey of disciplined listening to social context, self, client, and God which transforms both the client and the counselor to love more fully and freely. Speaking with honesty and vulnerability, Muse reflects about social justice issues and personal shortcomings that make the journey difficult. He offers resources to address the difficulties from his life experience, his deep reflections about the pastoral counseling encounter, his mysticism, and his Eastern Orthodox faith. These resources can make the journey rewarding. Indeed, if we listen, they can set our hearts into flame.

    Denise Massey, Ph.D., Associate Professor of Pastoral Care and Counseling, McAfee School of Theology

When Hearts Become Flame is a very valuable addition to the paucity of literature on psychotherapeutic encounter in which the author tries to describe and reveal the psychotherapeutic meeting as communion in Christ. The question "What makes counseling pastoral? (or what makes psychotherapy Christian)? "is solved here not technically, but by placing psychotherapy in an entirely different context of thinking about life. The main and decisive thrust here is understanding the therapist's work as service to neighbor, which places a very high demand on the therapist's personality. Also important is his personal experience, especially his experience of life in the Church and the experience of working on his own soul. But most important is his readiness for change himself, seeing each patient as another chance for salvation sent to him by God. All this is fully inherent in the author of the book and is revealed in its content.

Elena Zagorodnaya, Editor, Moscow Journal of Psychotherapy

Dr. Muse shares insight and wisdom gained over the course of his life's journey as a pastor and psychotherapist trying to follow the Light wherever He leads. Some profound and very useful insights are found within these pages.

Dr. Albert Rossi, psychologist, St. Vladimir's Seminary

When Hearts Become Flame invites those unfamiliar with the ancient healing traditions of the Christian East and how these are lived out in the modern context of pastoral counseling, into the depths where science and faith are not at odds, and the Christian tradition of healing is supported by contemporary theories of mental health. Using part travel log, part private journal, and part textbook, the reader is invited to encounter the author as one who offers himself to his clients, his students and to the broader community. It is through this self-offering that he witnesses to the nature of pastoral counseling as a trialogue between God, counselor, and client. In this way, the book reflects and reveals the work of a pastoral counselor prepared to encounter the person of the client: prepared to hear and discover rather than diagnose and treat. The only logical way to teach what he does is to share who he is, and in so doing, he invites each of us to share who we are as we minister to those we serve.

Philip Mammalakis, Ph.D., Assistant Professor of Pastoral Care, Holy Cross Greek Orthodox School of Theology

Stephen Muse has written an important book on pastoral counseling from the perspective of Eastern Orthodox theology. One of his key ideas is engaging in healing work with an intense awareness of the presence of God and the image of God in Self and Other. Spiritual seekers from various traditions will learn from Muse's insights.

James Newton Poling, Professor of Pastoral Theology, Care, and Counseling, Garrett-Evangelical Theological Seminary, author of *Deliver Us from Evil: Resisting Racial and Gender Oppression*, and *Render unto God: Economic Vulnerability, Family Violence and Pastoral Theology*

When Hearts Become Flame

Other books published by the Orthodox Research Institute include:

Metropolitan Panteleimon (Rodopoulos) of Tyroloë. *An Overview of Orthodox Canon Law.* Edited by Protopresbyter George Dion. Dragas

Fr. David G. Bissias. *The Mystery of Healing: Oil, Anointing, and the Unity of the Local Church*

V. Rev. Fr. Sebastian Dabovich. *The Holy Orthodox Church: The Ritual, Services and Sacraments of the Orthodox Church*

V. Rev. Fr. Sebastian Dabovich. *Preaching in the Orthodox Church: Lectures and Sermons by a Priest of the Holy Orthodox Church*

Protopresbyter George Dion. Dragas. *The Lord's Prayer according to Saint Makarios of Corinth*

Protopresbyter George Dion. Dragas. *On the Priesthood and the Holy Eucharist: According to St. Symeon of Thessalonica, Patriarch Kallinikos of Constantinople and St. Mark Eugenikos of Ephesus*

Protopresbyter George Dion. Dragas. *St. Cyril of Alexandria's Teaching on the Priesthood*

Byron J. Gaist, Ph.D. *Creative Suffering and the Wounded Healer: Analytical Psychology and Orthodox Christian Theology*

Alphonse and Rachel Goettmann. *The Spiritual Wisdom and Practices of Early Christianity*

Archimandrite Kyprian Kern. *Orthodox Pastoral Service.* Edited by Fr. William C. Mills

Fr. Stephen Headley. *Christ after Communism: Spiritual Authority and Its Transmission in Moscow Today*

Fr. William C. Mills (ed.). *Called to Serve: Readings on Ministry from the Orthodox Church*

Vladimir Moss. *The Theology of Eros*

Rt. Rev. Dr. Archimandrite Andrew (Vujisić). *Orthodox Interventions: Orthodox Neptic Psychotherapy in Response to Existential and Transpersonal Psychology*

When Hearts Become Flame

An Eastern Orthodox Approach to the διά-Λογος of Pastoral Counseling

Stephen Muse, Ph.D.

Rollinsford, New Hampshire

Published by Orthodox Research Institute
20 Silver Lane
Rollinsford, NH 03869
www.orthodoxresearchinstitute.org

ISBN 978-1-933275-48-2 (Paperback)
ISBN 978-1-933275-49-9 (Hardcover)

"We must learn to feel addressed by a book, by the human being behind it, as if a person spoke directly to us. A good book or essay or poem is not primarily an object to be put to use, or an object of experience: It is the voice of you speaking to me, requiring a response."

WALTER KAUFMANN

Table of Contents

Acknowledgements

"Christ our God, you are the true yearning and inexpressible joy of all who love you." These words from the anonymous prayer said following reception of Holy Eucharist serve well to express my gratefulness for all those unnamed persons in my life whose yearning for God, whether known or unknown, has provided incentive for relationship in my life that has caused my heart to burn as we walked to Emmaus together. All of you, however poorly recognized and appreciated have been light-bearers.

A few are especially important and deserve mention for having been significant in my journey toward appreciating the significance of the διά-Λογος that provides the central meaning to the reflections offered in this book.

Memory eternal to my first Amma, my mother, Jean, who taught me about faith, hope, love, courage, confession, grace, emotional transparency, freedom and Jesus, praying beside me on her knees when I was four years old. She endured enormous suffering throughout my life. At her funeral, her beloved physician, Dr. Goldner, an internationally acclaimed surgeon, told me, "Jean was the sickest woman we have ever treated at Duke Medical Center. It broke my heart that nothing we ever did helped her." When Dr. Goldner learned my grandfather had sold his house to pay for her bills, he never charged another dime for his services for the rest of her life. Such gifts remain in the heart forever, all helping to reveal Him.

My wife and dear partner in Christ, Claudia Ioanna, who for some 30 years now has loved, challenged and supported me in ways that only God will be able to fully acknowledge. Your incisive comments often amaze me in their perspicacity to reveal what it takes me a whole paragraph to say. Your attunement in love and simplicity to the Holy Spirit's gentle intimations I have recognized and acted on immediately on enough occasions that I am not surprised when of a sudden, another gentle, unadorned spontaneous suggestion emerges from your lips bearing the mark of the Spirit's uncoercive yet undeniably true voice.

For my children Gregory, Christi, and Kelly who have been my teachers as you were growing up, struggling to be authentically yourselves (and sometimes avoiding it!). You have forgiven my failings and loved and treasured me beyond what I deserve. You are my co-pilgrims through whom God has taught me invaluable lessons about love, mercy and privileging the 'between' of relationships that allows each person the freedom to be who they are.

For Dan Durway and Bill Bennett, the pastors of my youth, who read my poetry and fed me delicious books that stretched my mind. You challenged the crusader in me with loving confrontation to recognize early in my life the invaluable lesson that "not everyone who doesn't think like you is going to hell." Stung by those words I went to my cabin and wept. What an incredibly important lesson and confrontation.

Ten years later, Tom Forman, the most important mentor of my mid-twenties would tell me, "Stephen, you'd kill a man for kicking a dog." and challenge me to come down to earth out of the clouds of my protective religious idealism into my body with attention and "join the human race" with mercy for other mere mortals like myself. What you showed me about the necessary link between mind and body in order for real heart to emerge has been foundational and liberating for my entire life, turning me toward the truth of Christ in a way that my mind alone could not fathom. After hearing you tell me on many occasions, "Stephen fill up those boots you are wearing," my prayer to God after Seminary was to "send me to a parish where no one will understand what I am saying unless I can translate it into my boots." God answered my prayer. I am more grateful with the passing of time for those eleven years of call and response with the parish I served as pastor in rural Pennsylvania. The title of the weekly sermon on the Marquee outside the church did not change for a decade, because I told the congregation, I am always going to preach about the same thing. "Love." It is the living of love that proves most difficult.

For Barry Estadt whose generously shared humanity and vulnerability demonstrated the truth as he once shared it, that "Christ did not come to change the world but to embrace it." Thank you for embracing me over the course of nine years in my Masters and Ph.D. programs, following some traumatic years of personal loss and conflict in the church. You gave welcome to my deeply held pain, confirming the power of co-pilgrimage that exists between mentor and mentee, client and therapist, supervisor and supervisee, and yes, God and humanity, which is the *sine qua non* for the possibility of transformation.

For Gerondas Ephraim, Ilia and others unnamed, whose presence radiate grace and tender dispassion, erasing the illusion of time between the first apostles and we who live two thousand years after them, you are living testimony of the power of presence working through faith to open the way for the action of Grace to prepare the heart to receive God's word, however simple it may be and however many times it may have been said before, as though for the first time and personally offered as a 'fit' for my heart.

For Natasha Kesmeti, Dimitrios Oreopoulos and Geronda Antonios Romaios who were διά-Λογος partners for several years. Thank you for reading my papers and sharing your lives deeply and intimately. Your language skills, immense learning and generous loving spirits have offered me community and hospitality that have been more essential than bread. I remain grateful to all of you.

For Jamie Moran and Canupa Gluha Mani, two warriors whose fight for truth and justice is rooted in love and is the central heartbeat of their lives. Your willingness to live and speak in your own voices and to walk the road of passion that does not shrink back from the 'wound of existence' has intensified my examination of the places where I am not yet freely given in love to Christ and all those whom He loves. I thank you.

I am grateful to my friends and colleagues, supervisees and clients and the hundred or so U.S. Army and Air Force Family Life Chaplains over the past twenty years through my work at the Pastoral Institute, Inc., who have shared your lives with me. Our dialogues and encounters have been grist for the mill for me to formulate many of the perspectives that have come to fruition in this book. More than that, you have been significant in the adventures of my heart that have turned me toward Christ with thanksgiving for the privilege of walking to Emmaus with you on so many occasions and suffering vicariously the unique questions which have been born in your hearts.

Finally, I am appreciative to the Orthodox Research Institute and Daryle Lamoureux for the exacting editorial labors he has provided to get the book ready for publication. I especially look forward to the dialogue with those readers who are moved by these ideas and may be inclined to discuss them further and offer contributions of your own. It is through call and response, "work in behalf of the people" that we live and pray unto the Lord in order to discover the mystery of Christ in our midst and through Christ, the mystery of one another and of all life. +

Stephen Muse
Columbus, GA
October 16, 2010
Feast Day of Longinos the Centurion

Preface

It gives me great pleasure to introduce this wonderful book by Dr. Stephen Muse, *When Hearts Become Flame*, to people, both clergy and laity, for a better understanding of our Orthodox way of thinking. Dr. Muse's book is truly an offering of love, which is both enlightening and inspiring, on the diakonia of pastoral counseling within the Orthodox Church. Dr. Muse is using his faith, in order to express himself with love by hoping for the healing of his patients.

"Faith, hope and love, these three abide, but the greatest of these is love." St. Paul's inspired perception of the ways the heart of God is shared with humanity comes to my mind as I read Dr. Muse's reflections on the vocation of pastoral care and counsel. I have known Dr. Stephen Muse, the author of this excellent and timely book for many years, and have seen his faithful devotion to the Church and to the Christian life. In his vocation as a therapist and counselor, I have also seen his love for his patients.

Dr. Muse served as pastor for 11 years in a Protestant church and was trained in counseling, psychology and marriage and family therapy. Now he serves within the Greek Orthodox Church as a pastoral counselor. Because of his experience, Dr. Muse is in a unique position to reflect on the role of pastoral caregiver for both ordained clergy and lay counselors. Integrating clinical as well as pastoral and theological expertise in offering care to wounded souls, Dr. Muse recommends pastoral counseling that unites the sacramental life of the church, supported and aided by scientific knowledge and skill on the part of the therapist. He writes of the counselor's approach, which is primarily one of love, and the sacred meeting between persons that is at the heart of the Eucharistic encounter.

"In practice such love involves the difficulty of balancing rational science with receptivity to irrational Holy Spirit-illumined perception with regard to identifying the 'fit' for a particular person in a given situation. This is a function of trialogue which entails the difficulty of meeting a person on what Professor Martin Buber called the "narrow ridge" between the a priori surety of mathematical models and the absolute limitless freedom of the uniqueness of the created world with all its paradox and uncertainty."

Regarding the training of pastoral counselors and caregivers, Dr. Muse believes that the foundation is the same as for the ordained priesthood and for all Christians — to find life in Christ through learning to love. The Holy Spirit is called upon in order that Christ be in our midst. The ground

out of which the living plant of integration of clinical theory and religious faith grows and is sustained occurs exactly at that point of intersection where God, Self and Other meet and at no other place. The work of supervision of pastoral counselors is the work of facilitating genuine human encounters in the presence of God.

I am pleased to offer my hierarchical blessing upon Dr. Muse's work, offered with humility and love, as he shares his personal reflections over thirty years of ministry as a pastor and psychotherapist. He persuasively points to the parallel between the liturgical ministries of the ordained priesthood intercessing for the people at the Divine Altar and the existential ministry of lay pastoral counselors and psychotherapists who make intercession before the equally sacred altar of every person who unburdens his or her heart in the counseling relationship. As St. John Chrysostom also observed, "When I leave the altar I go to the altar of my brother and sister.

This sacred relationship is what Dr. Muse clarifies for the reader with grace, passion and a knowledge of the presence of Christ at the heart of the existential meeting of persons. This relationship becomes

Emmaus where the presence of Christ is newly revealed. This encounter, as Dr. Muse points out, is the core of pastoral counseling and has similarities to the sacramental life, specifically the Divine Liturgy where hearts become flame. The way to becoming person, as he writes, "is through hell with and for the sake of the other." The prayer of intercession and bearing the cross is, after all, central to the interpersonal communion among human beings in Christ.

I pray that this book, which provides an Orthodox perspective, will help promote a greater interest in the riches of the Orthodox Church, and most importantly that pastoral counseling can be used in the Sacrament of Confession as we minister to the Faithful in the Orthodox Church. Furthermore, I pray that it will be an inspiration to others involved in this endeavor, both clergy and lay, to provide their own contributions which will help to emphasize Dr. Muse's affirmation that the heart of διά-Λογος is indeed a personal encounter with our God who meets us as he promised "Wherever two or more are gathered in my name" in such a way that we recognize one another, not merely as created beings, but as brothers and sisters in communion with God, bearers of an immortal Spirit in earthen vessels.

May the Good Physician of our souls and bodies, the Lover of mankind, who is the Source of all good and perfect gifts, bring the seeds He has liberally sown throughout this fine volume to fruition among his beloved people.

Metropolitan Alexios of Atlanta,
Greek Orthodox Metropolis of Atlanta
October 28, 2010
Feast Day of the Holy Protection of the Theotokos
Atlanta, GA

Foreword

The Only News I know
Is Bulletins all Day
From Immortality.

The Only Shows I see —
Tomorrow and Today —
Perchance Eternity —

The Only One I meet
Is God — The Only Street —
Existence—This traversed
(Emily Dickinson, 1827)

The tiny gem I am quoting can reasonably become the anthem of a Christian faithful, provided that it is accompanied by the necessary interpreting statements: that all worldly news are valued to the degree it reflects the struggle with the thirst for eternity, that all those whom we meet bear "the treasure (of the Only One) in clay jars" (2 Cor. 4:7). Without such a theological interpretation the poem runs the risk of lethal misunderstandings about contemplating the world.

But what of mental health professionals? Should they share the above declaration? "Obviously," I can hear, "if they are religious." But can they adopt such a credo in the name and on behalf of their science? Is that faith a strictly personal matter or is it legitimized to penetrate into their helping behavior?

Stephen Muse, an experienced clinician and a man of strong faith, does not let himself fall into the trap of pseudodilemmas. What he does is allow his Christian Orthodox commitment to inspire all his theoretical insights and therapeutic work. And at the same time, he gives the secular world what is due (Matthew 22: 21), against artificial ideological entities like "orthodox psychotherapy." He does so by combining a solid scientific knowledge and practice with that sensitivity of the heart which derives from the genuine spiritual life which blossoms in the Church.

The author's stance proves of much more importance if we recall the polarities of his American context. Nowadays a therapist breathes inside a culture of technocracy which tends to make the awe for human mystery shrink into neurotransmitters and symptom-focused counseling advice. At the other extreme, for someone who feels the zeal of recognizing this mystery and serving it in the name of the Lord, a religiously labeled enthusiasm waits in the corner to devalue secular knowledge. In both cases, the Church gets degraded to the status of a sect instead of being a leaven.

A special kind of caution is required here. Following the poem, to see immortality as the only news we know and God as the Only One we meet makes faith. At the same time, to reduce psychological sciences into religious language and techniques makes fundamentalism. It seems to me that we need to be trained assiduously on the games of earthly life in order to win the battle for heaven. This means that mental disorders and the psychopathology of everyday life should be explained as outcomes of the deep heart of the human mystery as it gets painfully distilled, or even distorted, through brain peculiarities, traumatic experiences, and morbid interactions.

Theological truth about human being does not carry with it a specific science as was the case in the scholastic version of the middle ages; rather, it respects the products created by the agony of mental health professionals, nonetheless bringing to them basic criteria for self-assessment. Those criteria are really "Good News" because they stem from the trilogy of Creation-Incarnation-Sacraments, landmarks which provide us with a blessed variety of endowments and which elevate human worthiness shortly below angels and (wonder!) indicate persons' potential to become gods by grace. Thus, psychological sciences are offered the opportunity to mirror this holy tradition, not to compete on par with it which would be irrelevant and unfair, but to get enriched and to realize that they by no means describe and explain exhaustively human nature.

At the other side, by attributing to psychological sciences all their dynamics and giving them their due, the Church and her ministers help themselves to remember that we still live in a sphere where "Caesar" and all secular consequences are inevitable and valid, which by the way refuels our eschatological longing. Moreover, we have to remind ourselves constantly that the ontological truth which is expressed by ecclesiastical theology can be lived and perceived by us only after it is projected on to and filtered through our human reality, which renders it able to be experienced as psychological truth. There is no way to escape from this — and no need, I would add — until the eternal day comes and no psychological realities survive for those who share the immediacy of the ontological Uncreated Light of His infinite goodness.

To think and behave as if there is nothing beyond this psychological reality leads the human person to impoverishment and suffocation; to adopt an aristocratic attitude that demands only an ontological-theological discourse does injustice to the amazing 'manifesto' of John 3:16. However, we all know that extremes are easier to reach; people are reluctant to walk the route of 'Theanthropinon,' of the coexistence and cooperation between God and us as authentic *persons* and not in the 'New Age' manner which fails to reach this depth. This is the real 'way less traveled' which leads to the destination of sanctity, which implements the mystery that was conceived before all centuries.

Muse dares to reveal the affective adventures that have shaped him in a book with scholarly issues meant to assist his professional colleagues. This initiative is generally considered inappropriate in the scientific community, unless someone is determined to turn his existential beliefs into practice. And this is the case with him who struggles to make his clinical work a testimony of his existential pains. He seems to teach us from the humility of the same level, to consider the readers as co-travelers on the same existential journey. He bends down respectfully close to the so-called client in order to discover the Lord's wonders inside him/her.

His aim is twofold, as he bravely writes: he wishes to address both clinicians and priests/pastors. The work and ministry of each of these groups benefit from different aspects of the human mystery. Through the various topics of the book, one can discern the central idea repeatedly put and revisited: Is our pastoral and/or clinical praxis really existential? Does it change us? Do we truly meet the other person and in doing so meet Christ?

Stephen's compilation reminded me of a famous Greek poet, Tassos Leivathitis, who had been marginalized and sent into exile because of his leftist ideas. He wrote:

> "O, Lord, my sin has been
> That I tried to decipher Your enigma
> To enter Your mystery
> And so I, the fool, was astrayed
> For Your big secret is me.

So therapists serve the unspeakable with speakable means.

Rev. Vasileios Thermos, M.D., Ph.D.
Athens, Greece, Sept. 23, 2010
Conception of St. John the Baptist

Introduction[1]

When making the sign of the cross, I am reminded of the heart of the Orthodox Christian faith, the Holy Trinity, as well as the spiritual anthropology that is inherent to this revelation through the incarnation of the second person of the Holy Trinity, Jesus Christ, whose two natures, one fully God and one fully human, are seamlessly joined together in one person. God born in the flesh and assuming all of human nature in Himself while remaining fully God opens up the Way that leads to raising flesh and blood into the spiritual realm of the uncreated eternal life of the Trinitarian communion.

In the icon known in Greek as *Philoxenia* or "Hospitality to Strangers," the Holy Trinity is represented in the form of the three unknown messengers to whom Abraham and Sarah showed hospitality around their table. These strangers turned out to be angels sent from God to announce the fulfillment of God's promise that Abraham and Sarah would bear a son and through him their progeny would be more numerous than the stars. In welcoming these strangers, Abraham and Sarah are reborn through the encounter, with Sarah receiving a new name, indicative of the promise of blessing and new life that would arise between them and come through them as a result of the call and response of their trialogue with the Holy One.

---

[1] Expanded from an article first published as "The Meaning of Psychotherapy" in the *Journal of Pastoral Care & Counseling*, Vol. 52(2); translated and published in Swedish in *S:t Lukasbrevet* 3/98, pp. 2–4, and in Serbian for the website of the pastoral care center in Belgrade.

Hospitality is something we generally associate with good manners and social upbringing. In ancient times, hospitality was more than that, a form of communication scripted by a timeless ritual of welcome, refreshment and dialogue. It was a means of discovering the world beyond the familiar, offering safety and sanctuary that are part of the unwritten covenant with the guest, even if a potential enemy, while under the roof of one's tent, befriended. It was a matter of life and death. The desert is a forbidding place. So is life without the welcome of hospitality.

When I first traveled to Arizona and visited a monastery out in the Sonoran desert, I was not sure at first why I did not want to vanish into the mountains as I usually feel like doing when I get around wide open forested spaces I have not explored. There were giant Saguaro cacti standing like desert sentinels for miles in every direction. Whirling dust funnels darted across the sands like Tasmanian devils, while ponderous, dry rocky peaks reached up to the sky in the distant background. Then it dawned on me — it was inviting and forbidding at the same time. The desert is parched.

In Abraham's day, if the host did not offer hospitality to strangers, giving them shade, water and food, they might die. There were no service stations or restrooms. Tents were often more than several days journeys away from each other, as were oases offering respite from the burning sun.

Hospitality still is a matter of life and death in our culture, but for different reasons. The privileged children of our modern age do not suffer for lack of water and food. They are thirsty for the Grace of being welcomed with the pure waters of deep attentiveness and nourished by understanding and compassion that emerge from real stillness and presence, which allow us to be unhurried with another person and hear them. That is why we see so many people stopping at our tents seeking the welcome of pastoral psychotherapy.

Pastoral counseling, like hospitality to strangers, is a reciprocal relationship. The people we pay attention to as psychotherapists are inviting us into the sacred tent of meeting that is their life and soul, where their most precious treasures are kept and their deepest shame and heartache buried. Depending on our behavior and the quality of our attention, interest and the respect that we show to them, they may invite us further into their inner world where they discover in the process renewal, healing and confirmation of the value of their own humanity and glimpse the presence of an Unseen Guest in our midst, making it possible for the dialogue to become transformative.

When we first begin counselor training, we are anxious and busy inside, feeling we must fix people and take away their pain. Good physicians have always known that true soul-healing is much more than that. D. W. Winnicott once remarked, "When the therapist is reacting, there is no room for the client's mind." It is a sober recognition that silence is as important to the pastoral counselor as it is to the hesychast in prayer. Both are call and response drawing from the unfathomed artesian well of Grace, the waters of refreshment and new meaning that restores life.

In the beginning, we walk into the house of people's souls as anxious repair persons feeling the pressure of a positive outcome on our shoulders rather than as privileged guests, mindful of the presence of the Unseen Guest in our midst. Our minds are too busy with theories, diagnoses and anxiety-driven self-doubts to experience the person really. We fail to notice the subtle states of breath, sensation, movement and feeling in oneself and in the other that mark the changing qualities of the relationship and the emergence of new meaning.

As we mature and become quieter inside, we really begin to notice people and to notice ourselves noticing them. We learn that much of life involves suffering that we can do nothing to alleviate. Rather it is the human suffering which rightly engaged produces maturity, strength of character, engenders hope, deepens humility, fans the burning coal of prayer into flame and evokes mercy and compassion for others flowing from what we ourselves have found need for and received because we have recognized our blindness, paralysis and need.

Being a good and responsive guest is what true pastoral psychotherapy, or *healing of the soul,* is all about. Very often we do not "fix" people. What we really do is walk the road to Emmaus with them, offering them the pastoral care of attentive call and response to their experience and witness of their longing. Our hearts begin to burn together as co-pilgrims on a common human journey, looking together at the world as it is without turning away into fantasy and avoidance, hoping in the goodness of life itself and the One who creates and sustains us, to reveal a way forward.

To the degree that we are truly open to this trialogical encounter, like Abraham and Sarah, we ourselves are changed in the process. We find that we move between being host and guest simultaneously. The hospitality we receive is of the most precious kind — entrance into the courtyard of another human soul in the presence of God. What we have to offer in return is the authenticity of our honest observations and the commitment to continue looking beyond our experience to encounter the unknown other who is always beyond our experience. Good psychotherapy is a humbling enterprise. Its essence is rooted in our acceptance of our humanity and our recognition of our dependence on God. Those become good priest-physicians who become humble and loving human beings, as harmless as doves, while being as tenacious and discerning as serpents when it comes to discovering and bearing the truth in faith.

In this respect, the good psychotherapist is always a student of life, who recognizes, as did the Apostle Paul, that the great medicines of life remain these three: faith, hope and love, but the greatest of these is love. The ancient Greek inventor Archimedes is said to have boasted, "Give me a fixed point and a lever long enough, and I can move the world." Theologically, when it comes to pastoral care and counseling, we might say that love is defined by St. Gregory the Theologian's observation of God's co-suffering love for humanity in Christ: "Whatever has not been assumed, cannot be healed," which becomes our fixed point. The lever is the combined action of the Grace of God and human persons together in dialogue, which not only moves the world, but transforms and redeems it as well. This is because it is a trialogue of love benefiting from God's presence between us.

Pastoral care and counseling are, from this perspective, seen to be far more than merely healing human physical, emotional and mental suffering and reconciling people's behavior and attitudes to cultural norms. What good is it if Lazarus is raised from the stink of sickness, decay and death only to suffer them all over again in a few or a million years? Or, even more importantly, what good is it to have vital physical health and a strong ego if the heart is not healed of the passions that impede fullness of Grace that lead to deification in Christ? Pastoral care and counseling from the Eastern Orthodox perspective always occur within the larger context of God's greater life revealed in Christ, the first-born of the dead, whose hope and desire is to raise all human beings, by their free choice, to the eternal life.

Along with the Trinitarian emphasis of the sign of the cross, which is signified by having the thumb and the first two fingers closed together and two fingers collapsed back onto the palm, signifying the human and Divine natures of Christ, there is an implicit spiritual anthropology of great import in this simple, oft-repeated gesture. When I touch my fingers to my forehead, the locus of *nepsis*, or mindful attention, and then sweep down touching again just below the navel at the center of vital physical energy, I am indicating the incarnation of the Godhead descending into flesh, uniting heaven and earth. I begin to know that I am flesh when the descent of consciousness permeates or "assumes" awareness of the sensation of the whole of myself in the present moment. Then rising up again from the bowels and making a horizontal bar across the chest from right shoulder to left shoulder, there is remembrance of the reconciling action of the Holy Spirit which is known through the feeling "in sighs too deep for words." As one of my mentors told me, and I have verified for myself many times both personally and professionally, "When mind and body unite, feeling appears." When all three parts of myself are active and involved, *I AM* and the call and response of prayer and of living begins.

Ending by placing the palm of the hand over the chest signifies my welcome of Christ and the intention to share His cross in my life in the world. This is the external movement of love which "bears all things" which is the fruit of nepsis and prayer. This yearning receptivity of the heart, which is the center of conscience, together with the vital energy of the body and the wakeful conscious attention of the mind united and all turned toward God and the world simultaneously, is the way of prayer and love and the path of formation of persons in the image and likeness of God. The heartbreak of failing to love as I am loved, and give myself to the world as a seed planted in the ground, as Christ did, becomes repentance which fans the flame of prayer in a circle that leads to intensification of the prayer which increasingly bids us to call out to Christ who walks upon the waters of creation and bid Him, "Lord love the world through me and permit me to love the world through You."

According to my understanding of the Eastern Orthodox experience, it is through trialogue, internally with mind, body and feelings integrated and active, in dialogue with God and engaged existentially in action in the world that we fulfill what Jesus, combining Deuteronomy 6:5 and Leviticus 19:8, acknowledged to be the heart of the law: "You shall love the Lord your God with all your heart and with all your soul and with all your strength and with all your mind, and your neighbor as yourself" (Luke 10:27). Pastoral counseling is an offering of the prayerful presence of one's own three dimensional being to the dialogue with the other in the presence of God. Whatever else she or he does, the pastoral counselor, the same as the priest at the Divine Altar, enters into call and response relationship invoking God's presence and seeking to be receptive to God's activity unfolding in the here and now with the intention of offering Christ to one another serving at the altar of the human heart.

The essays contained in this book take their point of departure and return from reflection on the question, "What Makes Counseling *Pastoral*?" in order to show that it involves participation of all three aspects of our human nature in dialogue with others in such a way that as in Emmaus, Christ, the Logos, appears 'between' us. It is not enough to be emotionally warm or conceptually accurate or physically energetic in and of themselves. The human person is an integrated presence of all three turned toward trialogue with God, self and others.

Taking my cues from Jesus' formulation of the heart of the law, it is clear that an Orthodox approach to pastoral care and counseling cannot be focused solely on the intrapsychic and individual person. Nor can social justice precede cut off from the wellspring of contemplative life in Christ, as Thomas Merton observed, without burning out or becoming the evil that we fight against. There is both a private inner discernment and ascetical struggle in dialogue with God and an existential and communal outward dimension which involves fellowship in confronting justice issues in society that contribute to the sickness and wellbeing of persons. These two domains must be considered together as mutually influencing one another in a circular causality.

I offer these essays and reflections as "five loaves and two fish" in hopes of stimulating my Eastern Orthodox brothers and sisters, who in one way or another have the vocation of offering pastoral care and counseling, to begin to reflect on what it is we Orthodox Christian mental health professionals actually do in pastoral counseling and psychotherapy that reflects and embodies who Christ is and what Christ does in the world. I offer it to the priests as an aid to sharpening pastoral counseling skills and appreciating their partnership with lay pastoral caregivers. And to my Protestant brothers and sisters in the American Association of Pastoral Counselors (AAPC), I offer these reflections as a 'taste' of the treasures of Eastern Orthodoxy which has afforded me new life and meaning for the last thirty years, as a person, pastor and psychotherapist.

Given the burgeoning field of counseling and psychotherapy and the growing new interest in its spiritual dimensions, the time is ripe for interdisciplinary Orthodox dialogue between priests and practitioners, monastics, theologians and scientists as well as with mental health professionals outside Orthodoxy. The field of pastoral counseling has been largely Protestants and Roman Catholics, who, since the founding of AAPC in the 1960's, have contributed half a century's worth of valuable reflections on the integration of theology and psychology in service to suffering persons. There is a great deal we can share with one another to know Christ more fully and learn how to serve better and celebrate human potential when it is in co-creative partnership with God to help alleviate human suffering.

During a visit to Russia a decade ago, I recall the sobering words of Fr. Anatoly, an experienced priest who questioned what would happen in Russia in the coming years as the plentiful harvest of newly minted priests graduated seminary ready to serve the minions knocking at the doors of Orthodoxy in Russia. I do not remember his exact words, but the gist of his colorful and passionate meaning was something like, "How will these priests, so revered by the Church in their long beards and black *riassas*, be trained, seasoned and matured so that they do not offer lunacy to the people?" His words are prophetic, and the time is ripe for fruitful dialogue and considerations as to how we can better train our clergy and lay pastoral caregivers to extend Christ's *diakonia* into the arena where we are all made in God's image and being formed into God's likeness by contending with the rough and tumble of life of the information glutted, technology-dominated twenty-first century. Though the essence of the struggle remains the same, the forms are new and the pace of outward change is faster and faster, calling for a priesthood that is both firmly rooted in the ancient path, yet "wise in the ways of the world" and skillful in navigating between them in order to serve a complex and hungry world that is increasingly mistrustful of religion as the place of fanaticism and unlove.

In Chapter One, I begin with some reflections out of my own personal context so that the reader does not experience my reflections as disembodied and impersonal and in order to make clear from whence I have staked out the foundation of my dialogical approach to pastoral counseling, rooted in the person of Christ. From here, I move to the central question that is the heart of the book, *What makes counseling pastoral?* Several following chapters expand on the nature of personal encounter as the primary epistemological foundation for pastoral counseling work in contrast to a technically driven, subject-object-bound approach that places method over person as in the medical model, seeking to know about God, the world and other people through categories and diagnoses without actually relating to them personally.

Chapter Four is devoted to distinguishing some of the differences between the practical wisdom of therapists derived from natural intuition, experienced self-observation, supervision and training in contrast with the charismatic gifts of illumination given to persons by the Holy Spirit, which are found in abundance among some remarkable Orthodox elders throughout history and in the twentieth century. Clearly, both forms of perception are at times involved in the therapeutic encounter, further evidencing the presence of a trialogical encounter between self, other and God that is the primary context for authentic pastoral care.

In Chapter Five, I offer some observations regarding the theological and theoretical foundations for training and supervision of pastoral counselors as well as an excerpt from one of my supervision sessions, giving a taste of the kind of trialogue and focus on the person of the therapist that takes place in supervision. Chapter Six includes reflections based on research and counseling work with hundreds of clergy who have come through the Pastoral Institute's Clergy in *Kairos* program as they contended with depression, health problems, burnout and professional boundary violations stemming from the peculiar combination of unacknowledged human need and the problems of parish ministry weighing on their conscientious shoulders. The danger of burnout is viewed as a function of departing from the path of Christian life, healthy human relationships, worship and ascetical life rooted in ongoing repentance and humility regarding one's own legitimate human limits as contrasted with workaholism and the accompanying spiritual deception arising from those clergy who are unconsciously seeking to "make a self" out of their ministry, which tends to fuel other problems. "Compulsive" cross-bearing that gradually wears the priest out is very different from Jesus' statement, "No one takes My life from Me. I give it freely."

Chapter Seven expands the discussion of care for the caregiver beyond clergy to include lay mental health professionals, physicians and therapists whose own care is directly related to vocational satisfaction and the quality of care we are able to offer others. This chapter explores the relationship between spiritual health, mental health and physical health and the neurobiological substrates of addictive compensations as these parallel the Eastern Orthodox teaching on healing the passions. At root, the work of caring for others is a kind of spiritual formation process, which when undergirded by the ancient Orthodox path of faith and worship, which includes neptic awareness, inner prayer, fasting, almsgiving, confession, fellowship and loving service to others in the world — creates optimal conditions for human growth and well-being.

In the final chapter, I address the sickness and sin of our collective life as it relates to unacknowledged and unaddressed social justice issues inherent to the actions and consequences of *logismoi*[2] which contend with us on a collective scale through what St. Paul referred to as "powers and principalities" at work in high places disempowering whole groups of people who remain invisible in societal structures. Addressing these issues depends not only on individual repentance and lifestyle changes flowing from this, but requires intervention in the form of a collective witness and stand beyond what any one of us alone is able to do, in order to address the symptoms of dissociation and despair that are part of what I call our collective post-traumatic spiritual disorder. Pastoral counseling involves more than individual person-to-person dialogue in the consulting room which tends to be focused on one person's health and well-being and that of our families. From the Orthodox Christian standpoint, there cannot be full health and well-being for the few if this comes at the expense of the many. Orthodox Christianity is not simply a path to individual salvation as American culture tends to view Christian faith and most

---

[2] Greek word for 'thoughts.' Patristic teaching distinguishes simple thoughts from *logismoi* that are inherently charged with a potential magnetic attraction which appeal to the unpurified desires of the heart. Without watchfulness and prayer, these capture the attention and eventually lead to sin and captivity of the heart by various passions which in turn block the activity of Grace.

other things through the deceptive individualistic mythology of the so-called "self-made man" in search of the "American dream" who achieves God's blessing by hard work, etc., etc. It should be remembered that Orthodoxy is not a Western form of Christianity, but one that emerged out of a different cultural history and communal life in which the focus on the individual might be more accurately stated: "We are saved together, but we fall alone."

Pastoral Counselor Training Epistle[1]

If I know the classical psychological theories well enough to pass my comps and can reformulate them in ways that can impress peer reviewers from the most prestigious journals, but have not the practical wisdom of love, I am only intrusive muzak soothing the ego while missing the heart.

And if I can read tea leaves, throw the bones and manipulate spirits so as to understand the mysteries of the universe and forecast the future with scientific precision, and if I have achieved a renaissance education in both the exoteric and esoteric sciences that would rival Faust and know the equation to convert the mass of mountains into psychic energy and back again, but have not love, I am still a zero.

If I gain freedom from all my attachments and maintain constant alpha waves in my consciousness, showing perfect equanimity in all situations, ignoring every personal need and compulsively martyr myself for the glory of God, but this is not done freely from love, I have accomplished nothing.

Love is great-hearted and unselfish; love is not emotionally reactive; it does seek to draw attention to itself. Love does not accuse or compare. It does not seek to serve itself at the expense of others. Love does not take pleasure in other people's suffering, but rejoices when the truth is revealed and meaningful life restored.

Love always bears reality as it is, extending mercy to all people in every situation. Love is faithful in all things, is constantly hopeful and

---

[1] With thanks to the Apostle Paul.

meets whatever comes with immovable forbearance and steadfastness. Love never quits. By contrast, prophecies give way before the infinite possibilities of eternity, and inspiration is as fleeting as a breath. To the writing and reading of many books and learning more and more, there is no end, and yet whatever is known is never sufficient to live the Truth who is revealed to the world only in loving relationship.

For now, we are modernists, traditionalists and post-modern constructivists who do not see the world as it is, but only as we are. When perfection is given, we will know directly in relationship without symbol or metaphor the squaring of the circle of the union of I and Other in the Eternal Embrace.

When I was a beginning therapist, I thought a lot and anxiously tried to fix people in order to lower my own anxiety. As I matured, my mind quieted and I stopped being so concerned with labels and techniques and began to realize that, in the mystery of attentive presence to others, the guest becomes the host in the presence of God. In the hospitality of genuine human encounter with the Other, we come face-to-face with the mystery of Christ who is between us as both the one offered and the one who offers.

Now I begin to understand that it is in seeking to know others, that I am becoming more fully known. In showing empathy and care for others, I am healed by God's mercy. When all the theorizing and methodological squabbles have been addressed, there will still be only three things that are essential to pastoral care and counseling: faith, hope and love. These three gifts of the Spirit are personal energies of the Living God and they remain forever. When we abide in these, we each remain as well, without comprehending how, for the source and *raison d'être* of all is Love.

CHAPTER ONE

I AM the Door:
The διά-Λογος of Pastoral Counseling[1]

England is the source of the majority of both mine and my wife Claudia's ancestors. My father's side has been identified as far back as the 1500's to my great-x*n* grandfather who is recorded among the faithful of Souldrop parish in Bedfordshire, Great Britain, a few hundred miles north of London. So what am I doing here in the United States, four centuries later as a Greek Orthodox Christian with a Russian Orthodox icon of St. Elizabeth the Grand Duchess calmly looking out from a corner of our living room? I had it painted for Claudia, years before we even thought of going to Russia and visiting the convent St. Elizabeth founded — and since then our first granddaughter, who is named "Elizabeth," was born.

St. Elizabeth was also of European descent — the granddaughter of Queen Victoria, and a product of the political marriage between Hapsburg Germany and England. Deeply moved by the Orthodox Christian Tradition she found in "Holy Russia," she converted to Orthodoxy in the Russian Church after her marriage to Grand Duke Sergei, the uncle of the future Tsar Nicholas II, whom her sister, Alexandra, later married. I know that journey as well. It was like coming home.

By virtue of being an American, I am a wealthy and privileged man. My personal bank account would contradict that, but the luxury, wealth and possibilities I enjoy as a middle class citizen of the United States, with respect to the majority of people in the world,

---

[1] Expanded and revised from an article first published in *OCAMPR E Journal* as "Gift From Holy Russia."

like it or not, puts me in the class of the aristocracy with all the responsibilities that entails;[2] responsibilities arising from the fact that
the aristocracy's privilege always depends on the work and sacrifice
of a lot of other people. In America, that includes the inherited benefits of possessing lands taken by deceit and broken promises from
the original inhabitants who have subsequently been treated worse
than any other people in the country. The legacy of slavery on top of
the unwillingness and/or inability of Americans to cohabit with the
indigenous nations, who could not conceive of anyone 'owning' the
land as it belonged to the Great Spirit, are indicative of the passions of
greed and the pride of unexamined entitlement that are lodged deep
within American consciousness.[3] What does it mean that a nation
can continue collectively to refuse to acknowledge the full humanity of another group of people simply for not being like us in their
skin color, cultural customs, political structure, religion, and social
norms? What traumatic effects result from rationalizing and justifying being able to 'own' people as slaves for economic benefits? What
spirit is at work behind the scenes of this history?

All of these betrayals and atrocities in the case of both the indigenous population and the transplanted Africans were justified
consciously or otherwise, because they were seen as 'other' whose
unlikeness to power-possessing Caucasians did not provide opportunity for discovery through authentic encounter with them. It is a
strange irony that America, the so-called "melting pot" of nations,
has from its inception struggled with the tension between colonialist
expansion and the expediency of assimilation of the 'foreigner' into
the dominant culture at the expense of their uniqueness (which, to
the degree that it is forced, amounts to attempted cultural genocide).

---

[2] Find your wealth compared to world's here: http://www.globalrichlist.com/.
[3] This is not to imply that Americans are worse than other nations in history in
this regard, but only that repentance must begin with myself and with my own
country. It is useless and fruitless to compare oneself or one's country with others for the sake of any sort of self-justification which is just a failure to be willing
to examine conscience and make changes.

Two-hundred and fifty years later, we still do not seem to have enough and last count were utilizing 14:1 as many resources per capita as the rest of the world *oikonomia*. Are we giving back to the world proportionally as much as we are taking? Our military spending is greater than any nation in the history of the world. Much of our soaring health care costs are for care that would be unnecessary if Americans were not overeating in increasingly vast numbers, malnourished on foods lacking nutrients and on a host of other material comforts that still do not prevent exponential rise in the use of heavily massmarketed psychoactive drugs to treat depression, anxiety and other forms of mental and emotional suffering that stem from poor nutrition, lack of exercise, overwork and the loss of meaning and purpose in people's lives that cannot ever be found without a genuine relationship of charity and interest in the people of the world with whom we all share the same planet, breathe the same air and are loved by the same God. This is a serious collective issue, because our American 'aristocracy' entails some serious responsibilities. *Much is asked of those to whom much is given.*

There were 75,000[4] casualties in one year in America from gun-related violence and 783,936 deaths from medical error and prescription drugs.[5] That is 278 times more than those who died in the 9/11 terrorist attack and 15 times more casualties than those occurring throughout our entire decade long involvement in the war in Vietnam (about 53,000), yet strangely these areas get far less public attention. Some 2,936,000 children in U.S. were reported abused and/or neglected in 1992.[6] The U.S. has the highest documented number of incarcerated persons of any country in the world. As many as one out of thirty per-

[4] Center for Disease Control – Atlanta, cited in J. D. Brenner, *Does Stress Damage the Brain?* (New York: W. W. Norton & Co., 2002), 169.

[5] G. Null, C. Dean, M. Feldman, D. Rasio, and D. Smith, "Death by Medicine," http://www.healthe-livingnews.com/articles/death_by_medicine_part_1.html (2003).

[6] National Victim Center, "Crime and Victimization in America: Statistical overview," cited in B. A. van der Kolk et al. (eds.), *Traumatic Stress* (New York: Guilford Press, 1993), 31.

sons in the U.S. are either in jail or have been in jail and on probation at some point in their lives.[7] This represents nearly 35% of the world's inmate population, which presents another enormous cost to the larger American society that reflects the inequities and hidden suffering still abounding among us. The invisibility of those beneath the radar of public consciousness are virtual 'untouchables' who cannot find employment and stable relationships which renders them even more vulnerable to crime and illicit drug use.[8] Even so, I am still a good bit safer as a middle class white Euro-American male than persons in the Third World who suffer all sorts of traumatic events at a ratio of 166:1 times greater than those of us in developed countries.[9] Wealth, safety, education and privilege, in a world where millions do not have any of these, is a situation peculiar to aristocracy, and we all know the dangers of having power without a continually repentant, self-confronting heart that acknowledges the inter-relatedness of all beings and the necessity for those with power to exercise it in service of raising up those who do not. This is the way of Christ who beckons us to follow.

St. Elizabeth, a.k.a. the 'Grand Duchess,' was born into the pinnacle of aristocracy and privilege of European royalty at its height in the late 19th century. Through no choice or fault or merit of one's own, we are each born into existence in certain conditions over which we have no control. Responsibility begins only as a person reaches a certain maturity capable of making conscious choices about how to respond to the conditions in which we find ourselves. Motivation for this emerges from deep within the heart amidst many inclinations as each of us searches, more or less intentionally, for answers to the questions "Who am I?" and "Why am I here?" "What is the meaning and purpose of my life on earth?"

[7] Roy Walmsley, *World Prison Population List*, 8th edition (London: King's College London. International Centre for Prison Studies, 2009).
[8] Delbert Elliot from plenary address at the AAPC National Convention Plenary speaker — Atlanta, April 21, 2001.
[9] International Federation of Red Cross and Red Crescent Societies, *World Disaster report, 1993* (Dordrecht, The Netherlands: Martinus Nijhoff, 1993).

Conscious choice is perhaps the key determinant that makes us different from robots. Love is only possible for one who *does not have to love* and thus can *freely choose to love*. A lifetime of choices defines us as persons as clearly as do our fingerprints and the genes in our DNA. How we come to terms with this responsibility for choosing how to respond to the sense and purpose of human life on earth from moment to moment is the subject of what the Eastern Orthodox hesychasts of the *Philokalia* speak of as "spiritual warfare." Freedom of choice requires a special kind of attention or watchfulness, which is the *sine qua non* for achieving mental sobriety that enables us to respond to God, the world, and each other in the way that human beings were intended. In other words, an aristocracy which does not engage in the Christian formation of continual repentance is an aristocracy that is unlikely to give back as much or more than it has received. It is an aristocracy whose choices *God cannot bless* if they are contrary to God's will. This is what we must understand clearly as Americans when we say and sing "God bless America!" or any other privileged nation.

There are two forces in constant tension within us: consumption and contribution. Left on our own without repentance, without seeking to respond to something greater than our own unchecked appetites, daydreams (whether personal or cultural) and self-calming philosophizing, we are mere consumers; vampires sucking the blood out of life for our own individualistic and privatistic whims, whatever outward form this may take. Struggling against the forces of consumption without repentance, when it does not lead to burnout, merely leads to becoming a zealot; Pharisees, activists or bureaucratic civil servants whose unexamined 'shadows' conceal suppressed forms of the very things such persons are fighting against on the surface, and these eventually emerge, often with a vengeance.[10] This is why

---

[10] As, for example, in Adolf Hitler who had Jewish ancestors that came to represent that in himself which was despised and hated and must be eliminated as his abusive father had succeeded in eliminating in his poor son the possibility of remaining in contact with his own conscience which is rooted in a child's own heart. Cf. Alice Miller's powerful work, *For Your Own Good*, which closely

the early Desert Fathers, like St. Anthony, proclaimed, "Whoever does not know himself cannot know God." And St. Isaac the Syrian, "He who knows himself is greater them him who raises the dead!" And as the Lord Himself observed, "Blessed are you who mourn, for you shall be comforted."

Psychotherapists observe, on a daily basis, the damage done in the world to ourselves and others stemming from unexamined (and undeveloped) conscience and the propensity to project onto others what we are unwilling to see and own within ourselves and our motivations. It is not enough to will to do good. One must also become aware of how forces existing within us in a kind of homeostasis cannot be alchemically changed without the admixture of a third or reconciling force that is not within human control to supply. This is the condition for spiritual mourning, for yearning and praying for aid from above with which every addict in a 12 step program is familiar. Recognition of one's helplessness to overcome an addiction or compulsion apart from seeking help from a "higher power" is a *sine qua non* for healing, but it is not simply a "higher power" that is needed so much as recognition of the need for dialogue with One who can penetrate the sickness of monologue, which is at the heart of all individual addiction as well as societal aggression.

This reconciling force of Grace received from God brings disparate forces into harmony, making it possible to participate creatively in giving back to life a return on the Creator's investment in each of us, which, as the Gospels remind us, is not without tremendous price. It can be as simple and personal as offering a glass of water to another "in Christ's name" or as complex as the Passion of Jesus Christ, which is an intentional self-offering on a scale beyond what we can intellectually comprehend. And yet, the one is in the other if they are both genuine, for as Mother Theresa notes, "It is not possible to do great things, only small things with great love." Small things may become great things according to God's purposes over time.

---

examines this phenomenon in Germany from a psychodynamic perspective.

From this vantage point, with our struggle to make conscious choices within the conditions in which we find ourselves, we are at every given moment developing a likeness that gradually becomes clear over a lifetime, either as disciples of Christ who, as the Orthodox say, "is ever in our midst!" doing this, or as enemies of Him whose Body is the light and life of all humanity. There is no middle ground. We will go in one direction or the other.

From a patristic standpoint, it can be said that though made in the *Image* of God with the potential to develop accordingly, I do not necessarily fulfill this calling to develop in His *likeness.* The Divine Image I am *given* includes a *potential likeness,* but to fulfill this potential *requires something of me.* God's Grace acts in concert with my conscious responsive choice from my unique vantage point in the world through the being that I am, again and again and yet again until the last breath. Everything hinges on these small moments of choice, hardly even visible outwardly, made over and over. It is a synergistic process and, as Bonhoeffer might say, one in which *there can be no cheap Grace.*

So we can say that spiritual growth is a function of the grace of God and the effort of human beings in response to that Grace over a lifetime. "Attempting to pray without attempting to struggle with personal passions in order to obey the Gospel commandments of love in all arenas is naïve, if not blasphemous. Christianity is not a belief system or a warm, fuzzy feeling. It is, according to the Book of Acts, an ongoing Way to eternal life that requires an integrated response from the whole person: mind, body, heart, in response to God. Treating it as anything less than that dilutes it to the point of non-interest. As the abbot of one of the great monasteries on the Holy Mountain of Athos observed, 'A God who does not deify man; such a God can have no interest for us, whether He exists or not.'"[11]

In this struggle to walk the Christian path, St. Elizabeth is a valuable co-pilgrim and encouraging example, affording hope and elicit-

---

[11] Muse, S. "Boundaries: The hazards of VIPS," in Muse, S. (ed.) *Beside Still Waters: Resources for Shepherds in the Marketplace.* (Macon, Georiga: Smyth & Helwys, 2000), p. 124.

ing gratitude in a variety of ways. That's what God's saints do. As living icons, they show us the love of Christ in both their life's example and through their prayers for the world, inviting us to respond until we too can say "surely goodness and mercy shall follow me all the days of my life and I shall dwell in the House of the Lord forever."

Evil happens in the world. It has from the beginning. It is one of the conditions in which we find ourselves without knowing why. The problem is not eradicating evil, for we too easily become the evil we fight. Evil has already been defeated by God in Jesus Christ, the "Lamb slain from the foundation of the world." If we could have done it on our own, there would be no need for Christ, but neither can Christ do everything on His own without human participation. Our response to evil must always be one of partnership with Christ by returning to the continual repentance, prayer and solidarity that constitute the Christian path, which means loving the world and those in it as Christ does. This entails allowing our hearts to break for love and to lay down our lives for those we love. The cross of Christ is offered to all who would follow Him to the Resurrection in the Kingdom of God, where the last shall be first and love will have ended the suffering of existential partisanship. Until then, "for a Christian, there are no answers to be found in looking for who is responsible for evil: it lives in every human heart. There will always be evil on the earth. Christ said, *In the world ye shall have tribulation, but be of good cheer, I have overcome the world (John 16:33)*. The question to ask ourselves in times of peril or sorrow is whether in the suffering that comes upon us we draw closer to God, strengthened in faith."[12]

Following the shock of her husband's murder, St. Elizabeth's life suddenly shifted depths. After visiting her husband's murderer in jail and forgiving him, she made a series of choices that led to her to relinquish her former interest in her own personal beauty, and

---

[12] Abbess Michaela, "Hope in the Fields of Kosovo," *The Orthodox Word* No. 205 (1999): 57.

she was extraordinarily beautiful, with fine clothes and expensive jewelry, of which she had the best. She began using the privilege and power of the monarchy and all her personal assets in order to serve the people. After becoming a nun she received blessing to establish the Martha-Mary Convent of Mercy which was a unique monastic establishment within Orthodoxy whose mission was to combine Mary's deep listening to God with Martha's active ministry to the poor and sick in the world. The sisters of the Martha-Mary Convent of Mercy were not officially tonsured 'nuns' but were 'consecrated' in a service composed specifically for them.[13] St. Elizabeth's temperament was consistently peaceful in the midst of increasingly desperate conditions, showing mercy and lifting others up around her, finding ways to celebrate life and bringing a touch of beauty into the midst of great degradation.

At the time St. Elizabeth lived, Moscow was called the city of a thousand churches. When my wife Claudia and I visited there a decade ago, hundreds of churches had been returned to the Church by the government, and they were slowly rising from the ashes of their desecration and disuse. During Stalinist times, we were told, some of the great churches, existing centuries before there were Europeans on American soil, had their doors removed and were flooded with water so "the people" could ice skate in them. At Optina Monastery, the Mount Athos of Russia, where Dostoevsky visited the holy St. Ambrose, after whom he modeled the starets depicted in *The Brothers Karamazov*, the Communists put pig sties over the holy elders' graves and turned the monastery into a retreat for the Communist elite.

We attended several worship services and had supper with two of the women who serve meals to pilgrims. There have been only one or two other occasions that Matushka Evgenia knew of in the past two years when Americans had made the four-hour trip outside Moscow to visit the monastery. There is a naturalness and quality

---

[13] Cf. L. Millar, *Grand Duchess Elizabeth of Russia: New Martyr of the Communist Yoke* (California: Nikodemos Orthodox Publication Society, 1988).

of genuine essence that pervades Matushka's face as she speaks. No
sense of affected "personality." It is very refreshing, and when the
tears fall from her eyes as she shows us the tiny room in the skete
formerly occupied by the holy starets, St. Ambrose, it is a witness of
love and faith more eloquent in its simplicity and genuineness than
a month of sermons.

While we are eating simple black bread and drinking tea with
scoops of preserves made at the monastery to sweeten it, Matushka
tells us some of its recent history. The monastery was returned to
them by the government a few years ago. On the day they received
word of its return, the icon of the Holy Theotokos with Christ in her
arms, in the main church where we had worshipped (packed together
like sardines for five and a half hours the evening before), began to
stream myrrh from her eyes. There have been many tears in Holy
Russia, of joy and sorrow. Russia is raw, elemental, sublime, secular, profane and holy all woven together, like the state of each of our
hearts in this world if we observe clearly enough.

Unlike Optina, St. Elizabeth's Mary and Martha Monastery was
in disrepair when we visited and it had not been fully returned to the
Church. The sanctuary was occupied by workers seeking to restore
it, and the few nuns who were on the grounds were anxiously await-
ing the time when they might receive it back. But, for now, they were
worshipping in a very small chapel in an adjacent building amidst
huge holes in the ground exposing pipes, broken out windows and
crumbling mortar in the formerly occupied monastic cells. It had
once housed the best medical surgery unit in all of Russia, where
care was given free to all, funded by the Grand Duchess's own assets
as well as donations that poured in from wealthy Moscow donors.

> In addition to the hospital the Convent had an out-patient clinic
> of six consultation rooms serviced by thirty-four physicians a
> week. All of them worked free of charge. In the course of a single
> year, 1913, 10,814 patients passed through the clinic. Like the
> hospital, the clinic had its own library… the convent pharmacy

offered free medicines to the poor, others could obtain them
there at reduced prices. There was also a dental clinic,[14]

a ministry for orphans, literacy and educational classes, along with
regular worship, prayer and time for silence.

Over the door of the entrance to the Church was a powerful mosaic of the head of Christ in the form of the icon called the "Image
not made with human hands." Most icons of Christ have eyes that
look straight forward. This icon had striking green eyes that looked
to the left with an expression that contained both gravity and sorrow.
What were they looking at now? Above the icon were words written
in old Slavonic. Our friend Lisa (for Elizabeth!) said she could not
quite make it out — something like "I AM THE DOOR. WHOEVER
ENTERS, MUST ENTER BY ME."

I felt a great sense of pathos in the cold air amidst the semi-desert-
ed ruins around us, as I listened to the impassioned and anguished
voice tones and facial expression of the nun as she spoke at length
in Russian to our interpreter about the situation at the monastery.
A vague somber sense of grief hung in my heart as the intuitive lens
of my imagination lingered over a time some 83 years before when
the Bolsheviks ascended to power by descending upon the Church
like locusts, ravaging it and murdering thousands of priests, monks
and Christians. It was, for me standing there, as if it had just recently
happened. The history I have read and poured over many times, hoping each time that it will not happen again the way I know it must,
seemed as if to include me, helplessly standing by unable to do anything about *then*, but strengthening the yearning to do something
now, with my life *where I am able*, so that they may not have perished
in vain. As with the Lord Himself, "the Church continues to be built
on the blood of the martyrs." The present can change not only the
future but the past if the past serves as a motivation for us to struggle
to awaken to love NOW.

---

[14] Ibid., 142.

Every week in the Divine Liturgy, just before he enters the Royal Doors to call upon the Holy Spirit to sanctify the elements, the priest lifts up the Chalice and Paten holding the bread and wine that is the Body and Blood of Christ given for us all, and making the sign of the Cross over the people with it, he intones, "For those who love us and those who hate us," and the people respond in one voice, "Amen!" The Grace of God, like the rain, falls on the just and the unjust alike. All receive it, but not all consume it worthily, so to speak, in a manner that transforms us into persons through whom God works such that it is true to say, "*It is no longer I but Christ who lives in me.*"

Here I was, standing on ground where a soul given increasingly to God and the good of humanity had walked, quietly seeking to heal the wounds of pre-revolutionary Russia and then doing the same afterwards among her enemies, until some brutal, stupid, demonic force that could not see and value goodness since it was associated with Him, intervened. In murdering St. Elizabeth, and countless others like her, these forces unleashed by the Russian Revolution cut off part of its own body as it continued to do under Lenin and Stalin who were responsible for the exile and deaths of some 60 million Russian citizens. Those who had any clear and independent association with Christ and the Church, who were seen as the true power behind the monarchy were at the top of the list of enemies of the new 'people's' state. Whatever may be said about the state of the Church and the value of a theocratic monarchy, the fact that the Atheistic regime saw the Church as so great a threat and went to such lengths to try and eradicate it from Russian soil and psyche is perhaps the greatest testimony to its importance to "Holy Russia." Alexander Solzhenitsyn observes,

> If I were asked today to formulate as concisely as possible the main cause of the ruinous revolution that swallowed up some 60 million of our people, I could not put it more accurately than to repeat what I heard as a small child: "Men have forgotten God; that's why all this has happened."

What is more, the events of the Russian revolution can only
be understood now, at the end of the century, against a backdrop of what has since occurred in the rest of the world. What
emerges here is a process of universal significance. And if I were
called upon to identify briefly the principal trait of the *entire*
twentieth century, here too, I would be unable to find anything
more precise and pithy than to repeat once again: "Men have
forgotten God." The failings of human consciousness, deprived
of its divine dimension, have been a determining factor in all
the major crimes of this century.[15]

Fr. Anatoly, a Russian Orthodox priest in his fifties, with whom
we had dinner during our trip, told us of a copy of a letter written by
Lenin, which he had seen with his own eyes. It had been circulated
among Lenin's followers a few years after the coup.[16] Lenin writes that
it is necessary to weaken the Orthodox Church by stealing its wealth
and executing the priests, hierarchy and leaders in whatever manner
needed to accomplish the goal of destroying its power. He wrote in
his calculating cowardice and secrecy that this letter should be destroyed after being read.

---

[15] A. Solzhenitsyn, *The Templeton Prize for Progress in Religion, 1978–1987* (Edinburgh: Scottish Academic Press Ltd., 1988), 116–117.
[16] Unlike the French and American revolutions, one of the enigmas of the so-
called Russian "revolution" is that so few people were initially involved. Why
did the Bolsheviks win? According to noted Russian historian Richard Pipes,
eyewitnesses at the time and for decades later viewed it as a *coup d'état* rather
than a people's revolution. In his short essay, *Three "Whys" of the Russian Revolution* (New York: Random House, 1995, 32–33) he points out "only slightly
more than 5 percent of Russia's industrial workers belonged to the Communist
Party in a country where industrial workers represented 1 or 1.5 per cent of the
population." That Lenin's methods were ruthless and preemptive is confirmed
by documents released recently by the Central Party Archives, such as a letter
handwritten by Lenin which calls for "urgent unleashing of terror" and "confirms that the 'Red Terror' was not a reluctant response to the actions of others,
but a prophylactic measure designed to nip in the bud any thought of resistance
to the dictatorship," p. 41.

One of the leaders of the Church who had two strikes against her — for being a member of the Romanov aristocracy by marriage, and for being regarded by the people as a saint for her work among the poor and the sick in her hospitals, food banks and shelters — was St. Elizabeth the Grand Duchess, Russia's own Mother Theresa. People would line the streets and bow on their knees when she walked by, she was so loved and highly regarded. And this was so even in a time when her sister, the tsarina, was hated for her German background, for her reclusiveness and her compete unreasonableness when it came to her support of the so-called 'monk' Rasputin, who alone seemed able to stop the bleeding of her hemophiliac son.

Refusing to escape when she had the chance, St. Elizabeth was removed from the convent and taken by train with some of her nuns to a place outside Moscow, where she was held for a month until being taken for a short walk where she was thrown down a forty-foot mine shaft along with the others in her company, followed by two hand grenades. The next day, amazingly, singing was heard in the mine shaft, and when the White Army eventually recaptured the area and dug the people out, it was discovered that St. Elizabeth had used her clothing to bandage the wounds of her comrades who had remained alive for some time. She was found part way up the mine shaft with her prayer rope in her hand in the attitude of prayer with two unexploded hand grenades beside her. One witness observed that her body showed no signs of decomposition — a sign of sanctity. Her body was taken to China and then finally to Jerusalem, where she was buried at the church that she had earlier built there in honor of St. Mary Magdalene, after a deeply moving visit to the Holy Land. Recently, her relics were returned to Russia to the Martha-Mary Convent, which has been restored.

According to Sr. Maria, whom we met while she was dusting and cleaning in the small chapel currently serving as the church for Sts. Martha and Mary Convent, "Elizabeth was always busy. Somehow in the midst of helping others constantly, she found time to embroider and make the environment beautiful." Sr. Maria eagerly told us that St. Elizabeth loved plants and placed so many around the altar (as is customary during the feast of Pentecost) that when Tsar Nicholas II visited the convent, he would say, "Elizabeth, for you it is always Pentecost!"

I gave Sr. Maria some incense from Mount Athos as a gift for use in the sanctuary, and we told her we would pray for the speedy return of the church to the convent. Her lined face bloomed into a gracious and broad snaggletoothed smile and then she turned back to her meticulous dusting.

We made our way down the street after our visit to St. Elizabeth's convent, to join Archimandrite Zaccheus, the priest of the OCA representation church in Moscow, for tea and, as it turned out, several toasts with Russian "wine" (vodka). He said, "If you are cold (it was about 9° outside), this will warm you. And if you are warm, it will cool you!"

Fr. Zaccheus showed us the bell that he had in his office, which was to be delivered eventually to the newly rebuilt St. Nicholas Church[17] in the U.S. which had been destroyed in the World Trade Center bombing. We told Fr. Zaccheus about the condition of Sts. Martha and Mary's convent. He said this was true for many of the churches, but a great activity was going on in rebuilding and restoring them all over the city. I asked him about the difficulty with the Slavonic over the icon on the Church Entrance. He responded immediately with the correct translation, "I am the door, and whoever enters here enters through Me."

Later that evening, during the Vigil for St. Nicholas, which we attended in the church in which Fr. Zaccheus serves, I was standing very still in the sanctuary among sixty or seventy others. My back and neck hurt and, not knowing the language or the typikon, I am never sure how long services will last in Russian churches. During my time

[17] St. Nicholas Orthodox Church was the only place of worship destroyed in the 9/11 attacks. Only two icons were recovered. Nine years later amidst the controversy over a new $100,000,000+ mosque to be built at Ground Zero, support to rebuild St. Nicholas Orthodox Church at a fraction of the cost stalled, amidst controversy, a strange irony.

there, I joked that if I am told the service is to be a half hour, I should
expect an hour and a half. If I am told it will last an hour and a half, I
should expect three. At Optina Monastery, when I had been expecting three and a half hours, it lasted five and one-half hours! The Rus-
sians were concerned that the Americans were too soft (and spoiled?)
for this! So they offered us beds to rest if needed.

As I stood there in the midst of the Orthodox service touched by
the strange and beautiful Slavonic tongue, I began to be very aware of
the struggle of forces at play in me. These forces are always present,
but much more rarely seen, because I tend to be unconsciously reactive, identified with one or the other of them, instead of simultaneously remaining present to the tension between like and dislike, will
and imagination, sensation, feeling and thought. To *choose,* one must
remain awake to the possibility that emerges when holding oneself
apart from identifying and surrendering to one or another of these
inner promptings. It requires an active attention.

There are two streams flowing through us. One carries us along
the path of the "old man of the flesh." It "happens" to us without our really having to be present. It is the "self-made" being whose life follows
the easy path of willful achievements, pleasure-seeking, self-calming
and is anthropocentric, concerned with image and seeking a false security through increased privilege, power, possessions and prestige.
The other path involves intentional watchfulness of the forces that
become visible when we struggle to maintain ascetical[18] boundaries.
It is dialogical, a relationship of prayer to God and presence in the

---

[18] Asceticism rightly understood is the struggle to become free of lesser forces
in order to be responsive to the greater force of Grace. Thus, asceticism is part
of the conditions freely accepted which provide a context for struggle or inner
separation from identifying with suggestions as they arise without discrimination. Cf. Tito Colliander's classic work *Way of the Ascetics* and Bishop Theophan
the Recluse's *Turning the Heart Toward God* and the chapter by Dr. Jamie Moran, "Spiritual War: The Relevance to Modern Therapy of the Ancient Eastern Orthodox Christian Path of Ascetical Practice," in S. Muse (ed.), *Raising
Lazarus: Integral Healing in Orthodox Christianity* (Brookline, MA: Holy Cross
Press, 2004).

world in which truth is more important than self-image, serving love more important than self-protection. This is the road to becoming fully human, the "new man in Christ," and it is one in which the "I" that I am conscious of cannot be in charge of the process. This path is triune in contrast to the dualistic tensions that dominate me as a carnal man. With surrender to Grace, we discover a state of being *in* this world, while not being entirely *of* it. If nations become what the critical mass of its citizenry are, then perhaps where there are not enough of those who truly seek the way that leads to "Thy will being done on earth," then nations can take a wrong path, led forward by collective projections onto a leader who personifies the forces that hold the nation in obedience, offering an alternative means to security other than God, and such forces can bring a nation to ruinous calamity, just as they can each person.

As Fr. Zaccheus reminded us, "There are two Russias. One is Holy. One is secular." Both seek to prevail. The same is true for each of us. There is both sinner and potential saint, depending on our choices in cooperation with the Grace of God over a lifetime. As the Lord enjoins, in this life we must "keep awake and watch, for you know not when the Master will arrive, lest you be found sleeping." We cannot enter the Bridegroom's chamber just because we want to, motivated by acquisitive egoistic passions or armed with scientific precision, for any other impulses less than pure love of the Bridegroom and those whom the Bridegroom loves. Such pure love is a function of the quality of attention that is shaped by the heart's deepest longing fanned into flame by a thousand moments of choosing to be present to the invitation of Grace knocking at the door of our hearts every second of our lives. It is the one who loves who is most awake to signs of the beloved and who loves the *Beloved* more than the *gifts* of the Beloved. I ask myself where I am at any given moment, open and desiring of Grace for its own sake, with all my heart, mind and body and evidencing this in love for my neighbor as for myself? To what degree am I dominated by my inner press secretary who seeks not God, but the use of God for egoistic purposes? Noticing the ebb and flow and processes requires that I actually be present. This is a subtle and somewhat extraordinary condition that does not automatically occur, but must be intentionally renewed as an act of freely devoted attention throughout the day. If motivated by love and desire for dialogue with Christ, it supports repentance and prayer, for prayer arises out of observing the human condition and looking to God for help and companionship. Prayer does not bear fruit apart from the reconciling action of the Holy Spirit breaking into my inner monologue as 'other.'

This is more than *knowing* about God. One must *encounter* God. Otherwise, religion remains in the realm of content and does not transform process. As St. Isaac the Syrian asks, *"Can these things be truly known from ink? Does the taste of honey pass over the palate from books? Therefore: Who will read these things and yearn?"* Such encounter is a gift and requires a response from me. I must repeatedly see how I fail to respond to Grace by loving as I am loved. This is repentance: "A broken and contrite heart, O Lord, You will not despise." From this ruin, I remain beloved to God and prayer strengthens, rising like a phoenix from the ashes of my failure and I get up again, like a child, learning eventually to walk the path God sets before me.

My back is beginning to hurt along with my legs and shoulders now. Little complaints arise from somewhere and are delivered to the central switchboard of my attention, hoping to attract some feeling of sympathy and enlist my will to find a way to "stop the pain of standing" and "ease the suffering of not being in control of when this will end" and other such forms of what, if accepted, would amount to self-indulgence and self-calming rather than wakefulness and prayer. I see once again that I am having trouble *being obedient to something greater than my own self-will.* How much of my life is built on shutting my inner eye and giving in to this impulse? Or as Peter once found himself doing and saying, "Jesus of Nazareth? Never heard of the man. Don't know what you're talking about! Leave me alone! I have no part of any of that. I am just a man warming himself by the fire confound it!"

Watching these forces turning like snakes in my mind, the words *Lord Jesus Christ have mercy on me!* keep sweeping through me with each turn of another knot on the prayer rope in my hand. I subvocalize the words of the prayer, trying to bring them down into the heart where my yearning is buried amidst the clamor. Somewhere within me there is a longing to be touched deeply by God. How to find this in the midst of all this distraction? There is a fear that I might have come 4,000 miles for nothing, and then again, a gentle returning to awareness of *Lord Jesus Christ have mercy on me a sinner,* like a slow drip, a spiritual IV to eliminate foreign invaders from infecting the heart.

"Can we stop now?" the little child in me whines, while another part calmly reassures, "Be still and continue making the effort to be present." The body is obedient, but the emotionality in me wants to bolt, taking the body with it. The melodious chanting is not enough. Something more important calling to me holds me in place, *waiting for God.* Although the pain is felt in the body, the *suffering* is experienced in the *imagination* where self-will has its throne and it does not matter from this place what the suffering is for or what it makes possible. But this 'I' is not in control at this moment. A deeper yearning has deputized a group of other 'I's' to mind the inner house, such as it is. Nevertheless, something else is needed to reconcile these disparate parts of will and desire which appear to be in battle with each other.

I had come to Russia to teach a course on sin and psychopathology to counseling students in the only program in Russia at the time that united Christianity and Psychology. Previous discussions with them were in and out of my mind as I stood there. We had been talking about relational healing, and I had surprised them by suggesting that the prayer, faith and the person of the therapist in conjunction with that of the client were key variables, rather than method, especially in terms of whether the therapist was a person of prayer, who went to Confession regularly and who was rooted in Orthodox Christian tradition. This was a difficult idea for some of the students to grasp, reared as they were in an atheistic environment, in a culture whose government for 70 years tried to twist, deny or eradicate every particle of its former religious understanding from the people.

On the other hand, it is not so different from my own culture, where all too often Christianity, Holy Scripture and the words of Christ serve as little more than an adornment for the ego and its interests, securing and justifying social prestige, privilege and the right to wield power and uncritically judge others in the name of our own culturally and racially embedded 'righteousness' or so-called 'manifest destiny'. The line between the evil of self-aggrandizing aggression and war unleashed by a democratic nation to prevent the worse evil of a totalitarian nation from prevailing is sometimes difficult to discern. All war, even when necessary and deemed just as a defense of the defenseless, is an evil to be avoided if at all possible. Weapons of mass destruction used to enlarge territory or co-opt resources for one nation at the expense of another are as much the wrong path for a nation as it is for an individual. No house divided can stand forever. No political or economic solution that secures peace and security only for part of humanity, can ever be secure. "Progress which is not aimed at the resurrection of all would be merely a succession of murders."[19] Repentance and self-examination that ultimately lead to justice and mercy are critical to our long-term well being, both personally and collectively as a nation.

Having met Fr. Zaccheus in a relaxed, personal setting and now seeing him here leading the service, I was reflecting on how he, like other monks and priests I have known, in doing the liturgical services, fulfills a certain role and is caught up in a web of much greater meaning. I am struck again by the silence that envelops the priest like a shroud as he quietly moves through the prescribed patterns. Emptying themselves of their own "personality" as they perform the Liturgy invites me toward a deeper prayerfulness as well. Personality invites personality, and prayer invites prayer.

It suddenly occurs to me how the person of the therapist, the therapeutic alliance and the faith and hope of the client(s) in pastoral

---

[19] O. Clement, *On Human Being: A Spiritual Anthropology* (London: New City Press, 2000), 124.

psychotherapy are all rooted in Christ as hypostasis, the ontological ground of being. This relationship is the unifying element of psychotherapy just as it is for our personal lives. All healing occurs διά-Λογος. Christ stands between the self and other as well as constituting the ground of being that unites the two in one embrace which allows for separate persons to be in dialogue. The ego-personality needs of the therapist are left aside as the priest leaves aside his "small" self to be Christ's representative with and for others, just as St. Paul who in his ministry of preaching, "decided to know nothing but Christ crucified."

The Liturgy or dance of the therapist is different than the priest and may involve a variety of forms of human interaction from playfulness, to quiet empathy, confrontation or instruction, but the critical variable is still the *person of Christ* in whom our own and every other personhood adheres and from which we receive life and meaning and value. One enters into therapeutic alliance with another person as one enters into prayer itself. The source is not, as St. John the Theologian reminds, "that we love but that Christ first loved us." It is this which guides and sustains the healing ministry of pastoral care and counseling whatever its context. Human value begins with belovedness to God which is a pure gift offered to each of us.

I sometimes ask married couples, "If you were in a special courtroom where your spouse was on trial and you had to prove his or her existence in order to save them from death and the only evidence you could offer that would suffice for this, was that you or someone else had done something for him or her that had nothing whatsoever to do with meeting your own needs, could you do it?" It's a very difficult question. Only God is capable of such pure, unselfish love and, thus, we *exist* not because we can think or feel or know or do or have or any other power under the sun, but solely because *God unselfishly loves us.* If God is not *person*, then neither are we, for we obtain value as persons only by faith in Him who first loved us and not by empirical validation of our existence from any other source.

The essence of an Orthodox Christian anthropology was becoming palpable during the worship experience as I took in what was happening around me through my eyes and within me through my heart. At *just this moment* as I am attending to the "appearing" of this new apprehension of *hypostasis* in relation to my thinking about psychotherapy, Claudia whispers in my ear that Lisa just told her that the Gospel reading for the day which Fr. Zaccheus is reading, is the words of Jesus from the Apostle John that have been the subject of our wonderings all day, *I am the door...*

Quietly the heart wells up and breaks open like a ripe pomegranate with a sense of Eucharistic presence spilling over my thoughts, warming them with the joy of a personal encounter, making the words flesh. Quiet tears flow as the heart implodes with grateful sorrow at the message, now becoming personal, that "*I am deep within you in the depths of your own heart, the true Image in which you are made and outside of you in the likeness to which each are called and all around you in the one Body of many parts to which you belong. I am in the time of your becoming and the eternity of your being. I am the Alpha and the Omega. I am the crucified and Risen Lord. Whoever knows Me in the humblest of forms: as the beggar outside the monastery gate or as the Anointed Tsar; among the forsaken and bereft in the Gulag or in the beauty of the Divine Liturgy celebrated amidst the splendor of the most beautiful churches in the world, knows the One who sent Me. It is through Me that all healing occurs. Apart from Me, you can do nothing.*"

The worshippers move forward now, converging from all directions like a Moscow traffic jam, to receive the sign of the cross made by the priest on each forehead, personally, one at a time, representing Him through whom each of us is uniquely and personally created capable of dwelling together just as Father, Son and Holy Spirit are uniquely one and three in love. The fragrance of the oil is breathed in, and it is like a grace that begins to spread throughout the body and mind. My heart is full and I am aware that, even at that moment, my mind is trying to snatch pieces of the experience to enlarge the ever burgeoning United States or Soviet Union of my Ego, thinking, "You are having a spiritual experience," or "Does this mean God is touching you specially?" This happens in a second along with the awareness of letting all this go, realizing it is secondary to the encounter which may not even leave a trace that can be captured and built into any sort of "tent" to "house the glory" of the moment as experienced. Like Peter on the Mount of the Transfiguration, the point is not to succumb to any deviation from orthodoxy (literally, *correct glory*) trying to enlarge the separate reality of one's own individual ego, even for the best of intentions, but simply to return to the Word coming from above: "Listen to My Beloved Son," *now at this moment. And the next.* For God is at every instance creating something new. In obedience to this, for a moment, I *become myself* without even knowing how. Why is it so difficult to gain freedom from my compulsive man-making-self in order to find in Christ a self not made with human will or defined by human opinion? God esteem is prior to and the ground for authentic self-esteem. Whoever settles for the latter, will lose both, but whoever surrenders to Divine Love, will find the latter as well, and it will remain with the soul forever, in the way God originally intended.

As I leave the church, I realize strangely that my body no longer aches ... or maybe it does, but it no longer matters, because there is no *suffering.* Leaving the church here in this strange land among strange people, I am strangely at peace as if among my very closest kin.

Jesus said, "If I be lifted up, I will draw all people to Me." So there is nothing strange at all in the fact that another scion of the English branch of humanity, a.k.a. an American, has found his way home to the Orthodox Christian faith which embraces and illumines all cultures and all races in all times in places without diminishing the uniqueness of any one person or nation, but rather completing and uniting them in one Body. For truly, "In Christ, there is no East nor West, no Greek nor Jew, no slave nor free, but Christ is all in all."

Lord Jesus Christ, by the prayers of the Holy Theotokos, and the holy martyr St. Elizabeth the Grand Duchess and all the saints both known and unknown who have loved You and, in so doing, loved us all, pray for us sinners who set our hope in Thee!

CHAPTER TWO

Finding the Fit:
What Makes Counseling Pastoral?[1]

*The one who enters through the gate is the shepherd of
the flock. The gatekeeper lets him in, the sheep hear his
voice, one by one he calls his own sheep and leads them
out. When he has brought out his flock, he goes ahead
of them, and the sheep follow because they know his
voice. They never follow a stranger but run away from
him; they do not recognize the voice of strangers.*

John 10:2–5

*The most important problem for Orthodox theology
will be to reconcile the cosmic vision of the Fathers
with a vision which grows out of the results of the natural sciences… Theology today must remain open to
embrace both humanity and the cosmos.*

Dumitru Staniloae

Some years ago at an OCAMPR conference at Holy Cross in Boston, Fr. Philotheos Faros suggested that it makes as much sense to
consider an Orthodox Christian psychotherapy as it does to think of
Orthodox Christian plumbing.[2] If he is right, it does not make much

---

[1] An excerpt from this article translated into Greek is in press, to be published in
2011 in the first edition of a new journal in Greece *Ψυχῆς Δρόμοι* (*Ways of the
Soul*), devoted to the dialogue of theology and religiosity with the psychological
sciences. Fr. Vasileios Thermos, MD, PhD, is the editor. This chapter is expanded
and revised from a presentation given at the 4th Biannual International Orthodox
Psychotherapy Conference in Florida, January 2008.

[2] Cf. J. Chirban (ed.), *Sickness or Sin* (Brookline, MA: Holy Cross Orthodox

sense to ask the question, "What makes counseling pastoral?" Are the
Divine Uncreated Energies and the natural energies of the created
worlds so far apart as this? Is the Church the only hospital we need
and, with the exception of certain genetically based or traumatically
induced metabolic disturbances, are priests the only psychotherapists capable and necessary, as Metropolitan Hierotheos (Vlachos)
suggests?[3] Is salvation totally distinct from physical, emotional and
psychological healing? Even Jesus asked the people questioning His
healing ministry, "Which is easier to say, 'Your sins are forgiven or
pick up your pallet and walk?'"

THE MORAL CONTEXT OF COUNSELING. From the Orthodox
Christian perspective, pastoral counseling involves addressing
both an existential dimension involving freedom of choice in specific
and unique circumstances as well as an ontological dimension of belovedness to God and creation in the image of God. Together these
constitute the arena of human struggle involving the developmental
possibilities inherent to the path of *theosis*, which is a response to
the redemptive call to love and the gift of being loved inherent in
Eucharistic Communion of Christ's Body and Blood given for the life
of the world. An Eastern Orthodox perspective I believe is in agree-
ment with the perspective of Professor Emeritus Merle Jordan, of
Boston University, who has suggested, "All psychotherapy is clinical
theology." Psychology and medicine are a branch of applied theology,
and the pastoral counselor must always 'test the spirits' of any given
theory or approach to see if they support the immense potential for
life that is offered humankind within the context of the Orthodox
Christian *kerygma*.

In 1976, Don Browning, then a professor of Religion and Psychological Studies at the University of Chicago Divinity School,

---

Press, 2001).
[3] Cf. H. Vlachos, *The Illness and Cure of the Soul in Orthodox Tradition* (Levadia,
Greece: Birth of the Theotokos Monastery, 1993) and *Orthodox Psychotherapy*
(Levadia, Greece: Birth of the Theotokos Monastery, 1994).

published a little book entitled *The Moral Context of Pastoral Care*, in which he put forth the thesis that "there is a moral context to all acts of care." Whether professional pastoral counseling and psychotherapy or the ordained pastoral ministry, there remains a need for a theological plumb line to assess their validity. Pastoral counseling by its very definition is a trialogue with God, self and others, or it cannot be *pastoral* counseling.

> "Pastoral care and counseling must be able to show what is 'Christian' and 'pastoral' about what the minister — or the pastoral specialist — does when he/she offers services. And pastoral care must be able to show that what it has borrowed from other disciplines will not corrupt the essential thrust of its own unique perspective."[4]

The importance of this discernment was underscored a few years later when sociologist Robert Bellah observed that American religious life had over the past half-century become increasingly a culture of the therapeutic, reinterpreting the meaning and value of love, marriage, family, personal growth and commitment in highly individualistic ways that often depart significantly from traditional Judeo-Christian values.

> The quasi-therapeutic blandness that has afflicted much of mainline Protestant religion at the parish level for over a century cannot effectively withstand the competition of the more vigorous forms of radical religious individualism, with their claims of dramatic self-realization, or the resurgent religious conservatism that spells out clear, if simple, answers in an increasingly bewildering world.[5]

[4] D. Browning, *The Moral Context of Pastoral Care* (Philadelphia: Westminster Press, 1976), 19.
[5] R. Bellah et al., *Habits of the Heart* (Berkeley, CA: University of California Press, 1985), 238.

In some ways, psychology had been a kind of Trojan horse subtly changing Christianity from within, after having been embraced for its obvious ability to offer consolation and assistance to persons malnourished by an impoverished civil religion. One need only observe the zeal with which proponents of various approaches view each other almost as competing faiths to understand the need for theological critique. As one observer noted,

> "The contemporary United States mental health field is characterized by competing schools — biological, social, interpersonal, psychodynamic, and behavioral — each of which has proposed different theories concerning the nature and origin of mental illnesses and emphasized various modes of treatment. So intense are the loyalties and emotions manifested by the adherents of these various schools that the mental health field appears from the outside to be more like an arena of conflicting ideological sets than a scientific discipline based on commonly shared theoretical concepts, methodological approaches, and incremental advances based on empirical knowledge."[6]

A decade later, an article appeared in *American Psychologist* suggesting "psychology is, in American society, filling the void created by the waning influence of religion in answering questions of ultimacy and providing moral guidance."[7] This was particularly interesting in that the author also noted that surveys consistently revealed mental health professionals to be "an atypical subpopulation in America today, with lower levels of religious participation and higher levels of agnosticism, skepticism, and atheism than the

---

[6] G. L. Klerman, "Historical perspectives on contemporary schools of psychopathology," in T. Millon and G. L. Klerman (eds.), *Contemporary Directions in Psychopathology: Toward the DSM-IV* (New York: Guilford Press, 1986), 23–24.
[7] S. L. Jones, "A Constructive Relationship for Religion with the Science and Profession of Psychology," *American Psychologist* 49(3) (1994): 192.

general population?"[8] Only 24% of clinical and counseling psychologists in a recent survey reported belief in God, and only 26% stated they valued religion as "very important,"[9] a not altogether surprising finding given the fact that mental health counselors in general have received little or no training in addressing the religious and spiritual dimensions of human concerns. Even though evidence suggests a significant relationship between the religious integration of the therapist and their capacity for clinical empathy[10] surveys of training directors of counseling psychology programs in the United States reveal that less than one out of five programs offered a course on religion and spirituality.[11] So the question arises, "What moral universe do I serve and how does it influence my practice of counseling?" Deborah van Deusen Hunsinger, Assistant Professor of Pastoral Theology at Princeton Theological Seminary suggests as foundational for pastoral counselor training:

> "I hope to show students that all one's work in pastoral care depends fundamentally neither on one's theoretical clarity nor on one's practical skill, but on one's relationship to God in Jesus Christ. Only the person who is centered in prayer can faithfully take up the work of pastoral care and counseling."[12]

---

[8] Ibid., p. 192.

[9] Studies by E. P. Shafranske et al. (1990, 1996, 2001) cited by K. I. Pargament, *Spiritually Integrated Psychotherapy: Understanding and Addressing the Sacred* (New York: Guilford Press, 2007), 9.

[10] S. Muse, Ph.D., B. K. Estadt, Ph.D., J. G. Greer, Ph.D. & S. Cheston, Ed.D., "Are Religiously Integrated Therapists More Empathic?" *Journal of Pastoral Care* Vol. 48(1) (1994): 14–23.

[11] D. L. Schulte, T. A. Skinner, & C. D. Claiborn, "Religious and Spiritual Issues in Counseling Psychology Programs," *Counseling Psychologist* 30 (2002): 118–134.

[12] *Princeton Seminary Newsletter*, p. 17, date unknown. Cf. D. Van Deusen, *Theology and Pastoral Counseling: A New Interdisciplinary Approach* (New York: Eerdmans Publishing Company, 1995).

How important is it as a matter of informed consent, to make clear with those who seek our services as mental health practitioners, the moral universe that we ultimately serve in our life and work as a part of informed consent since it is likely to be influential in subtle ways? Even with the best of intentions, there remains an ongoing stance toward others and the world in Christ, which, though it remains hidden in part even from ourselves, we must hope and acknowledge that God is at work in spite of our conscious and unconscious attempts at compartmentalization of religion and psychology which are far more integrally related than our conscious minds can or should try to separate. From the Orthodox perspective, it is more like Bob Wicks' story of teaching his pastoral counseling class about integration of spirituality and psychology. A student from Africa raised his hand and said, "We don't integrate psychology and spirituality where I come from." "And why is that?" Dr. Wicks asked. "Because we never separate them in the first place." This is indicative of a non-Western, non-Descartesian viewpoint which is more consonant with the Eastern Orthodox approach.

> There is, in the ultimate reality of things, no non-spiritual life that is closed off to the Holy Spirit... The world that is called profane is in reality a profaned world and man is responsible for that. We have expelled God from this world: we do it every day. We chase him from public life by a Machiavellian form of separation between our private lives — pious and good — and the domains of politics, commerce, science, technology, love, culture and work, where everything is allowed. All these domains of human work depend upon the creative work of man, seized, modeled, and inspired by the Spirit of God.[13]

The person of Christ remains central to both the counselor who would function pastorally in her/his role of psychotherapist as well

---

[13] Fr. Boris Bobrinskoy, cited in J. Jones, "Confronting Poverty and Stigmatization: An Eastern Orthodox Perspective," http://www.incommunion.org/articles/resources/confronting-poverty-and-stigmatization (March 2006).

as in the way in which counseling and psychotherapy are conducted. For this reason, in the United States, the field of pastoral counseling has produced an extensive literature over the past half century among largely Protestant and a smaller number of Roman Catholic clergy and lay mental health practitioners who formed the American Association of Pastoral Counselors in recognition of the specialized ministry of pastoral counselors. The challenge of Fr. Dumitru Staniloae quoted above remains a vital one for our time. As it begins to wrestle with recognizing the value of pastoral counseling outside the ordained priesthood,[14] the Orthodox Church has an opportunity to address in a fresh way questions arising in our twenty-first century context related to religious pluralism, bioethics, gender, sexuality, ecology and human potential, while remaining true to the "Way, the Truth and the Life" of Jesus Christ, who is the eternal link between humanity and the Unseen Creator. It is the pastoral counselor's peculiar task and vocation to draw from the contributions of natural sciences, the patristic witness and Orthodox Christian *kerygma*, to serve the ends of the Church which are to love the world as Christ loves the world and gave His life for the sake of the world.

As an Orthodox Christian with academic training in counseling psychology focused on pastoral integration, having previously served for over a decade as an ordained Protestant minister, and for

---

[14] Currently, the Orthodox Church *de facto* recognizes the vocation (*diakonia*) of "lay pastoral counselor" as it has set apart several lay persons who are qualified according to the guidelines of the American Association of Pastoral Counselors to integrate clinical and pastoral domains in the work of counseling and psychotherapy. (Cf. AAPC.org for further information on qualification, etc.) There remains unclarity within the Orthodox Church regarding the particular distinction between non-ordained 'pastoral' counselors who work on the border between clinical and pastoral functions in service of the ends of the Church versus secular psychologists and mental health counselors who do not. In the beginning of its organization in the 1960's, all pastoral counselors in AAPC were required to be ordained. This requirement was later changed with the proviso that the counselors would maintain rootedness in their respective religious tradition and receive sponsorship by the appropriate hierarchical governing body.

twenty five years as a pastoral psychotherapist and trainer of pastoral counselors working with hundreds of clergy from all denominations, I have found great richness and challenge in asking the question, "What makes counseling pastoral?" and "What makes a counselor a pastor?" Admittedly, these are not questions one would ask of a plumber, but they are central to the vocation and practice of pastoral care and counseling which increasingly occurs in our day and time in the Orthodox Church outside the ecclesiastical priesthood among a small but growing group of lay mental health practitioners in ways that are certainly not relevant for plumbers in their work. Many of these mental health professionals have expressed the desire to have more formal training and venues for collegial discussion on how to be effective and congruent with their Orthodox Christian faith in their ministry of pastoral care and counseling and to be able to better serve the Church.

Does it make sense to ask if a counselor, steeped in Orthodox Christian ethos, worship, formation and worldview, all other things being equal, handles the practice of psychotherapy in general more effectively than someone who is not?[15] And is there anything about counseling and psychotherapy itself, independent of the person of the therapist, that lends itself to being corrected or improved by being informed by Orthodox Christian perspectives and illumined by the Grace of God? Further, to what extent is it possible to approach non-Orthodox Christians with the riches of Orthodox Tradition in a way that respects their freedom and does not subtly impose upon them from any sort of imperialistic cultural supremacy, yet neither withholds anything that may be given freely "as the rain falls on the just and unjust alike" from the treasury of blessing of Orthodox Christianity?

BEYOND THE TAUTOLOGY OF EMPIRICAL DATA AND THEORY. In a now famous debate with Werner Heisenberg, who was in-

---

[15] Cf. S. Muse, B. Estadt, J. Greer & S. Cheston, "Are Religiously Integrated Therapist More Empathic?" *Journal of Pastoral Care* Vol. 48(1) (1994): 14–24.

sisting that only empirical data should be included in a theory, Einstein responded, "It is quite wrong to try founding a theory on observable magnitudes alone. In reality the very opposite happens. It is theory which decides what we can observe."[16] The 'deep things of the Spirit,' which are the basis of Orthodox faith and life and which gradually form a person, affect what he or she can 'see' just as does the gender, family of origin, culture and world views of the times we live in as well as the diagnostic criteria of the DSM-IV and mandates of licensure boards. There is a shared life and human essence that is common to all on the earth regardless of all these variables just as each of these and all together constitute a dimension that is utterly unique among all.

According to Professor Martin Buber, these two inseparable dimensions are designated by the two fundamental aspects of human relationships: I-Thou and I-It. From this perspective, *all* data-gathering and diagnosis involve distortion and objectification of persons. Only the relationship of love and freedom responsive to the Holy Spirit beyond time and space and beyond the will and desire and possibility of an individual person to create, approaches the other in such a way that Christ is sacramentally present, by Grace, between the two in the mystery of *meeting*. This means that healing in its fullest dimension is not and can never be *merely technical*, and Christianity cannot be correctly viewed as primarily a technical methodology or 'psychotherapy' but rather as a love relationship, albeit with special boundaries to support the specialized work involved. This context has the utmost implications for the practice and calling of pastoral counseling and psychotherapy as well as for the conduct of ordained pastoral ministry and the Sacraments.

GRACE THROUGH SACRAMENTS AND GRACE THROUGH RELATIONSHIPS. In his Church history, Eusebius tells a story passed

---

[16] P. Watzlawick, *How Real Is Real?: Confusion, Disinformation, Communication* (New York: Vintage Books, 1977), 58.

on by Clement I of Rome, concerning St. John the Theologian in
which the Apostle, under obedience to the Holy Spirit, prophetically
entrusts a young homeless adolescent he sees in Ephesus to the local
bishop's care. The bishop baptizes him and offers him the Sacraments
of the Church and then leaves him to his own devices with the result
that the young man becomes a notorious gang leader. Some years
later, the Apostle, already an old man, upon hearing the words of the
bishop describing what has happened to him, jumps on a horse and
rides out into the desert to find the young man in his encampment,
where he risks his life approaching him. According to Eusebius, he
then "interceded for him with many prayers, shared with him the
ordeal of continuous fasting and brought his mind around by the en-
chanting power of words, and did not leave him we are told, until he
had brought him back to the Church."[17]

This story of the relationship between the Holy Spirit, the Sacraments and ascetical disciplines of the Church and the importance
of developing a therapeutic alliance through dialogue and personal
sacrifice invites the question: "How are the Uncreated Divine energies present in and mediated through the Holy Mysteries of the
Church by way of the activities of the priest related to the Grace of
God given in and through those lay mental health providers who offer pastoral care and counseling to suffering persons without being
ordained? Many, if not most, psychological problems may be considered essentially to have spiritual etiologies and not all priests are
able to 'heal' them, though the Sacraments administered by them
remain effective regardless of the state of the priest's moral and/or
ascetical fidelity. Healing is a communal activity of the Church. A
related question is "What is different about the relationship and effect of Grace conferred in ordination to the priesthood on persons
as contrasted with the Grace offered through unordained Orthodox
Christian mental health counselors, physicians and others seeking to
serve Christ through diakonal ministries as lay persons? Must one be

---

[17] Eusebius, *The History of the Church* (London: Penguin Books, 1989), 83–85.

an ordained clergy for counseling to be legitimately considered as effective pastoral care? How does the Grace offered in the Sacraments by a priest who 'cannot heal' compare with the Grace offered through the prayers of a God-bearing elder who is unordained? Or within the context of a counseling relationship in which the Holy Spirit's activity is clearly evident by way of the results even though the counselor is neither ordained priest nor a holy person?

PSYCHOLOGIZING THE SPIRITUAL AND SPIRITUALIZING THE PSYCHOLOGICAL. In California, some years ago, a young man came to his pastor complaining of depression and he was given counsel to read Scripture and pray more. After he committed suicide, the family sued the minister on the grounds that he failed to refer him for evaluation for depression to a physician or psychiatrist. The family won the suit, thus raising the bar in terms of what clergy must know about the current mental health field in order to provide appropriate standard of care for medically and psychologically treatable syndromes.

At the other end of the stick, psychiatrist Gerald May related an example in which a pastoral counselor sent a woman to him for consultation, with whom he had been working for over a year. He had diagnosed her with depression and sent her to a physician who had placed her on antidepressants, but she had only grown worse. After one session with her, Dr. May sent her back to the counselor suggesting that she had a "hunger for God" that was not being addressed and that she needed spiritual direction. This suggestion was followed up with the result that the woman's depression quickly cleared up and she did not need medicine any longer.[18]

Clearly, both priest and lay mental health counselor work in an arena which, being concerned with the human person, necessarily must be concerned with both the Uncreated Divine Energies as well as those of the natural world, with psychopathology, sickness and

---

[18] Gerald May, MD, from a lecture, "Spiritual Guidance and Clinical Care," attended by the author at Valdosta State University in Georgia (1993).

with sin[19] as well as health and growth and meaning. Pastoral counseling involves intuition and science, prayer, care and spiritual discernment as well as diagnostic precision. Both the gifts of the priestly
office and those of the lay pastoral caregiver are activated by faith,
hope, love and vulnerability in the present moment to the activity of
Holy Spirit acting in concert with the collective data of established
bodies of knowledge and those as yet unknown to science. Each area
demands a special kind of discipline and is confirmed and guided
by a special kind of integrated knowing in the context of a caring
relationship. Each calls for the same quality of ascetical sobriety and
attention that are part of hesychastic prayer in order to facilitate the
person finding a fit that is *just right* in his/her life situation.

FINDING THE 'FIT': TWO DIAGNOSTICIANS. I would like to offer
two bookends to frame our discussion. The first comes from Dr.
Michael Crichton, a physician, explorer, and raconteur, who in his
autobiographical journal *Travels* includes an account of scientific precision that is important to consider as we begin investigation of this
question of the relationship between faith and science in the practice
of psychotherapy. He poses the following as a 'thought experiment.'[20]

> Think of a person you know well.
> Now make any correct descriptive statement about that person.
> *George is an even-tempered man.*
> Now consider that statement. Is it really correct?
> The chances are, as you consider it, you will begin to re-
> member times when George lost his temper, or was upset about
> something, or in a bad mood for some reason. You will think of
> the exceptions.

---

[19] Cf. J. Chirban (ed.), *Sickness or Sin: Spiritual Discernment and Differential Diagnosis* (Brookline, MA: Holy Cross Orthodox Press, 2001) and S. Muse (ed.),
Raising Lazarus: Integral Healing in Orthodox Christianity (Brookline, MA:
Holy Cross Orthodox Press, 2005).
[20] M. Crichton, *Travels* (New York: Alfred Knopf, 1988), 403–406.

So you must admit the statement is not quite accurate. You could modify it to say, *George is often an even-tempered man,* but that is actually just evasive. That word 'often' merely says the statement is sometimes correct but sometimes not. And since it does not tell when the statement is not correct, it is not very helpful.

So you would have to be more explicit, to give a fuller statement.

George is usually an even-tempered man, except on Mondays when his favorite football team lost the day before, or when his wife had a fight with him, or when he gets tired and cranky — usually late in the week — but not always — or when his boss gives him a hard time, or when he has to rewrite a report, or, when he has to go out of town ... or when ... or when ...

Pretty soon you see that your descriptive statement is turning into an essay. And you still have not covered all the things you know. It is still not complete ... In fact, it is hopeless to try to make a complete statement about George's ever-changing temper. The subject is too complicated. It was doomed from the start.

So let's start all over.

George is neat and orderly.

That is unquestionably true, you think. George is always neatly dressed, and his desk is always tidy.

But have you ever seen the workbench in his garage at home? What a mess! Tools scattered all around. His wife is always after him to clean it up. And what about the trunk of his car? All kinds of junk in there that he never bothers to clean out.

George is usually neat and orderly.

But by now you can see where this modification is eventually going to end up — in another essay.

So let's make a different statement, one that is both concise and complete.

George has gray hair.

That does it, you think. He has gray hair and there is no question about it.

Of course, not all of his hair is gray. Most of it is, though, especially around the temples and the back of the neck... Then, too, even if George has gray hair now, he did not a few years ago. And at some time in the future, he will no longer have gray hair, he will have white hair. So this is only a correct description of George's hair right now, at this moment in time. It is not a description of George in some universal, invariant way.

Let's try again...

George is a man.

Well, yes. But 'man' is rather unspecific; it is really a culturally determined word, when you get right down to it. At birth, he was not considered a man. You have to attain a certain age and position in society to be considered a man.

George is a male.

Now, that is unarguable. George is, and always was, a male. There is no way to dispute that. It is a true statement about George; both now and in the past. It is an eternal verity. It is an accurate description of the reality of George.

Of course, by 'male,' we mean that he has an X and a Y chromosome. But we do not know that for sure, do we? George might have an extra chromosome. He might only be *apparently* male...

And so on.

There are two points about this exercise in making statements about George. The first is that every single statement we make about George can be contradicted. Why is that?

It's because our statements about George are only approximations, simplifications. The real person we call George is always more complicated than any statement we have made about him. Thus, we can always refer to that real person and find in him a contradiction to what we have said.

The second point is that the statements about George that are most securely held are also the least interesting. We cannot say anything comprehensive about his moods or his neatness or his complex behavior. We are on much safer ground describing the simplest aspects of his physical appearance: hair color, height, sex, and so on. There — with some qualifications of measurement error and changes over time — we can be sure of what we are saying.

But only a tailor would take pride in this fact. And, indeed, a tailor might. After making many fittings for George, and adjusting the patterns at each fitting, the tailor might eventually be able to cut a suit of clothes for George entirely in his absence, and when George came in for a final fitting, the finished clothes would fit him perfectly!

This is a triumph of the art of measurement, but the clothes that fit so wonderfully are draped over a creature that the tailor may not know at all. Nor is the tailor interested. He could not care less about other aspects of George. It is not his job.

On the other hand, what interests *us* most about George are not his measurements. We are most interested in precisely those other aspects, which the tailor, by definition, does not care about. We find it far more difficult to define those other aspects of George than the tailor does to define George's measurements.

The tailor can do his job of description perfectly. We, on the other hand, cannot really describe George at all.

Now, since the tailor is so good — so clearly successful — at what he does, we might be tempted to ask the tailor, "Who is George?"

The tailor will answer, "George is a forty-four long."

And if we protest that this answer is not really satisfactory, the tailor will reply with assurance that he is unquestionably right about George, because he can cut a whole suit of clothes that will fit George perfectly the moment he walks in the door.

This, in essence, is the problem with the scientific view of reality. Science is a kind of glorified tailoring enterprise, a method for taking measurements that describe something — reality — that may not be understood at all …

It would be crazy to think that reality is a forty-four long. Yet it seems as if that is what Western society has done. For hundreds of years, science has been so successful that the tailor has taken over our society. His knowledge seems so much more precise and powerful than the knowledge offered by other disciplines, such as history or psychology or art.

Elder Porphyrios, the Chaplain of the Polyclinic Hospital in Athens, who did not receive a formal academic education, and used a different form of measuring, responds with equal exactitude, yet much more effectively in relating to the real person in a specific situation. The elder's 'client', a young priest, writes:

I was going through a trial that I had never experienced before ... of great length and great intensity, which threatened to tear me apart both physically and spiritually. I was vulnerable because the wound came from somewhere where I had innocently expected support or, at the very least, understanding. I was at a complete dead end, and I did not know what to do, because I saw a totally unacceptable solution in all the choices open to me.

In the days that followed, the situation became explosive. I could put the whole thing down to one event, and I did not know if it was from the devil or from God. I met my spiritual father and told him my dilemma. If it came from God, I was prepared to accept it, however much it would cost me; if, however, it came from the devil, I was determined to fight it to the end. My spiritual father, a man of rare genius, humility and love, was both forgiving toward those who had created the problem for me, while at the same time, pointed out what must be done (something I had difficulty in accepting). However, when faced with my dilemma, he stopped. He did not offer me his opinion but said: "The person capable of answering your difficult question is Elder Porphyrios. I don't know what you'll have to do, ask, phone, search, until you find him. He will solve the puzzle for you. Afterwards, come back and we'll talk about it again. Until then, I can't tell you anything on the matter."

I expressed my fear that, with what he had to say, he might tie down my freedom. He replied that Fr. Porphyrios is discerning and never ties anyone down; on the contrary, he respects the freedom of others. He also gave me the telephone numbers of three people who knew him.

From that moment on, armed with this 'referral' from my spiritual father, I started the search to uncover Elder Porphyrios. At the time, the elder did not have a permanent abode. I phoned two of the people who had contact with him, but got no answer. Fortunately, I found the third, who was more than willing to put me in touch with the elder as soon as he could. Days, even weeks, passed by and I kept phoning my stranger, but he did not have any relevant news.

Until...late one afternoon, as I was walking home from work engulfed in the sorrow that had burdened my soul for months, I suddenly felt something unexpected within me. The clouds of sorrow dissolved, a bright warmth comforted me with calmness, and I felt like singing.

I secretly made the sign of the cross over myself, again and again and whispered full of disquiet: "Lord have mercy!" I knew myself well enough in such situations. These kinds of problems needed time for me to get over them; the sorrow always declined gradually. Since I was at the very center of my trial, what did this sudden and unexpected shift from sorrow to joy mean? However, a few minutes later, that joy vanished, and the sorrow returned. This strange happening was to repeat itself in the days that followed. The mystery was solved when I was informed much later that my stranger, who was to become an exceptional friend, had contacted the elder and had given him my name, and it had been placed on his prayer list.

In the meantime, I impatiently waited to see the elder. At last, one spring morning, I heard a lady's voice—it was the churchwarden of the Chapel of St. Gerasimos at the Polyclinic Hospital. She told me that Elder Porphyrios would be able to see me at 10:00 AM in the chapel. I went down to Omonia Square immediately. Various emotions inundated me on the way: hopeful expectation, uneasiness, curiosity, reservation. What could an elderly, poorly educated monk possibly say about my problem!

I arrived at the chapel and waited. When my turn came, I went up to the confession room. A small-framed little old father was waiting for me. I was impressed as soon as he approached me. I kissed his hand and sat opposite him. He looked at me from behind his glasses with a couple of bright blue and lively eyes. Throughout that moment, I felt that his gaze was piercing my soul. I felt that this person knew me already. I noticed, at the same time, that his lips were whispering something, and I realized that he was praying continuously. He gave the impression that he both was and was not present, that he was both here and elsewhere at the same time.

He opened his mouth, and I heard his voice for the first time — refined, calm and charming. "Well then, what do you want to tell me?"

I remembered my spiritual father's advice and put my problem to him very briefly, no longer than five minutes and then I fell quiet. The elder listened thoughtfully and sighed every now and then. I had the feeling that he was suffering my pain more than I was. Then I was bombarded by a host of novel surprises. The elder analyzed my character with great care. He described and gave reasons for both my faults and my merits with such accuracy that even my own parents could not have come close to it. I saw my own self for the very first time, as I really am and not as I would like to be. This self-revelation was a moving experience for me. It gave me the impression that I was born, or rather re-born. Afterwards, the Elder came to my problem. He shed light on it and explained it from all points of view. Both from my point of view and from that of the other people who were involved. With great sympathy, he pointed the correct and mistaken moves taken by myself and by the others, whose characters he also described. Then he assured me that the event that led to the dead-end dilemma was a temptation from the devil. He advised me about the way to face it. My spiritual father had suggested the same method.

Then he caught hold of my hand and took my pulse and pointed out my bodily sicknesses. This diagnosis was a summary of the sicknesses discovered by my doctor years before; it was also an explanation for them. Finally, he blessed me by making the sign of the cross over my head and said with much love, "Well, get going now and we'll talk again the next time we meet."

I got up, kissed his hand. Overcome with emotions of wonder, peace and joy, I went towards the door. There, I turned right around and stood still, looking at him as though thunderstruck and trying to comprehend all the unbelievable things that had just happened to me — things that challenged my innate disbelief and rationalism. The elder looked at me, smiled and said, "Why did you stop? Just do what I told you." I replied, "Elder, I didn't stop because I felt it was difficult to do what you told me, but rather to express my surprise. What you have told me to do is exactly what my spiritual father advised me to do. But, while I had some inner difficulty with him, with you, the way you explain the problems, I have no difficulty at all with continuing, not in thought, not in my heart, not in will. On the contrary, I feel that I would have rejected all other solutions other than the one you gave. It fits me perfectly, like a glove. I shall carry it out with pleasure." A broad grin lit up the elder's face, which shined with joy, and added: "Go, go on now."

I bowed to him and left. As I went on my way, spiritually enchanted by the discovery of a real *starets*, I realized the most wonderful thing of all the things that he had surprisingly revealed to me. With unrivalled pastoral skill, the elder was able to calm my troubled soul, in a brief amount of time, and to make

me joyfully desire what I had rejected just a short while before:
God's will regarding my complicated problem.[21]

Can you imagine going to someone who did not feel anything for
you, who was not suffering some kind of pain because of your pain?
Or can you imagine your priest and confessor taking all of the *Philokalia* and the Bible — everything we value in Orthodox tradition and
downloading it into the most sophisticated computer in all creation
that synthesized it and sifted it and organized it perfectly? And then
you go to the confessor and tell him, "Father, I'm in trouble in my
marriage and I don't know what to do." And your priest consults this
computer, which goes click-click-click: "Thou shalt not be divorced
except under these conditions" according to canon law — ding-ding-
ding! Here's your penance. All applied legalistically, formulaically,
without pastoral discernment and care for the specifics of your situations and disposition? Horrible! Because the essential ingredient of
compassion is missing, along with a precise and detailed understanding of the person's situation, even though there is perfect measurement in an idealized, abstract form. Measuring humanity by the idealized form, whether religious or scientific, is just another form of
oppression when compassion, mercy and practical wisdom necessary
to find the exact fit are missing.

I should have called these two bookends 'foils,' because the place
where most of us live is in between the two. Rare are persons like Elder
Porphyrios who are so responsive to the Holy Spirit that they 'see' the
exact fit that sets someone free and it is recognized immediately. I think
it must also be acknowledged that Grace, working through the client's
faith, provides the powerful anesthesia of therapeutic relationship of
love and acceptance that opens the heart to receive the medicine.

Secondly, science is not nearly so useless as Dr. Crichton makes
it seem in his amusing anecdote; however, abstracted from the con-

---

[21] C. Yiannitsiotis, *With Elder Porphyrios: A Spiritual Child Remembers*, trans.
Marina Robb (Athens, Greece: Holy Convent of the Transfiguration of the Savior, 2001), 28–33.

crete situations of our lives, knowledge, even spiritual knowledge, can be far off the mark. While it can be admitted as Elder Paisos of Mount Athos suggests, "Whoever thinks that he can come to know the mysteries of God through external scientific theory, resembles the fool who wants to see Paradise with a telescope," it is also true that science should not be ignored for what it does have to offer in its own sphere of competence in the created word. Anyone who thinks he ought to treat diseases and psychological illness merely by praying while ignoring all that science learns diagnostically through microscopes, MRI's, genetic research and painstaking intersubjectively reflective and mindful dialogue, had better be quite sure of being in attendance of the Holy Spirit! Even Elder Porphyrios began to read scientific journals to complement his direct noetic vision.

GRACE, FAITH AND THE PERSON OF THE THERAPIST. Without a humble attitude and presence that includes loving sensitivity and respect for the other, vulnerability and ascetical fidelity to the Holy Spirit, any one of us, whether armed with the latest science or even genuine spiritual experience, is capable of missing the mark of responding to the uniqueness of a person. This can be either by lack of real meeting with them, losing major aspects of a person as we fit them into the Procrustean bed of our theories or by too imprecise a fit creating a similar problem, resulting from the counselor's own untransformed passions and unconscious countertransference which distort receptivity to the person and her/his disposition of soul and circumstance of life. In the compulsion to fix another, we can unwittingly make the error that Elder Paisios suggests of "trying to clean mucous from a baby's eye with a wire brush." Sincerity of intention and precision in and of themselves, whether scientific or spiritual, do not guarantee effective pastoral care and counseling which is inherent in discerning the exact 'fit' for a person and a given situation.

Secondly, there is reciprocity to healing in which the counselor is also affected. Aboriginal elders, represented by Lila Watson, observe, "If you have come to help me, you're wasting your time; but if you have come recognizing that your liberation is bound up with mine, then let us work together." I believe this existential stance expresses the true relationship within the Orthodox Christian Community and the world — one not of any sort of individual or collective triumphalism, whether overt or more subtle, but rather a clear recognition of the oneness of all humanity which shares a common Creator and a common mutually responsible life. I tell my students, "If you have not been changed by your relationship with your client, then you have not met the person yet." This is because real 'meeting' is never imperialistic in which I who *am* or *have* or *know,* do unto you who *are not* or *have not* or *know not.* Rather it is a co-pilgrimage[22] in which both are changed by the encounter with the Lord who appears in our midst, whether recognized or not, whenever we love one another in this way. Healing and discovery of our true life result from authentic meeting with one where we discover Christ in our midst. As an Orthodox Christian, I believe that it is Christ alone who makes such meeting possible, whether recognized or not — a reality rendered dogmatically by the doctrines of the Incarnation and the perichoresis of the Holy Trinity, which may be considered prototypical and a *sine qua non* for marriage, friendship in community as well as the healing relationship. Healing and growth occur in concrete, specific situations with persons whose essential uniqueness is preserved and enhanced by the mutual self-giving to the other which preserves, liberates and enlivens the whole community.

It is evident in the action of Elder Porphyrios with the young man that Grace and faith are at work. His intervention is noetic, involving direct perception and occurs in this instance, from a dialogue with God about the person, rather than only with the 'client' himself. In effect, the elder is sharing in God's dialogue and 'meeting' with the person whose heart and circumstances the Spirit has searched and known perfectly and, therefore, he is privy to details that the man

---

[22] I am grateful to Barry Estadt who embodied this in his presence, teaching and supervision. Cf. B. K. Estadt, M. Blanchette & J. R. Compton (eds.), *Pastoral Counseling* (Englewood Cliffs, NJ: Prentice Hall, 1983).

has not shared with the elder, but which are known to God. Due to his own ascetical fidelity, continual repentance, faith and vulnerability, the elder is made aware of the diagnosis through the Grace of the Holy Spirit. Shared Christian faith and love enable a depth and quality of therapeutic alliance that could take years to approach from the natural side and could never quite reach apart from the Divine Energies and the actions of Grace. Elder Porphyrios was evidently one of those God-bearing elders whom Metropolitan Hierotheos Vlachos suggests in his books "can heal spiritually" not by virtue of ordination, but by the charism of the Holy Spirit working synergistically and trialogically through their prayers. While this happens to some extent with people through natural intuitive means inherent to the created world, as most counselors have witnessed, the fact that it more consistently occurs through someone like the elder, and in ways that go beyond our current understanding of natural law, appears to signify a certain qualitative difference between the 'God-bearing' dispassionate elder and the ordinary parish priest or lay mental health practitioner in whose life passions continue to fragment the self's motivations causing blindness to the spiritual eye. This has enormously significant implications for the training of pastoral counselors and caregivers who must consider their religious foundations of ascetical struggle, worship, prayer and repentance as primary to an ongoing formation process to be effective pastoral counselors.[23] Yet this is largely neglected by counselor training programs which concentrate on psychological theory and methods as primary.

---

[23] This is not to say that God's Grace is not also at work invisibly between a counselor whose heart is not healed and a client, neither of whom may be Orthodox. This question, along with the relationship between the content and spiritual process that is shared by the Christian kerygma and other religious traditions, involves a number of important and difficult problems that are beyond the scope of this book. However, a helpful theological framing of the question of Grace and life in Christ operative outside of the formal bounds of institutional Christianity, while yet being in Christ, can be found in a book recommended to me by Metropolitan Anthony Bloom in response to my questions to him in this regard. J. Danielou. translated from the French by Felix Faber, *Holy Pagans of the Old Testament* (Wales: Helicon Press, 1960).

Elder Archimandrite Sophrony identifies traditional Orthodox Christian spiritual disciplines of prayer, watchfulness and ascetical fidelity as integral to the formation of persons capable of accurately diagnosing and offering care to suffering persons:

> Eventually the mind sees not the physical heart, but that which is happening within it — the feelings that creep in and the mental images that approach from without … When the attention of the mind is fixed in the heart it is possible to control what happens in the heart, and the battle against passions assumes a rational character. The enemy is recognized and can be driven off by the power of the Name of Christ. With this ascetic feat the heart becomes so highly sensitive, so discerning, that eventually when praying for anyone the heart can tell almost at once the state of the person prayed for.[24]

Science alone, no matter how good it is, cannot come as exact to finding what is needed for a person as can the Holy Spirit; however, this is not a justification or an excuse, as some use it, to refuse all psychotherapy and help except when it comes from a presumed clairvoyant elder or from an Orthodox priest who may have little or no counseling experience and applies canon law from the 9th century "like a wire brush to the baby's eye" in an attempt to heal the person in the 21st century without recognition that the unique circumstances require *economia* and discernment and so contributing to their situation becoming worse than it was before. It would have been better in such a case for the person to have received assistance from a qualified lay counselor who might not even be Orthodox but who brings love and humility to his or her work with others instead of the naïve presumption that 'one size fits all,' or that monastic strictures can be applied to married persons 'living in the world' however dogmatically accurate, without

---

[24] Archimandrite Sophrony. *His Life Is Mine*, trans. Rosemary Edmonds (Crestwood, NY: St. Vladimir's Seminary Press, 1977), 114.

taking time to know the penitent more deeply in order to identify the unique approach that is a developmentally appropriate and timely 'fit.'

Absolute trust in the validity of the eternal Church and the elusive "Patristic Consensus" or "mind of the Fathers" should not be used as an excuse to refuse training in science in favor of concentrating only on prayer as if prayer and science were mutually antagonistic. It is not science or psychology *per se* that is the problem, but rather persons using psychology to usurp religion's place or religion as a reason not to conduct scientific study, of which we should be appropriately critical. In the same way, we should be vigilant that Christian Tradition is not reduced to a self-help psychology or that priests remain ignorant of their own unconscious issues and/or basic standards of care in the field of counseling and psychotherapy.

In my journeys, I have found holy grace-filled elders who had no use for psychology as well as those who found it of immense benefit and sought to draw from both. This alone shows me that God does not leave any stone unturned if it can help restore life. Both the simple and unlearned shepherds, as well as the learned Magi, found their way to the birth of the Christ by different means appropriate to each. Where there are physicians available, God works through them, and where they are not, even the rocks and stones themselves can break open to reveal healing waters and Balaam's donkey can prophesy. St. Basil's parable of the bumble bee remains instructive for Christians in this regard: "Visit every flower and take just that which is needed from each to return to the hive and make honey." All the fruits of the garden of the cosmos are available to humanity. Only the tree that leads to knowledge obtained through monologue instead of trialogue with God and Creation is forbidden in order to protect creation from the suffering brought into being through the damage inherent to this path.

MEDICALIZING OF COUNSELING FIELD. When pastoral counseling and psychotherapy ignore the intuitive noetic dimension of Orthodox Christian life evidenced in persons like Elder Porphyrios along with the disciplines of ascetical fidelity, worship, prayer and spiritual direction, seeking to find legitimacy solely through the technologies of science, a different problem results. We are seeing this in the medicalizing of the counseling field under the sway of business models and the technologies which regard persons as reducible to a set of body parts or brain states, like a car engine, which are (or should be) responsive to a specific set of healing ingredients identified by research methods, in order to get the desired results. Yet meta-analysis of 40 years psychotherapy research[25] is clear in showing that the medical model cannot begin to explain the data of outcome studies in psychotherapy, which involves body and soul as an inseparable entity. Specific 'ingredients' of therapy account for less than 1% of variance in therapeutic outcome while the contextual variables of the person of the therapist, the quality of therapeutic alliance, etc. account for at least 40% of the variance.

It is appropriate for Orthodox Christians to be critical of various limiting reductionistic scientific assumptions implicit in the methodologies and theories of psychotherapy just as we must be discerning of theological heresies that dilute or distort the fullness of Orthodox faith. Persons are unities of body and soul. Psychotherapy cannot afford to ignore medicine, and medicine cannot afford to ignore the spiritual, psychological and emotional dimensions of persons expressed by their physical illnesses which are only fully engaged in the mystery of a love relationship involving Divine Grace.

> "Although the human body in its biological reality, is subject to laws that govern the functioning of every living organism, the body cannot be treated like just any other living organism, since it is the body of a human person from which it cannot be dissociated without losing its very nature … By refusing to consider the spiritual dimension of human persons when we seek to alleviate their physical ailments, we do them immense harm."[26]

[25] B. Wampold, *The Great Psychotherapy Debate: Models, Methods and Findings* (London: Lawrence Erlbaum Associates, Publishers, 2001).
[26] J. Larchet, *The Theology of Illness* (Crestwood, NY: St. Vladimir's Seminary

For these reasons, I prefer a practical approach to the question of "What makes counseling pastoral?" Counseling is pastoral to the degree that it clears obstacles from the way of a person fully embracing the path of deification in Christ. Practically speaking, this means that whatever approach is taken, it avoids sacrificing the unique life and circumstances of persons to the dull blade of reductionistic abstract representations whether these are in the form of scientific precision or moral absolutes with regard to doctrine, ritual and/or canon law or to cultural fads and political pressures that support ideological biases. Application of science and practical theology to a person's unique life and circumstance requires much more than a cookie cutter, manualized, technical approach or uncritical acceptance of prevailing cultural norms and religious dogma. Above all, it requires faith, hope, love and humility, which, according to Grace, render these medicines effective. (Contrast this with Jesus' criticism of some of the Pharisees whose way of applying religious doctrine from unexamined lives created further burdens for their 'clients.')[27]

In practice, such love involves the difficulty of balancing rational science with receptivity to irrational Holy Spirit-illumined perception with regard to identifying the 'fit' for a particular person in a given situation. This is a function of trialogue which entails the difficulty of meeting a person along what Martin Buber referred to as the 'narrow ridge' between the *a priori* surety of mathematical models and the absolute limitless freedom and uniqueness of the created world with all its paradox and uncertainty. Counseling is pastoral to the degree that it evidences respect for the limitless complexity and uniqueness of each person in the sight of God for whom every hair is numbered and every sparrow that falls from the tree is noticed. The I-Thou relationship Buber speaks of is what reinvigorates and changes us through the miracle of 'meeting.' Because Christ is in the midst of this 'meeting' as in Emmaus, it is transformative and reorienting in

---

Press, 2002), 14.

[27] Cf., for example, *Matthew*, chapter 23 and by contrast *Acts* 15:10.

contrast with merely 'improving' or relieving psychological or physical symptoms.

Without such trialogue in which 'I' and 'Thou' are linked by 'love' — the Eternal Thou of Christ who is forever in our midst wherever such dialogue occurs — whatever our theoretical orientation and motivation, it seems to me we are approaching the counseling relationship merely technically and thus it remains monological — I-It. This inevitably leads to approaching clients and speaking of them, as the former American Secretary of Defense Donald Rumsfeld did in his offhand comments during a briefing, when he referred to our soldiers as 'fungible'[28] — 'replaceable parts'. This, indeed, is the view of a tailor, for whom the ontological mystery and existential concreteness and irreplaceable value of each human person is reduced to a mere commodity or 'case'— ciphers in an abstract schema inevitably serving utilitarian interests, whether military, corporate, religious or otherwise, which are a denial of the dignity and worth of persons made in the Image of God for whom Christ offers Himself in sacrifice. As Martin Buber has warned, "Monologue is Lucifer." It is only through what he called "the dialogue of meeting" that we become human beings or, as Jesus pointed out to His disciples, "Wherever two or more are gathered in my name, there *I AM* in their midst." Such a dialogue becomes a trialogue as is expressed in the familiar Orthodox liturgical praise, "Christ is in our midst!", which invites the response, "He was, is and ever shall be." This is true existentially only to the degree that, as Christians, we do not refuse to 'meet' even our enemy in the love of Christ who is 'between' us.

By reducing people to 'fit' a model, however accurate as an abstraction, the value of the human person is sacrificed on the altar of an illusory precision rather than rising to life in mercy on the Way which invites the growth and transformation of the other through the self-sacrifice and loving service of the counselor in dialogue with the other until that 'fit' is discovered, which is 'Truth

---

[28] Secretary of Defense Donald Rumsfeld — Thursday, April 15, 2004 2:17 PM EDT.

and Life' for the person in his or her particular circumstances. The pastoral counselor's task of remaining receptive and available in non-judgmental compassionate interest to the particular person in the here and now, rather than driven by the theoretical agenda, is well-described by the British psychoanalyst Wilfred Bion, who observes, "the psychoanalyst should aim at achieving a state of mind so that at every session he feels he has not seen the patient before. If he feels he has, he is treating the wrong patient."[29] By avoiding the necessity for 'not knowing' — the sacrifice of certainty on the part of the caregiver that is a prerequisite for this path — the greater life of soul is always sacrificed for the sake of the smaller life of ego in order to have power and control over life rather than to enter into it as Passion-bearers as Christ invites. Clinging to power and control, whether in religious or scientific form, is at the root of every refusal to approach the other in love and mercy as a mystery forever beyond my ability to fully diagnose or 'know' on my own through my own limited personal experience. As we have done unto the least among us, including ourselves, in flesh and blood, so we have done unto the Lord. Attachment to imposing the letter of the Law brings death. The Spirit, by contrast, "which, like the wind, blows where it will and no one knows whence it cometh or where it goes," cannot be contained by the dead letter or by mathematics, and yet these all receive their life and being from it.

Eric Fromm, in his lovely book *The Art of Loving*, captures this with his arresting image of the scientist who can name and categorize every aspect of the butterfly pinned to the page, except for its life, which can only be known through the freedom of love while it is alive, flitting from one flower to the next. For me, the answer to the question, "What makes counseling pastoral?" is simply the 'fit.' This is because the sheep will only obey the shepherd's voice. The right approach is the one that actually works to set people free. The yoke

---

[29] Cited in D. Wallin, *Attachment in Psychotherapy* (New York: Guilford Press, 2007), p. 329.

that is 'easy' and the 'burden that is light' is the one that fits EXACT-
LY — the one made ONLY for you or for me; the one that allows us to
'hit the mark' for which God intends us in a given situation and over
a lifetime. If not for the imagery of sheep and shepherd that perme-
ate Christian history, the English word 'pastor' would not be so rich
with evocations of spiritual care and comfort. The gist of what I am
saying is rooted in what this imagery is meant to convey about our
relationship to the Good Physician of our souls and bodies and about
the redemptive process of Salvation that results from it.

When asked the purpose of lifelong ascetical struggle and the
employment of various spiritual disciplines, St. Anthony is said to
have responded, "To become yourself." This same understanding is
implicit in the question St. Silouan the Athonite asked the Cauca-
sian ascetic, Fr. Stratonicus, in their remarkable conversation preserved by Archimandrite Sophrony.[30] In this, St. Silouan asked the
renowned elder a question that might well be the most important
question for a counselor in training to ask his supervisor or for his
supervisor to ask him or her. "What is perfect speech?" Fr. Stratonicus was suddenly speechless and in humility deferred to the much
younger Silouan, who responded, "Perfect speech is to say only what
the Holy Spirit bids us to say." St. Seraphim of Sarov's observation
to his disciple Motovilov, "Acquire the Holy Spirit and thousands
around you will find their salvation," became the heart of the book
by I. M. Kontzevitch entitled *Acquisition of the Holy Spirit in Ancient
Russia*,[31] which, as its title suggests, shows the Holy Spirit's activity
in us as constituting the 'Way' of Christian development that leads
to fullness of life or *theosis*. The definition of what makes counseling
pastoral is that it is redemptive in this way, not because it addresses
a disorder specified in the DSM-IV, but because it takes its approach
and developmental goal from Christ who opens the way to deification. The implications here for the training of Orthodox Christian

---

[30] A. Sophrony, *St. Silouan the Athonite* (Essex, England: Stavropegic Monastery
of St. John the Baptist, 1991).
[31] Platina, CA: St. Herman Alaska Brotherhood, 1989.

priests and counselors who would be good spiritual physicians are obvious in that they involve both the fullness of Orthodox worship and ascetical life as well as the rigors of self-examination, scientific study and the emotional intelligence, intuitive art and skill of interpersonal relations.

The litmus test or plumbline by which I would evaluate the pastoral effectiveness of counseling is the degree to which it contributes to and facilitates the formation of a *person* in Christ by clearing away obstacles to the fullness of life in the Church and the indwelling of the Holy Spirit, which is evidenced in one's love for the whole world without distinction, "for those who love us and those who hate us." In this sense, the Orthodox Christian psychotherapist is midwife, gardener and cognitive and emotional masseuse seeking to facilitate and cooperate with the healing and developmental processes of God to bring redemptive life to those whom God has created and loved at great price to Himself, as we see in the cross and passion of Christ depicted in the Gospels.

Epistemologically, science (dealing with the created world) and religion (dealing with the interaction between the created and the uncreated worlds) are both empirical to the extent that each requires a specific methodology for engaging the data of their subjects and both rest on unseen faith convictions about that data which are inseparable from existential stances in the world that flow from them. For example, if I believe that I can examine the natural world and explain it without God, I am taking a faith stance to interpret empirical sensory data which will ultimately have implications regarding the meaning and purpose of life and the ethics of how I live as a result of this meaning. If I see the same data with the faith conviction of its origins and life in God, a different set of values and actions will emerge through a different interpretation of the 'data' which is indeed, if Einstein is correct, changed by the lens of the theory through which we see the data. From the Orthodox perspective, the primary hermeneutic or interpretive lens for seeing the world as "declaring the glory of God" does not arise from within the created world itself, but from beyond it, from the uncreated world of the divine energies through the revelation of the Holy Spirit, which acts with increasing clarity as the heart becomes purified through Grace.[32]

In the same way, only those actions that facilitate persons facing self, other and the existential conditions of life through the illumination of the Holy Spirit, can be said to be 'according to the science of sciences' of the patristic physicians of the soul as portrayed in the collection of the *Philokalia*. Orthodox Christianity has measured effectiveness empirically, not so much through brief, time-limited, modern, devised, double blind, randomized, controlled studies but rather over millennia-long periods of history replete with anecdotal examples from huge catchment areas involving millions of subjects. In this way, a replicable formation process of human development is detailed in the patristic writings and history evidenced by the fruits of the Holy Spirit in the lives of persons who people come to regard as 'saints.' Orthodox Christian history is in effect a two-thousand year 'drug trial' far more rigorous than the tiny time-limited studies pharmaceutical companies use to get new medicines on the market. Significantly, Abram Hoffer, MD, Ph.D., the first psychiatrist to conduct randomized, double blind, controlled studies in psychiatry in the U.S. insists that "it is always through anecdotal evidence that discoveries of science are made which are only then confirmed in double blind controlled studies."[33] For this reason, he ceased long ago to bother with such studies as he is more interested in furthering the field through practical results made through discovery in unique individual cases.

---

[32] For an accessible discussion of the difference between the scientific approach to reality and the process of purification of the heart stemming from Grace in Orthodox tradition, cf. Kyriacos Markides, *The Mountain of Silence: A Search for Orthodox Spirituality* (New York: Doubleday, 2001). For a more in-depth encounter with ancient sources, cf. G. E. H. Palmer, P. Sherrard, and K. Ware (trans. and eds.), *The Philokalia: The Complete Text: Vols. I–IV* (London: Faber and Faber, 1995).

[33] Personal correspondence with the author responding to the question of why Dr. Hoffer no longer conducts such randomized trials in his work.

Documents and writings of the Church from the Gospels to the ancient desert Abbas and Ammas and modern saints acquire respect because of the trustworthiness that accrues to them from those in whom the Holy Spirit testifies to their value through specific and concrete details in people's lives. Over time, they eventually become the empirical validation or canon of the Church's 'medicines' of Word and Sacrament, ascetical methods and guidelines for living. Heresy can be viewed as a form of 'medicine' or treatment which is incomplete and, therefore, likely to lead to different results. This is not to say that there is only one starting point on the Way which is the same for everyone, but insofar as Christ seeks out the lost wherever we are, the starting point for the one true Way that leads to life, can only begin in the place where "I AM." As Geronda Antonios Romaios of Holy Gregoriou Monastery on Mount Athos has observed, "There are as many ways to Christ as there are people,"[34] thereby recognizing the unique life circumstances and calling that must be appreciated and taken into consideration for each person.

When Orthodox Christians sing in the Liturgy, "We have found the true faith," it is, therefore, not a license to confuse the Living Christ with His representation in "orthodoxy" for a static form or model that obviates the uniqueness or freedom of other persons to find Christ in their situations, for Christ is "in all places and fills all things." He is larger than the institutional Church as He was larger than the Temple and the Orthodoxy of the Law "made by human hands" in Israel. Thus, the Russian theologian Khomiakov's perspicacious remark, "We know where the Church is, but we do not know where it is not." Or as one Old Calendar traditionalist bishop wisely cautioned a young zealous priest, who like James and John (whom Jesus called "the sons of Thunder") asked if they should "call fire down" on those who were casting out demons in Jesus' name, but not affiliated with them (Luke 9:54), when he was decrying the absence of Grace in the new calendar churches "who do not believe like

---

[34] Related from personal conversation with a friend of the author.

us!" — "Where there is no love, there is nothing to discuss." This is
a corrective to pride and authoritarian fundamentalism masquerading as faith in zealous persons who have unwittingly sacrificed the
Grace-infused love relationship of faith for religion as an ideology
which all too quickly yields the fruits that render us enemies of the
very Source of love we proclaim to serve. By absolutizing the Truth of
Orthodoxy (which is Christ) as a form, however correct, it serves to
separate us from others rather than unite. Such zealotry for the truth
serves the same self-protective function at the process level as do the
various characterological defenses which insulate persons from actually being vulnerable to encountering others. We remain walled off
from our own depths, clinging to a religious abstraction rather than
encountering the living Christ whom we cannot see except in the
faces and in the lives of our brothers and sisters, including those who
seem to us for whatever reason "the least of these." We do well to
remind ourselves that where there is no love, there is also no truth.

A WORKING DEFINITION OF PASTORAL COUNSELING. Counseling is pastoral to the degree that it

- emerges out of an existential stance that accords absolute and
  limitless freedom to the person to choose her/his own way while
- bringing to bear science, humble faith in God as healer and
  respect for the mystery of the person whose self (life) as the
  Apostle Paul observes, is forever beyond any diagnosis "hidden with Christ in God"[35] and which
- evidences a love that endures all that is part of an eternally
  open-ended dialogical relationship with the other
- rooted, as the Apostle John observes, not in the fact that I love
  the client, but that God first loved each of us as is set forth in
  the Gospels as revealed through the Holy Spirit at work among
  the cloud of witnesses who make up the Church Universal.

---

[35] Col. 3:3.

In terms of the relationship between science and religion, or whether there can be such a chimera as an "Orthodox Christian psychotherapy," which was my starting point, there is an acknowledgement of faith in the opening words of the Gospel according to St. John, which states that God in Christ is the Uncreated Logos who is iconically represented in all physical creation which is brought into being through Him. Science and religion are thus ultimately expressions of one Source.[36] Just as the Uncreated Essence of God is one with the Divine Energies by which Grace illumines and vivifies all creation as fire does iron so that the two are virtually indistinguishable and yet distinct, so the Created order never becomes God by essence, but yet by Grace is fully penetrated by the Spirit and brought into Communion with the Logos. Holy Communion is ultimately a love relationship, not a technical, mathematical operation or magical action. Freedom and love are forever existentially in tension in the created Word. God remains at work in history and through the choices of each man and woman who constitute the "royal priesthood of all believers"[37] called to serve God's purposes. Taking up the cross in one's own life and circumstances is according to Jesus, the means of sharing the Passion of Christ and entering into the heart of God's love for the world. As each of us groans and sighs under the influence of the Holy Spirit while we "work out our salvation in fear and trembling," creation itself groans and sighs until it is in harmony with its Creator, and the Lamb and the Lion are able to lie down together in the new Jerusalem through the reconciling power of the Holy Spirit who ultimately makes such a 'fit' possible. The Holy Spirit is the Counselor who brings about the 'fitting' of our yokes and provides our wedding garments in place of our garments of skin that give us entrance into the Divine wedding feast.

---

[36] Cf. the excellent analysis in this regard of Professor Alexei V. Nesteruk, *Light for the East: Theology, Science, and the Eastern Orthodox Tradition* (Minneapolis: Fortress Press, 2003).

[37] I Peter 2:9.

ABSTRACTION, **E**XTRACTION AND **D**ISTRACTION: **T**HE **F**AIL-URE OF **H**UMAN **P**RESENCE. One of the fathers of object rela-tions psychology, the physician D. W. Winnicott, was once asked by a group of pastors, "When can we tell if someone needs a psychiatrist or will benefit from a pastoral conversation?" He liked the question I am told, and his response was a simple one, easily understandable to most psychotherapists, but perhaps strange at first hearing to his audience. "If when you are having a conversation with the person you are bored, then they need a psychiatrist. Otherwise, whatever you do, they will receive some benefit from the conversation."

What was he getting at? Boredom is a manifestation of the distur-bance of human *presence*, and the attentive person can quickly notice a deeper problem when there is a disturbance here. Depending on its severity and etiology, loss of presence is the cardinal symptom of severe mental illness, of captivity by addiction and of severe trauma. It is a measure of the severity of every psychological and emotion-al problem that plagues humanity, including spiritual illnesses de-scribed by various patristic authors in their analysis of the struggle with untransformed passions afflicting soul and body which are es-sentially psychosomatic energies diverted from the spiritual harmo-ny[38] of fully alive persons.

Where there is schizophrenia, dementia and psychosis, damage to human presence is primarily one of *abstraction*. The person may be mentally preoccupied with solving world problems or obsessing and ruminating over having committed the unpardonable sin, yet cannot even manage to take a bath. Or they may be so severely de-pressed that they have lost initiative and the ability to concentrate, to make choices and to feel ordinary pleasure in living. The life has 'gone out of their eyes' so to speak. Drawing from St. Maximos the Confessor's spiritual anthropology in referring to the mind (*nous*), soul (*epithymos*) and the incensive power (*thymos*), we can say that

---

[38] Cf. H. Vlachos, *The Illness and Cure of the Soul in Orthodox Tradition* (Levadia, Greece: Birth of the Theotokos Monastery, 1993) and Palmer, Sherrard and Ware (eds. and trans.), *The Philokalia Volumes I–IV* (London: Faber & Faber, 1995).

for these persons, the deeper intuitive *nous* is separated off from the *epithymos* and *thymos* due to their illness. Their 'I', cut from integration with body and soul, leaves them to wander "like the Gentiles, lost in the imagination of their minds." Suffering in this way, the person loses both the will and the ability to act in an integrated way along with the ability to be interested in and contribute to genuine human dialogue.

In the case of addiction and the afflictive emotions or 'passions', as they are called in Orthodox Christian anthropology, the damage is primarily one of *distraction*. A kind of hypnosis holds sway in the person due to being attracted to various forms of titillation which overcome the soul by drawing off energies of the body in such a way that the soul is momentarily beguiled by the search for further stimulation which leads to a more serious condition, which St. Isaac the Syrian diagnoses as a form of spiritual beguilement leading to spiritual blindness for "the knowledge of God does not reside in a body that loves comforts." In this condition, the body and/or the false self dominate the soul through a group of '*I*'s' that are semi-autonomous in the psyche, rather than being obedient to the Spirit through the soul when it is protected both by discernment of the *nous* and the incensive power or 'holy anger' of directed *thymos* which is able to stand guard and help maintain ascetical fidelity to real life which involves facing things as they are with the full sense of one's physical presence. When this hypnotic distortion repeatedly occurs, captivity or addiction result and the path to theosis is impeded in contrast to the state of health which occurs, as Jesus observes, "When your *eye* (*nous* at one with heart) be single, your whole body will be full of light."[39]

We are particularly vulnerable to the disruption of distraction whenever God-given blessings in harmony of creation are isolated and concentrated like opium taken from poppy flowers or the distillation by marketing forces inundating us from the unreal worlds of

---

[39] Luke 11:34.

television, magazines and entertainment news programs or through
the ephemeral fame and vainglory derived from "the praise of men"
stemming from other false personalities whose empty praise is
sought to maintain the buoyancy of the false self, instead of the soul
being nourished by the authentic joy of giving glory to God through
real encounters with others in the world. Orthodoxy, which is *ortho*
(correct) + *doxia* (glory), means, in effect, to glorify God and live
in harmony with all of creation in contrast with glorifying the individual false self at the expense of the shared life of all persons and
nature in community.

To the degree that we fail to give glory where it is due in this way,
and thus experience intrinsic joy in living, the freedom of a person
to choose life becomes so impeded that the *nous* is gradually blinded
with the result that the soul is further fragmented and distracted in a
downward spiral of increasing pain and suffering. *Thymos* now begins
reactively to serve a new master who is not the true lord of the household.[40] Personal presence is gradually lost; either to the instinctive
processes of the body in the case of addiction, or to the compulsive
cravings of the personality in the case of passions of vainglory, pride,
self-justification and such, which infect the soul leading to various
other forms of bodily sickness that reflect the unhealthy condition
of the soul. Both of these situations can exist in persons who would
not be recognized by society as mentally ill, yet from the standpoint
of life in Christ, could be said to be essentially "heartless." Or as C. S.
Lewis diagnoses our human condition in his book *The Abolition of
Man*, such a state constitutes being "a man without a chest" — only
instinct and intelligence without a heart of flesh that can love and be
loved and willingly bear the burden that comes with this. When this
affects the people of a community or nation as a whole, such spiritual

---

[40] Even though the sheep are temporarily held under sway of this master, "they
will not follow him," i.e. they cannot be set free to become themselves, because this
can only occur in response to the one Master who is True. The *Imago Dei* remains
in effect, regardless of the degree of illness, and there is hope of eradicating the
oppression, whatever its source, and restoring health and salvation.

sickness can go unnoticed because of the kinds of disguises that arise as camouflage for the larger systemic illness.

For example, when society serves Mammon while insisting that it is serving God; when it refuses to address the sins (traumas) of the past, such as slavery and genocidal practices against indigenous people as has happened in America, history itself is written in such a way as to prevent our discovering the truth[41] and finding healing. Christianity is co-opted and displaced by forces of worldly empire[42] retaining only the form of religion but lacking its moral integrity and force. This requires spiritual warfare on the societal level as it were "against powers and principalities," as St. Paul counsels. Pastoral care and psychotherapy are needed on a much larger scale in the form of social action rooted in repentance and love prompted by individual conscience in our daily lives, seeking support through the worshipping community solidarity. It involves a recognition that ultimately your and my personal health and well-being and our faithfulness to Christ are inextricably linked with our faithfulness in the stewarding and protecting of creation on behalf of all persons and creatures, not just the few who benefit from it at the expense of the rest.[43]

A third form of loss of human presence is *extraction*. This occurs when the injury is primarily to the soul through some kind of severe trauma. This involves a severing or compartmentalization of the soul from bodily and mental life, a fragmentation of the person captured well by the African saying, "When you hurt a child, their spirit moves outside them." When severe, such as sexual molestation of children and post-traumatic stress resulting from prolonged combat exposure,

---

[41] Cf. S. Muse, "Post Traumatic Spiritual Disorder and the False History Syndrome." http://incommunion.org/articles/essays/post-traumatic-spiritual-disorder-and-the-false-history-syndrome (2007).

[42] Ryan LaMothe, Ph.D., "Empire Matters: Implications for Pastoral Care," *Journal of Pastoral Care and Counseling* Vol. 61(5) (Supplement 2007): 421–437. Cf. also James Douglass, *JFK and the Unspeakable: Why He Died and Why It Matters* (New York: Orbis Books, 2008).

[43] Cf. J. Diamond, "What's Your Consumption Factor?" *New York Times*, January 2, 2008, www.nytimes.com.

recent studies confirm actual brain damage in the form of shrinkage of the hippocampus in the limbic system of the brain,[44] indicating the seamless connection between body and soul. What damages one damages the other as well.

In all three instances, depending on the intensity and repetition of the injury and/or the duration of suffering, the result of extraction, distraction and abstraction means further starvation of the soul by interfering with the metabolizing of the necessary 'food' which is received only through dialogue in the I-Thou relationship with other persons and with the natural world as person. This has to do with full *presence*: body, mind, heart and soul. From this vantage point, we can say that a pastoral conversation is above all else an authentic human encounter and counseling is pastoral whenever there is a genuine meeting in love so that Christ appears in our midst and 'I-It,' to borrow on Martin Buber's gift to us, becomes 'I-Thou.' This is the field in which the 'fit' is to be found which brings healing to the troubled soul and which prepares us to become fully alive as human persons in and through the call of God in Christ to each of us to become Passion-bearers.

PASSION BEARING AND PASSION AVOIDING. When we consider the question "What makes counseling pastoral?" in light of the pre-requisite for human I-Thou presence, we are ultimately asking "Does counseling enable persons to be Passion-bearers rather than Passion-avoiders?" Does counseling help persons face reality and love the world as God in Christ loves us by responding to the Holy Spirit in faith? So much of human pain is the result of an evasion of our true vocation and our calling as the "royal priesthood" to be who we are and where we are with total self-giving abandon. In the final analysis, every evasion of *presence* in the here and now, if not healed and brought back into integration, amounts to a refusal of love, an

---

[44] Cf J. Bremmer, *Does Stress Damage the Brain?* (New York: W. W. Norton & Co., 2002).

evasion of heart, a denial of faith in the goodness and value of life. This is shown forth clearly in the Passion of Christ who refuses to shut His eyes or turn His full presence away from the hell to which His incarnation and love leads Him, on behalf of the world. In His humanity, He recognized the desire to do so. "If there be another way ... take this cup from Me ..." Yet, in His obedience to God who will not give up on the world, He prayed, "Nevertheless, Thy will be done." From this mysterious and awesome refusal on God's part to abandon the world, however hellish it may become, comes the Gospel of our redemption.

Where illness, addiction or trauma are the reason for evasion of Passion, people obviously require a variety of different approaches, psychological, medicinal, behavioral and spiritual, more so than merely moralistic exhortation or attempts at more 'inspiration' or merely taking a pill. Nevertheless, depending on the degree of severity, we can separate those persons who function in society successfully while still evading real Passion from those who are too ill to do either. The writings of St. Mother Maria Skobtsova offer a vivid diagnosis of various ways that seemingly healthy Orthodox Christians evade Passion-bearing through misappropriation of religion to serve individualistic purposes.[45]

This can occur when we prefer the heady wine of authoritarian and fundamentalist grasping at religious truth as a hedge against having to take existential risk of enduring hardship and making sacrifices in a particular circumstance for a particular person as did St. John the Theologian with the young man who had, through neglect, fallen to criminal behavior. Or it can be through misappropriated ascetical struggle. As St. Basil suggested, in this way we can become a demon through a zeal which reduces Orthodoxy to a religion that amounts to yet another technical means of becoming empowered to resist the existential limits imposed by God and Creation. Asceticism for the purpose not of fidelity to a love relationship with the Person of God

---

[45] Cf. M. Skobtsova, *Essential Writings* (New York: Orbis Books: 2003).

and humanity, but rather as individualistic self-seeking divinization is a form of sorcery, a kind of spiritual capitalism aimed at securing one's individual salvation while leaving others wounded on the side of the road in the process. Surely this misses the mark.

Passion-evading can also appear in an aesthetic version in the form of liturgical myopia where fanatical, officious concern for the exactness of performing the liturgy eclipses the dialogical relationship between priest, people and God, which is the 'work of the people.' Love through and *as the Church in the world,* not perfected ritualistic performance *apart from the world*, leads to the eventual sanctification of the world through the presence of those who have been transformed in and through the Church. In other words, as St. John Chrysostomos observed, "When I leave the altar, I go to the altar of my brother." It is not that we avoid Church with excuses "that I have to bury my father" or "I have taken a wife" or "I have to examine my fields," but rather that all these activities are means through which we become who and what we are intended to be only by realizing them to their fullest *through* the Church which is Christ who sanctifies all things. For God does not dwell in houses made by human hands any more in the twenty-first century than in the first. It remains true as St. John the Theologian of love pointed out, "Those who would worship Him must" still "worship in Spirit and in Truth."

T HE YOKE THAT FITS IS THE EASY YOKE. When Jesus says, "My yoke is easy and My burden is light," I take this to refer to it being an *exact fit* for each of us — that He is making it possible for us to become our real and true selves. When I evade the mark toward which I am aimed, my 'vocation' — and this includes my cross in life which is Passion-bearing with Christ — I am inevitably, as Jonah discovered, swallowed by the unconscious manifestation of that which I have avoided. Passion-evading leads to being overcome by what I have rejected, now in the form of a passion that has assumed the proportion of the great Leviathan which takes possession of me fueled by the power of the very untransformed energies that would otherwise have become part of my authentic aliveness in Christ. By virtue of avoiding my cross, I forfeit the freedom to become myself. I miss the mark. My yoke does not 'fit'. As the Lord said to Saul when he was avoiding his own passion-bearing through presumptuous self-righteousness and the idolatry of religious ideology, "It hurts to kick against the goads." I remain captive in the belly of the whale, as it were, until I am spit out, and hit bottom like the Prodigal in the pig sty where I am offered a chance to 'come to my senses', turn again, and set off in the direction of my Father's house, carrying my cross and beginning to recover from the wounds inflicted by my avoidance.

All these forms of 'illness' are the result of not finding the right 'fit' or 'yoke' between the divine call to communal life and the world as I experience it through the infection of my sins and afflictive emotions that create spiritual blindness and passion-evading failure to love. Refusal of authentic dialogue with the world is a refusal of genuine relationship with God in favor of the monologue of individualistic self-justification, self-comforting, self-protection and attempted self-divinization. It is a refusal of love and a betrayal of Christ. Another way to speak of it is in the form of hypocrisy or as Jesus diagnosed in some religious counselors in His day regarding their unexamined countertransferences, they were "whitewashed tombs full of all sorts of dead men's bones. You bind heavy burdens on others that you would not help with your little finger."[46]

Spiritual health is to be in the 'likeness' of God who has opened the door to the fullest human potential by creating humankind in the Image of God's own being and providing a bridge to communion with God through Christ whose cross of love plunges from heaven through earth into hell where, as my friend Dr. Jamie Moran has emphasized in his Passion writings,[47] the battle is decided afresh in every human heart with every human choice for the sake of the whole world. Either we are set aflame by the Holy Spirit and burn with

---

[46] Matthew 23:4.
[47] (In press) in Russian and Greek as a two volume set with the title *The Wound of Existence.*

Christ's Passion for the world or we die in coldness from the evasion of Passion.

In each moment, we declare with our actions whether we are for Christ or against Him. I tell my clients, "Your work in therapy is to speak so that your body confirms the truth of your words, just as in life we confirm the truth of our hearts by our actions." Anything less is not capable of any real change, for words that arise from the lips, without the heart and soul and body united, are empty and do not create transformation. They have no love; no heat. Love is costly. It burns with pain for the world's suffering. As Jesus said to His disciples, "If you love Me, you will obey My commandments." Or perhaps in other words, "Act so that your behavior confirms the truth of your faith." This is transforming, for it amounts to a living existential prayer uniting word and deed that invites the action of the Holy Spirit to complete in relationship with each one of us and all of us together, what no one of us alone can accomplish.

THE NECESSITY FOR PROTECTING FREEDOM OF CONSCIENCE. Since most of us do not approach clients with unilateral, direct, noetic perception into their lives such as given to Elder Porphyrios by the Holy Spirit in the example above, nor do we possess an exact science that can be used to approximate this, we rely on the dialogical encounter keeping ever before us the triadic contextual reality, which German Protestant Theologian Dietrich Bonhoeffer described as:

> Because Christ stands between me and others...I must release the other person from every attempt of mine to regulate, coerce and dominate him with my love. The other person needs to retain (his/her) independence of me; to be loved from what (s)he is, as one for whom Christ became man, died, and rose again, for whom Christ brought forgiveness of sins and eternal life. Because Christ has long since acted decisively for my (neighbor), before I could begin to act, I must leave him freedom to be Christ's; I must meet him/her only as the person that one

already is in Christ's eyes. This is the meaning of the proposition that we can meet others only through the mediation of Christ. Human love constructs its own image of the other person, of what (s)he is and what (s)he should become. It takes the life of the other person into its own hands. Spiritual love recognizes the true image of the other person which he has received from Jesus Christ; the image that Jesus Christ himself embodied and would stamp upon all (persons).[48]

There must be a willingness to "first do no harm," while also being willing to offer one's "five loaves and two fishes" to the best of one's ability with faith in the providence of God and the freedom of conscience of the person to receive what is offered in like spirit. This is a respect for God as the primary healer while the psychotherapist is midwife to the process. Too light a penance or too heavy and a person has an obstacle placed before him/her. There must be an exact 'fit'. How to discern this? One hundred thousand people die annually in the U.S. from medicines rightly prescribed. Imagine what happens when they are wrongly prescribed. How many suffer from good religion wrongly presented or understood or when *kanonoi* are offered by well-meaning priests acting as spiritual fathers who lack adequate self-awareness and pastoral care training. Above all, freedom must be preserved through love. Russian Theologian Nicholas Berdyaev observes how difficult this is in practice:

We live in a time when people fear the freedom of conscience, they shy away from it, and they resent the burden of freedom, the burden of responsibility. I believe that the question of the freedom of conscience is essential for Christianity and must be raised with the greatest clarity and the greatest radicality. Freedom should always come before authority. Everything is decided in the life of the spirit, in the spiritual experience. The Holy

---

[48] D. Bonhoeffer, *Life Together* (London: SCM Press, 1954), 22–23.

Spirit does not act like the forces of nature or the social forces. The hierarchical organization of the Church, which is historically unavoidable, the constitution of the canons, are secondary phenomena, and not paramount. The only paramount phenomenon is the spiritual life and what is discovered in it. It is the spiritual life that keeps the Church sanctified.[49]

A CONTEMPORARY EXAMPLE OF FINDING A FIT IN FREEDOM. A deeply pious woman from a Protestant tradition suffered extreme humiliation and physical abuse from her mother for years as a little girl. The mother was mentally ill and also a kind of witch. My client, who is of part native American ancestry, has had the gift of inner visions since childhood. God has ministered to her over the years, helping her survive her childhood and later an abusive marriage with an alcoholic husband who controlled her and cheated on her and restricted her freedom in a variety of ways, through a rich internal dialogue in which she regularly responds to divine promptings in a very personal dialogical way. Her life and relationships evidence numerous confirming examples of the vitality of this relationship through the impact of her prayers, faith and love in ways that people from all walks of life, from homeless, drug-addicted and traumatized to well-educated and emotionally stable persons, respond in life-enhancing ways.

She has been a long-time member of a Bible believing fundamentalist Protestant church, and when she sought the pastor's help over the years for her marriage difficulties and the pain and loneliness she was suffering, she was always counseled according to Scripture and told to stay in the marriage. By her loving service, eventually her husband would be saved. He did eventually stop drinking, but he became even more cruel to her than before.

In our work together for the first year, she dealt primarily with the damage to her sense of self and her nervous system resulting from

---

[49] Nicholas Berdyaev, quoted in a talk given by Fr. Alexis Struve at the Annual Conference of the Episcopal Vicariate of Great Britain and Ireland, May 2007, entitled "The Freedom of the Spirit of the Church is Sacred."

her childhood abuse, which was extensive, sporadic and ongoing and included physical abuse, emotional abuse, sexual molestation and the parentifying burden of protecting a parent with mental illness. As she began to tolerate the uprising of dissociated grief and pain of those early years into her body, she began to experience first a throat problem and later a periodic paralysis and numbness on the left side of her face. Physicians could not find a medical reason for this. Her mother had repeatedly slapped her while she obediently knelt before her, having learned to be numb while mother unleashed the fury and hatred she projected onto her from the self-loathing she had absorbed from her own abuse as a child. As she worked her way through this pain and immense grief, the facial paralysis cleared up and has not returned. Throughout the process over the past two years, she became more and more interested in Orthodox Christian ethos and tradition, which I shared with her as an integral part of our work.

After I had returned from a trip to Greece and to Mount Athos, near the end of one of her sessions, she asked me what it was like to kiss a piece of the true cross. My response to her sincere and deeply felt question was as though I were back there again, and I wept quietly without saying anything further. The place we 'met' at that moment was the place where Christ's presence between us caused both our hearts to burn in love as He drew us each deeper into the mystery of faith. My response was prompted in part by the sincerity of her faith which opened a channel of Grace. The client's sincere need in partnership with God's Grace can even make Balaam's donkey speak in a helpful way! As with so many other encounters over our time together, by the Grace of God, I have at times often wondered who was helping whom, for her faith and humility never ceased to move me deeply. It was clear from the beginning of our work together that she was seeking *pastoral* counseling because this was the context in which she felt safe to face the unbearable feelings and feared meanings she had avoided for the previous 40 years. Without God and trust that God was working in between both, she could not have risked the vulnerability to make the journey.

One day after a session when she had been struggling with the long and chronic pain of her abusive marriage, I said to her, "You don't have to keep letting your mother strike you." She had been unconsciously tolerating physical and emotional abuse from her husband as if she 'deserved' it the same way as she did as a child with her mother and protecting her church and pastor who repeatedly enjoined the biblical mandate against divorce, as she had her mother as a child, all at her own expense. Believing that one must embrace the cross consciously in freedom rather than compulsively and unconsciously as a form of continuing our childhood traumas, I felt moved to give her the above quotation from Nicholas Berdyaev. She found it deeply encouraging, and something transformative occurred for her as she felt that she could no longer stay in the marriage with integrity. She prayed about this, and God gave her a way out by her husband's own decision that they "had nothing in common" and she could leave.

As she worked her way through this decision in the coming weeks, facing the initial fury of her children who had grown up trusting in the mother's resolute adherence to the Bible, she prepared to be brought before the whole church eventually and condemned in public, as was the custom of her church in a divorce. A long-time trusted friend, also in the church, advised her, "Don't tell Pastor. He will hurt you." She decided she had to tell her pastor "not just for my sake, but for those women who will come after me." As she spoke of this in anticipation, her chin jutted out ever so slightly like a determined small girl preparing to face Goliath, and I gently called her attention to this. She laughed quietly in recognition that it was so, though she said she had not noticed until I mentioned it. It reflected a certain insistence on her own part to "prepare for the strike" stemming from compensatory emotional power, rather than surrender to the truth and putting her trust in God which had been her sure path in the midst of a life of uncertainties.

A few weeks later, as I was working on this talk of which she knew nothing, I had shared with her some comments from the spiritual father of a friend of mine in Greece who sent me translations of a recent talk he had given in which he spoke of God not being interested in our sins but in our repentance and love. She read them and, feeling great joy, sent me the following email. I asked her if I could share it at the conference because of the obvious relevance to the theme of my presentation and she agreed without reservation.

Stephen Muse,

Sometimes when you begin to speak or send me words like this or tell me the sayings of the Spiritual Fathers a fear rises in my heart that I won't catch on, or understand. It feels like I begin to run trying to catch a moving passenger train, trying to grab hold and jump aboard. I listen very hard. Try to catch and digest every word — it's almost like hearing something foreign, something I've never heard before, something I've missed all my life and my soul's been searching for. Something old and ancient, something that's come at great cost, something that rings so true in your heart that it settles in like it had always been there. And, it rings so true it becomes a part of you.

That's how I feel. Most of the time I cannot pronounce those great Saint's names (and that is a struggle for me), yet I am trying to consume what has been placed in front of me (like a little starved girl placed at a banquet table — a Holy Table). Sometimes I cannot remember which Saint said what (and I am working on that), but I do know this — that it fits in my heart. And it is a good fit! A 'fit' meant to be.

Perhaps when pastor brings me before the Church words that God has in-trusted to my heart from the hearts of others will come up from the well springs He has inside of me! Then I won't have to *"stick out my chin"* right? *Ha!* (You see much! And well!) Maybe the Spirit of God will let me say words that will ring so true that some will find them to be a perfect 'fit' also. Perhaps.

The 'fit' she speaks of is the essence of what I believe makes counseling pastoral. In the context of our work together, this letter is yet one more of so many, many small 'confirmations' of an Unseen Hand that is present in the loving dialogue between persons confirming the triadic nature of pastoral counseling. It is the arena established by our Common Creator whose love for the world is evidenced by accepting the helplessness of human incarnation and ultimately risking His own life in the face of the uncertainty of human response to His love. His sacrifice for us is given only in the hope that we might be drawn with Him into the work and privilege of meeting God in the 'between' where heaven and earth meet whenever we approach one another in "fear, faith and love" as in the Holy Eucharist. At this crossroad between the ontological and the existential, which is where the holy road of the Passion of Christ always leads, we are ever pilgrims and sinners; confident and hopeful in the love of God, yet mindful that it is "not I but Christ who lives in me," who acts 'between' us in and through the mysterious depth of freedom in human conscience which Christ gives His life in order to preserve and invites us to do the same.

CHAPTER THREE

Heart of Faith:
An Epistemology of Personal Encounter[1]

It is one of the laws of life that new meaning must be lived before it can be known, and in a mysterious way modern man knows so much that he is the prisoner of his knowledge. The old dynamic conception of the human spirit as something living always on the frontiers of human knowledge has gone. We hide behind what we know. And there is an extraordinarily angry and aggressive quality in the knowledge of modern man; he is angry with what he does not know; he hates and rejects it. He has lost the sense of wonder about the unknown and he treats it as an enemy. The experience which is before knowing, which would enflame his life with new meaning, is cut off from him. Curiously enough, it has never been studied more closely. People have measured the mechanics of it, and the rhythm, but somehow they do not experience it."

Sir Laurens Van der Post[2]

The world only if shared exists.

Tassos Leivathitis

The Sonoran desert was in full bloom as I drove down the dirt road known as "St. Joseph's Way" on my way to St. Anthony's Monastery

---

[1] Expanded from an article first published in *OCAMPR E Journal* as "Heart of Faith."

[2] L. Van der Post, *Patterns of Renewal*, Pendle Hill Pamphlet Number 121, (1962), 3.

in Florence, Arizona. The dry March heat was pleasant, and the new landscape captivating for an East Coast dweller used to the verdant hardwoods of Pennsylvania and the evergreen pines in the steamy heat of southern Georgia. Now I found myself alert and without too much resistance, standing through the all-night vigil of the Annunciation, which began at 12:30 AM and concluded at 8:30 AM with the fresh light of the desert morning greeting us as we emerged from the fragrant oil lamps and icon-illumined darkness of the sanctuary.

On this trip, I was able to speak briefly with Geronda Ephraim, whom I had met for confession before on several occasions. He is a former abbot of one of the monasteries on Mount Athos, and the last living disciple of Elder Joseph the Hesychast, who is one of the remarkable elders responsible for the renaissance of spiritual life on Mount Athos after a period of declining numbers. Elder Ephraim has begun some twenty or so monasteries for men and women all over the United States that follow the same typikon (or rule of life) as on Mount Athos.

On this occasion, I was able to make my confession and, for the first time, to venerate some of the monastery's relics, which I discovered include a piece of the True Cross from a fragment kept for millennia on Mount Athos along with a bone fragment from St. Mary Magdalene. I had never had the opportunity to venerate these relics before, and I did not know which of these ancient treasures the monastery had. When the small fragment of the cross, embedded in a larger wooden cross, was placed in my hands, I held it to my heart and tears flooded through me in a great wave washing through my chest. For a second, there was no difference between 33 AD and 2001 AD. I was standing with the Theotokos and the beloved disciple before the cross with all the pain of love that recognizes I too have a part in hurting this One who loves me and the entire world enough to lay down His life for us.

It was of particular interest to me that I felt this while being tired and physically sick at the time. There was even some residue remaining of the mood of self-hatred that I had been contending with, left over from irrational blame of myself for not being able as a young child to heal my father and mother of their severe and chronic illnesses, which had been unconsciously aroused in me again by current family circumstances and the build-up of vicarious trauma[3] from contending with the pain and difficulties of the persons in my pastoral counseling practice who in some ways are a kind of 'parish' for which I am responsible. This coupled with pride and self-will operating in my life in the present had been part of my discussion with geronda earlier. The elder had suggested, "The devil has used your childhood pain to deceive you and attack your prayer." It was a one sentence response offered in his characteristic humble and unadorned simple way without any emotional pressure to accept or reject, and it hit the mark.

It was true. Like a tag-team match of wrestlers, pride, concupiscence, gluttony, vainglory, accidia, rancor, greed and despondency had joined together like the Lilliputians, entwining me in enough small threads of oppression that I was being robbed of my sense of belovedness to God and with it, the inclination to pray the Jesus Prayer, substituting thinking instead—a bad mistake. Beginning with the provocations of one and then joined by another and another, sometimes invisible and sometimes deliberately evoked through a kind of insolence that does the thing I hate because I hate it and ought to be better than that, a very subtle and dangerous form of pride! Losing my purchase in prayer, my undisciplined attention had once again begun to run amok, hither and yon, enticed into the forest to be attacked by the bands of roving *logismoi* looking for some lost pilgrim to devour.

Like an orphan running away from the structure of boarding school, without any particular place to go, I had wandered off the path into trouble, attracted by memories of past sins and hints of

---

[3] *Vicarious trauma* refers to the impact upon therapists that occurs through empathic connection with persons who have been traumatized, creating a similar resonance in the therapist's nervous system. *Secondary trauma* is distinguished by the fact that it is an actual experience of trauma secondhand, by physician, family members or friends of the traumatized person. *Compassion fatigue* is a more general and less acute form of burnout that can result from overwork and forms of vicarious trauma.

those yet uncommitted, shimmering in the counterfeit golden promises reflected from the treasures of God deep in my own heart. I was
looking in the wrong direction for what is always found at the source,
giving life to all the world. My home and ordinary aspects of my life
were being taken for granted and repeatedly undervalued as my spiritual heart became hardened and I began yet again the fruitless search
for the stimulating taste of the apple that would bring me compensatory satisfactions. It is a common trap. Elder Paisios of Mount Athos,
in his straightforward and earthy way, writes:

> The one who neglects his prayer and duties unjustifiably and
> works all the time (building pyramids for Pharaoh)[4] is es-
> tranged from God, becomes wild, constantly and cruelly hitting
> his guardian angel with kicks of disorder, until he finally drives
> him away. Then, he accepts the devil as his ruler, who immedi-
> ately makes the following changes: 1) abolishes the prayer rope,
> replacing it with worldly worry beads, and 2) does away with
> spiritual study completely, replacing it with worldly magazines
> and newspapers. In the end, the devil conquers him and he suf-
> fers internally and desires to be entertained, like Saul did,[5] when
> he was alienated from God and demon possessed.[6]

Finding solace in some mirage of life other than where I am and
in some form other than who I really am is an invalidation of God's
love and presence and of my own being as well. Seeking life in a form
other than the one God has given me is a form of spiritual deception
that is dangerous because, as Metropolitan Anthony often reminded
those who sought his counsel, "God can save the sinners that we are,
but not the saints we pretend to be." In order to attack us, the devil
must first weaken our spiritual immune systems by infecting us with

---

[4] Cf. Ex. 5.
[5] Cf. I Sam. 16:14–23.
[6] Elder Paisios, *Epistles* (Souroti, Greece: Holy Monastery of the Evangelist John
the Theologian, 2008), 218.

the snake oil of this delusion rooted not in dialogue with God "just as I am" but the thought that I should postpone dialogue with God until *after* I can become good enough to be worthy of such a meeting. This is the other end of the stick of pride, which already presumes to be worthy of dialogue and so remains in a monologue of self-love out of envy and vainglory. Both result from what I call "eating devil's food" — that is, feeding on the comparison-fueled notion that "unless you are God, you are worthless." Invalidation and hatred for self and humankind arise from this, which is a mark not of Christ but of Satan. This kind of devil's food subverts Christianity from within the soul so that it has the form of religion but none of its power. Instead, it becomes a means of "getting better" in order to be loved one day, when, in fact, it is just the reverse, an eternal love proposal from God for humanity as God created us. It is not how much we love God that is the determining factor of our lives, but that God first loved us (I John 4:10) that is the primary context. Eucharistic food is offered because we are *already* cleansed by the Word of Him who loves us in our incompleteness, our error and yes, in spite of the pain we cause others and God. Because God knows what we truly are and can become when we feed on Eucharist rather than devil's food. It is because of God's love for us as we are that St. Anthony's pithy observation concerning the purpose of spiritual struggle, "to become yourself," makes so much sense.

This state of inner discontent had been affecting my counseling work in ways that probably were not perceptible on the surface, but I knew I was not giving people the quality of simple, attentive, interested, not-knowing presence that the mystery of Christ in our midst invites us to when our hearts are light and open and we are obedient as best we are able, for which our hearts most yearn. I had become "burdened with cares of the world," both my own and the accumulated pain of my clients, a common infection of those who listen to other people's sins and personal traumas. My own sinful inclinations and the accumulated stress of working with hundreds of other souls who have sought to lay down some of their burdens in my office combine at times to make all sorts of strange brews capable of causing a recurrence of the familiar pain of a small boy who could not heal his parents of their illness and pain and developed his own conscious and unconscious ways of avoiding that burden.

That is one reason I so value weekly Divine Liturgy, periodic pilgrimage to the desert and confession; to be shorn like a lamb of the layers of accumulated mental and emotional thorns and brambles that have begun to choke my hope and prayer, threatening to steal the joy of God's salvation from me. In the Orthodox Christian Church, we soon learn that the shame and humiliation of the ego felt in confession are sure signs of the working of the medicine of Grace reaching the heart as the crust of self-will and vainglory are sloughed off in the moment of returning to God. It is only when the ego lowers its head to the floor in shame that the heart realizes in sorrowful joy how it is being lifted up by the inspiration of the Holy Spirit blowing on it freshly from the lips of the Risen Lord, before whose icon we kneel and from whose hand we receive blessing and in whose Word we find abundant life. Strange it is that we wander away over and over again, betraying the treasure of our spiritual life in Christ. Yet, as St. Paul himself observed, there is ever a danger that "the good that I would do I do not and the evil that I hate, that I do!" Surely, we cannot expect more from ourselves then he, and so we take consolation in the saint's words, for real faith is always put to the test by shouldering the cross in this world; the cross that pays the price of being capable of loving and being loved, precisely because *we are free not to.* We are not robots. From the beginning, God paid an enormous price for this — *the lamb slain from the foundation of the world* — and each one shares in this who wishes *to become real,* for it is love that uses itself up for the sake of the Beloved that evidences the miracle of redemption. "You have freely received; therefore, freely give," says the Lord. It is life of which He speaks, and in this living and dying, we are born to the eternal life of real personhood.

This freedom is why I frequently tell my counseling students, my clients, and remind myself, that it is necessary for the child to put the compulsive cross down so that the adult can freely pick it up. For as

Fr. Vasileios Thermos crisply observes, "Love without freedom and freedom without love are pathological situations and need therapy."[7] When a child lives with alcoholic parents who are not consistently available or, in my case, with a father who suffered the craziness and violence of periodic paranoid schizophrenia and a mother with chronic physical illness leading to deformities and amputations, the child learns in various ways, without realizing it, to place his/her own needs on the back burner, even to the point of becoming unaware of having needs, in order to be responsive to the parents and the unpredictable environment. This is not spiritual, but rather a form of dissociation with a neurophysiological basis. It is compulsive, not free. When the child grows up, these unconsciously learned habits of relating to others create situations where the adult may continue caretaking habits that serve to starve the inner being of the essential nutrients of love and intimacy. The child, who eventually becomes a priest or counselor, finds the theological explanation of self-denial and love for others as a convenient way of explaining the compulsive cross that he finds himself carrying. But there is a fly in the ointment.

How is it that Jesus, who carries the greatest burden in the world, who, as Archimandrite Sophrony points out, is at the very nadir of the upside down pyramid holding up the world from the depths of hell, can say to others, "Come to Me all you who are heavy-laden and I will give you rest, for My yoke is easy and My burden is light" (Mt. 11:28)? Does this make sense? It does when we realize that Jesus's yoke is easy because it *fits Him exactly*. It is His calling. His burden is light, because He carries it *freely* with His whole heart. The problem with cross-carrying that stems from childhood neglect, abuse and trauma is that it is compulsive. The fly in the ointment is that it is not freely embraced. It is not a response to a call of the Spirit, but a reactive, developmental response designed to preserve the child's precarious position in his/her family of origin by meeting his parents'

---

[7] V. Thermos, *Thirst for Love and Truth: Encounters of Orthodox Theology and Psychological Science* (Montreal: Alexander Press, 2010), 39.

and family's needs rather than, as it should be, the parents meeting the child's legitimate needs for nurturing and interest. In this way, the child is not free to carry his/her cross as an adult. This is one of the core issues that must be addressed in order to adjust the yoke and lighten the burden of clergy and helping professionals who burn out. It begins with telling the deep truth of one's pain and hurt and the secret sins that collect around the false martyrdom that grows up on the shoulders of the parentified child. Ironically, it is this truth-telling "so the body confirms the truth of the words" that begins to shift the center of gravity of the person from compulsive cross-carrying that is actually a form of egotistic self protection, to one in which the adult freely takes up and bears the cross given him or her, no longer as a means of survival, but as a self-offering in love.

There is a saying among the Omaha nation, "If you speak from the heart, you will be answered from the heart." I believe it is also true that if you listen from the heart, people are more likely to hear their own hearts speaking. Both depend on a sense of belovedness that allows for shedding the unnecessary baggage of emotional reactivity, unforgiven debts, worries and all manner of the afflictive, unredeemed passions that choke the joy of life. The priest or counselor listens best who has been listened to her/himself deeply in such a way that she/he has experienced unburdening the heart to another, facing one's own pain and receiving the medicine of Grace and love. The more often, the better, for just as we need to shower and brush our teeth regularly from daily life, the same is true emotionally and spiritually. We cannot have mercy toward others without experiencing for ourselves, and we will not recognize the value of deep listening unless we have experienced being on both sides of the equation often enough to know how much we ourselves are in need of mercy and have received mercy.

This is why I believe the most important preparation for doing the work of pastoral counseling is being loved. This creates the right foundation for honoring the ascetical yoke of prayer, repentance, confession, worship and obedience to the commandments of Christ, which are one and all a response to love. Any 'no' to something, resulting from

Christian life is in order to preserve a greater 'Yes'. Ascetical boundaries, like the professional and ethical boundaries that make therapy possible, have nothing whatsoever to do with 'getting better' or 'being good' but are all a response to preserving and protecting the great love which is the soul's deepest yearning. Only a guileless and humble heart evokes the same in others, and this comes from being in relationship with the Source, not on the basis of a false and compulsive imaginary self, but in the hope and simple innocence that all children once knew in their lives. As the Lord has stated, He is the vine that gives life to Creation and we are the branches. "Cut off from Me, you can do nothing."

As the fragment of the cross was placed in my hands, my confusion and cloudy mental state parted like lightning through dense fog. Weeping and holding this sacred relic to my heart, there came a kind of subtle whisper from the more peripheral layers of my mind like a nudge: "How do you know this is really a piece of the True Cross?" I was aware at that moment of the power to shift my attention to entertain this question, "How do you know this is genuine?", but it would have meant forfeiting the emerging sense of heartfelt remorse and closeness to the Lord's sacrifice which was flooding through me as a result of an *encounter*. Elder Paisios of the Holy Mountain says that provocations from the demons are like airplanes that suddenly pass into the air space of the psyche, but it is not necessary that we build them a landing field in the heart. Let them pass on through. Sometimes, the neutral activity of the scientific, logical intellect (the *dianoia*) is used by an invisible spirit to lure the attention away from a deeper noetic encounter which brings the mind into the heart.

Repentance, born of Grace and working through faith, is beyond me to create for myself. I see that my *assent* is needed when such moments of Grace are given. It is definitely a relationship and not an invasion. God never preempts human freedom, but gives everything in order to draw persons toward real freedom which is to be responsive to the Holy Spirit. En route to this mystery, one must learn to wait with patience and alertness until such moments come as the Apostles did at Pentecost. This is part of the training of all-night vigils. The seed of the Word is planted in the heart, and at a moment when we do not expect, God may command it to bloom. We must have oil in our lamps and be ready to enter when the door unexpectedly opens. Oil comes from having paid attention and kept watch for the treasure for which one's heart yearns.

A friend of mine told me the story of his visit to Mount Athos, where, upon his initial arrival, he was present for most of an eleven-hour vigil service that was in process. At the end, the abbot asked him, "How did you like our service?"

"A bit long."

He responded, "Ah, but did you notice that you became quiet only in the ninth hour and that it was only in the eleventh hour that you began to enter into the mystery?"

"When the Son of Man comes again, will He find faith on earth?" While it is not within human power alone to preserve the warmth and sweetness of Grace when it is offered by God, as St. Paul's lament poignantly evidences, the heart begins to know the anguish of losing it. Then prayer and watchfulness are born in earnest, and the soul springs forth like the bride in the Song of Solomon, running through the streets of our lives, barefooted, single-mindedly seeking her Beloved, who in humility and purity, has turned back at the first hesitation in receiving Him.

Mental skepticism, which is the core of the scientific method, is capable of serving many masters and for different purposes. Albert Einstein observed that reason is a "very strong muscle, but it must never be in charge." This is reserved for the heart. It is, as the hesychasts have repeatedly confirmed, in the deep heart which reveals itself in stillness when the mind is in the heart, that real discerning intelligence is found. Reason and the scientific method have made it possible for human beings to land men on the moon, discover penicillin, transplant organs, develop cybernetic technology and map the human genome. But reason has also served in the attempted genocide of Bushmen, Armenians, Native Americans, Jews, Tibetans and countless other populations along the way, enabling us to exterminate quickly and cleanly any physical trace of the soul's incarnation of the Divine Image. What I discover is that there is an invisible and subtle influence that can co-opt my deep noetic attention, capture my will and then enlist my reason in service of a different spirit. While a very valuable tool, in and of itself, reason is incapable of bringing us to faith or, in spite of Immanuel Kant and Pascal's commendable efforts, to bring us to ethical *intent* by pure reason alone. There is a deeper, more direct, intuitional knowing that must be purified of *phantasia* in order to be responsive to God's presence. Faith, hope and love, which are tested by living in the world, reveal the heart's intent through the stands we take and the boundaries we keep. These are the medicines that gradually effect this transformation in dialogical relationship with God as person in and through life with all whom God loves.

Faith is not something 'I' think myself into or *do* by myself independent of a love relationship with the Ontological Source of personhood, the *hypostasis* of Christ. The transformation which faith makes possible when the heart repents in the presence of the Living God results from a personal I-Thou encounter that is even more real than the common, everyday, casual, social exchanges that we routinely experience more superficially among friends and family most of the time.

> The very conception of sin obtains only where the relations between the Absolute God and created (hu)man assumes a purely personal character. Otherwise, we are left with nothing but some intellectual assessment of the perfection of forms of existence. Sin is always a crime against the Father's love. Sin occurs when we distance ourselves from God and incline towards the passions.[8]

Reason alone and the skepticism demanded by scientific enquiry cannot plumb the depths of the *conviction of things unseen*. Faith is not

---

[8] A. Sophrony, *We Shall See Him As He Is* (Essex, England: Stravropegic Monastery of St. John the Baptist, 1988), 20.

a monological process, something one can do on one's own, with one's own power. It is a response to the Holy Spirit speaking in the heart. If being born as a human being, witnessing a universe expanding, a consciousness growing, flowers blooming and men and women offering themselves for love at the expense of their own lives, does not offer the possibility of faith, neither will seeing someone raised from the dead or any other so-called 'miracle.' Faith comes from another domain and brings with it eyes to see the world from *a heart of love as personal.* This cannot be created or established by any scientific fact or inquiry, nor does it exist as mere mental thoughts unmetabolized by heart and soul and left unexpressed in actions. "They love Me who obey My commandments." Even the devils believe that Christ exists. In fact, they *know* it. Nevertheless, they do not existentially embrace Christ in life. So they can be said to be essentially *without faith* and *without love.*

> Being a believer has little to do with mentally assenting to, or verbally declaring doctrinal truths whose existential promises we have no experience of, and whose sacred power has not won us over, dwelling in our depths and upholding our action. The heart 'believes' when it trusts in its action a road on which mountains will have to be moved, and camels will have to pass through the eye of a needle. Belief is what we are prepared to do, to give, to risk, to lose, for love.[9]

The question that posed itself to me as I felt my heart open to the mystery of the holy cross, disguised at that moment as if it were an objective examination by reason, originates from a source that ultimately precludes faith. In fact, as Archimandrite Sophrony observes,

[9] J. Moran, "Spiritual Warfare: The Relevance to Modern Therapy of the Ancient Eastern Orthodox Christian Path of Ascetical Practice," from an address delivered at the 12th Annual Conference of the Orthodox Christians Association of Medicine, Psychology and Religion. Holy Cross Greek Orthodox Theological School, Brookline, Massachusetts (2002). Printed in S. Muse, *Raising Lazarus: Integral Healing in Orthodox Christianity* (Brookline, MA: Holy Cross Orthodox Press, 2005).

"In the impulses and actions which our reason justifies, we cannot see 'sin.'"[10] This is not reason's fault, but the fault of the impulse or 'I' that co-opts reason for this purpose, replacing the heart of faith with a heart of stone, made cold by demonic *unfaith*.

From this perspective, like the angels who fell with Lucifer, even if I were to be with God at the very moment when the universe was first created, it would still not be possible to come to faith through this means, because certainty and the absence of all questions due to perfect knowledge, are the only things that could satisfy that motivation or intention which is attempting to use reason to arrive at faith (or subtly, to avoid surrendering to it). This kind of satisfaction is possible only for God Himself! Thus, *pride* is hidden behind the seemingly 'neutral' skepticism of reason which withholds personal involvement until a guarantee (aka control) is wrested from the deep heart of love and given to the cold heart of the mind outside or 'above' the heart — the place of prelest or spiritual deception.

This reluctance to love until there is security is rooted in self-preservation and always resists God and the surrender that love invites. The activity of demons and of evil itself, though without faith, are *purposeful* precisely because the reality of God has rendered a meaning and purpose to life independent of the nihilistic forces which work against it.

> Nothing that is unclean — which means proud — can draw near Him. Pride is abomination, the opposite of Divine goodness. Pride is the principle of evil, the root of all tragedy, the sower of enmity, the destroyer of peace, the adversary of divinely-established order. In pride lies the essence of hell. Pride is the 'outer darkness' where (hu)man loses contact with the God of love. "They loved darkness (John 3:19)." Repentance alone can deliver us from this hell.[11]

---

[10] Op. cit., 34.
[11] Op. cit., 29–30.

If at the moment of my encounter with the "true cross" I had ignored the heart of faith to respond to the wolf disguised in the lambskin of reason's skepticism, it would have been because I was preferring *knowing* over *loving* and *being loved*. I would have remained in monologue, by myself, rather than being affected by encountering the presence of the *other*. It would be a denial of the I-Thou encounter and whoever is not willing to risk love until one is God, is *Satanic*. "*Knowing ever more and more and yet never coming to faith*" applies well to the impulses that prompt us to investigate and philosophize at the very moment of standing on Holy Ground being invited into relationship with God. At such moments, repentance, worship, awe and love are the only threads that are worthy of being woven into a wedding garment in preparation for the Divine Feast to which we are being invited.

Standing in the presence of the only begotten son of the Living God and asking, as Governor Pilate did, pathetically, noncommittally, dismissively, "*What* is truth?" at such a moment is demonstrative of a reluctance to be vulnerable to personal encounter that is a function of a state of pride and fear that ultimately leads to despair. Pilate's critical examination of the *living human document*[12] standing before him, when he ironically said, "*Ecce homo*, Behold the man," failed to recognize the true proportions of the Godman because he preferred to deal with *what* he already thought he knew instead of risking personal encounter with *Whom* he did not yet know, but could have. Without faith, Pilate was blind to the deepest mystery of life, the *ontology of personhood*, which reveals that life is fundamentally *relational* and trialogical. *I am* only in the relationship of loving and being loved in this community created by the Father, Son and Holy Spirit. There is no eternal life in me as an 'individual' *I* apart from others. That would be the hell of "an eternal fall into nothingness."[13]

---

[12] Cf. C. Gherkin, *The Living Human Document: Revisioning Pastoral Counseling in a Hermeneutical Mode* (Nashville TN: Abingdon Press, 1984).

[13] Any punishment of sin is the consequence of making the choice of withdrawal from the commonwealth of God's love. In monologue, a person already begins to suffer the 'judgment' inherent to that freedom of choice which Professor Christos

The ontological and existential gulf between the relational 'person' and the existing-by-itself 'individual' is infinite unless bridged by the hypostasis of Christ who brings me into relationship with all others in love, including my enemies. This is why, as St. Silouan of Mount Athos observed, the sign of a Christian is "love for one's enemies." Love is not a feeling or something I 'do' but rather constitutes an existential turning toward the dialogue wherein Christ arises "wherever two or more are gathered" not by way of abstracted reason, but by way of reciprocal personal encounter such that in the very midst of the encounter, Christ is revealed through the shared life between them as contrasted with privileging one over the other, which leaves one of the persons unconfirmed in his/her humanity.

This way of understanding love is a kind of Copernican revolution from our ordinary individualistic humanistic perspectives, but it is essential to the revelation of God as Triune. Geronda Antonios Romaios of Holy Gregoriou Monastery on Mount Athos captured this very simply for me[14] when, echoing St. Maximos the Confessor, he said, "If you say that you love someone but there is even one person on the earth that you do not love, then you do not love the one you say you love." Martin Buber expresses the same thing forcefully and elaborates further.

> Feelings accompany the metaphysical fact of love, but they do
> not constitute it; and the feelings that accompany it can be very

---

Yannaras describes as an eternal fall into nothingness: "Sin is a self punishment which the human person chooses freely, rejecting communion with God, rejecting that which it has been called to be, rejecting Being, which is existence 'according to nature' and 'according to truth, and preferring to miss the mark' with regard to the 'natural' end of its existence and fall away from Being... Sin is the moral content of nothingness as an existential fact, the measure of the annihilation of existential fulfillment, which is a ceaseless fall into non existence which is never wholly accomplished, since the person is still preserved even in his ultimate self-destruction." C. Yannaras, *Person and Eros* (*To prosopo kai o eros*) published in Athens 1987 and English translation by Holy Cross Orthodox Press 2007, p. 294.
[14] Personal correspondence with the author.

different. Jesus' feeling for the possessed man is different from
his feeling for the beloved disciple; but the love is one. Feelings
one "has"; love occurs. Feelings dwell in man, but man dwells
in his love. This is no metaphor but actuality: love does not
cling to an I, as if the You were merely its "content" or object;
it is *between* I and you. Whoever does not know this, know this
with his being, does not know love, even if he should ascribe
to it the feelings that he lives through, experiences, enjoys, and
expresses... For those who stand in it and behold in it, men
emerge from their entanglement in busyness; and the good and
the evil, the clever and the foolish, the beautiful and the ugly,
one after another become actual and a You for them; that is,
liberated emerging into a unique confrontation. Exclusiveness
comes into being miraculously again and again — and now one
can act, help, heal, educate, raise, redeem. Love is responsibility
of an I for a You: in this consists what cannot consist in any feeling — the equality of all lovers, from the smallest to the greatest
and from the blissfully secure whose life is circumscribed by the
life of one beloved human being to him that is nailed his life
long to the cross of the world, capable of what is immense and
bold enough to risk it: to love man.[15]

Pilate's mistake is too often our own. I fail to plumb the depth of
the mystery of the other and the world in which I live, even though I
may study it and write books about it, because I refuse the dialogue of
meeting. I try to know the other and the world only through knowledge about it. By standing outside and apart from the other, privileging my own (or the other's) perspective instead of the 'between' that
unites us in mutual responsibility and opens up the possibility to be
affected by the other, I am refusing to meet with Christ. By remaining bound by the frame of reference which presumes to know the
other as it were monologically only as 'object' seen through my own

---

[15] M. Buber, *I and Thou* (New York: Charles Scribners & Sons, 1970), 66.

experience and world view (the "log in my own eye") or diagnostic lenses and theories without entering into the vulnerability entailed in the mutuality, I remain outside of Christ and outside of my authentic self which can only come into being to the degree that I am in authentic relationship with others. Love involves a willingness to bear the discomfort and confusion that arises when the other's voice has claim on me to comprehend its difference from my own; when his or her being matters equally as much as my own and is part of the same life we both equally share. To 'get' the other requires using what I already know and am comfortable with only in order to get beyond it. As with God's own being, whatever we can know and say about God is not God. The same is true for the 'other' and for one's own self. All three have an apophatic dimension. The self that is observed is not coterminous with the self that is doing the observing, nor is the other who is observed coterminous with the experience of the observer.

The willingness to be responsible for and to be affected by the belovedness to God of the other person is the doorway into relationship with God who *is* love and continues to be love forever, no matter what the cost. By remaining in monologue, skeptical, without commitment to encounter with the other, I fail to find the pearl of great price — "the hidden person in the heart" (I Peter 3:4). The human problem is the problem of love, and it cannot be solved apart from the heart of faith in God whom reason alone cannot fathom, but exists only to serve.

Jean Paul Sartre's famous statement "Hell is the other" is certainly one part of the equation as we experience human relationship from the side of our projections onto others of what we resist seeing in ourselves that ends up scapegoating others as it did Jesus. But it is equally true, as Ernesto Cardenal notes, that "human beings are not, as Sartre observed, a meaningless passion, but a passion whose meaning is love."[16] This love which bridges the distance between persons is the Logos active in and through each of us. This is expressed beautifully

---

[16] E. Cardenal, *Abide in Love* (New York: Maryknoll, 1995), 25.

in one of the prayers of thanksgiving following Holy Eucharist, in the words "Christ our God, You are the true yearning and inexpressible joy of all who love You and all Creation praises You."[17] Love is this 'between' which is epitomized by the perichoresis of the Holy Trinity, which, through Christ, is opened up to humanity. Combining Sartre's realism with Cardenal's recognition of the presence of Christ as love, the Orthodox epistemology of encounter can be stated as "the quickest way to the becoming a person is through hell for the sake of the other." This is how far God is willing to go to encounter humanity, to the point of being rejected and traumatized by the meeting. Because God is willing to be affected to the full depth and breadth of humanity's created 'otherness,' and suffering the fate of not tampering with human freedom, a possibility is opened for humanity to be affected to the depths by God's uncreated 'otherness' as well.

The epistemology of personal encounter is initiated through God's activity in Christ who unites both human and divine nature seamlessly in Himself and is present wherever two or more gather in His name. This is why it can be said that the fundamental conditions for human life on earth and the foundation of the vocation of both priesthood and pastoral counseling is one ensuring perfect freedom and love, which are the grounds for the possibility of *personhood*. This is only possible if God is person. The worst human suffering, regardless of the type of illness, is loss of meaning and purpose of life which is at heart an illness of spiritual alienation; from God, self, others and the whole created order. It is why Alexander Solzhenitsyn can say, "If I were asked today to formulate as concisely as possible the main cause of the ruinous revolution that swallowed up some 60 million of our people, I could not put it more accurately than to repeat what I heard as a small child: 'Men have forgotten God; that's why all this has happened."[18]

---

[17] Included among the prayers said following reception of the Holy Eucharist in the Divine Liturgy.

[18] A. Solzhenitsyn, *The Templeton Prize for Progress in Religion, 1978–1987* (Edinburgh: Scottish Academic Press Ltd., 1988), 116–117.

It is in dialogue with others where God appears in between, making it a trialogue that healing occurs and meaning and purpose are restored, for as it is beautifully stated from the Hasidic perspective, *Human beings are God's language* and *The Spirit seeks a body through speech*, through the call and response of dialogue. Early Christian voices recognized the power of dialogue which is captured both in the worship experience of the call and response of the Divine Liturgy as well as St. Basil's observation in the 4th century that the Church is a hospital and the priests are psychotherapists. Both the spiritual formation of becoming fully human as well as the healing power of psychotherapy are always διά-Λογος. Whenever 'I' encounter the 'Other' as beloved 'Thou,' the heart begins to kindle like the burning bush with a fire that does not destroy as it becomes a trialogical encounter, an Emmaus road experience where the revelation of Christ appears in between, creating something new for each person. It is because of many such eucharistic moments as these that we are then on the road to becoming fully human and free to love as we are loved.

Theoria, or the vision of Christ at supper at the conclusion of the Emmaus road encounter in the Gospel according to St. Luke, is never monological, but always dialogical encounter that is a kind of invocation that moves to trialogue as in the encounter of the priest before the Divine Altar in partnership with the people. In the same way, the theophany of the transfiguration of Jesus on Mount Tabor in the presence of His disciples was not a time to build tabernacles to try and enshrine the experience of the moment, as Peter imagined, "not knowing what he was saying" but rather one in which to continue to be part of the living encounter, to be still inside, to 'listen,'[19] and be in dialogical call and response of relationship with the Son of God. The same is true for every person we seek to be in relationship with. As Martin Buber observed, "The human being to whom I say, 'You' *I do not experience.* But I stand in relation to him, in the sacred ba-

---

[19] Stillness of listening is the essence of hesychasm in which the one praying has become all ear, listening for the Beloved's voice in the emptiness of heart without word or image.

sic word. Only when I step out of this do I experience him again. Experience is remoteness from you."[20]

This trialogue is, I believe, the foundation of an Orthodox Christian approach to pastoral counseling. At every point along the way, my inner press secretary is taking pictures of such encounters, building a photo album of experiences that can be grasped only with the mind and lived only by pressure of will, without the grace-full fluidity of love. Yet God and every other is always *now*, doing a new thing, arising out of nothing as a new creation. The real self is never merely the self of collected experiences which our minds can re-member and observe, but includes the self, who like every 'other' remains beyond our experience, "hid with Christ in God" (Col. 3:3). This self is grown and nourished by God 'in secret' as it were, outside of our conscious experience. Any attempt to know this, by stand-ing outside of it, is a form of vainglory and pride — attempting to build a tabernacle to house the glory of God as object rather than in personal encounter. The real self is true, without hypocrisy, without division between word and deed, an action arising only in the act of personal I-Thou encounter without any attempt to measure or add anything to one's image in the process. The Self is the interaction of love in relationship with others, not a static kind of experience-worship which is a form of idolatry, like Narcissus staring at his re-flection in the water unable to move as a result, an eternal frozen fall into the nothingness of a mere reflection.[21] Like Heisenberg's

---

[20] M. Buber, *I and Thou*, 59–60.

[21] "Thou shalt not make for thyself a graven image. Thou shalt have no other Gods before me," and "Thou shalt not use the Lord's Name (I AM WHO I AM) in vain" can be understood to relate not only to God who meets us from beyond us, but God who enlivens us from within, as the breath does the dust in the Genesis account of the creation of humanity. This mysterious meeting-place or 'tabernacling' of dialogue between God and the dust from which person arises, remains ever a gift and beyond comprehension. No amount of 'graven images' or man-made tabernacles are capable of replacing this 'self' that is always in motion in response to the perichoresis or self-emptying 'dance' of love among the Holy Trinity.

uncertainty principle in which you can't tell the speed and position of an electron at the same time because of the wave-particle duality, in the same way it is not possible to observe the self in the act of responding to the Spirit. We can only collect an album of the traces and reflections left by the movement of life as it lives through us. Experience is always in the past.

Like in the parable of the Pharisee and the Publican, the self-representations that I the Pharisee present to God and the world in the form of my inner press secretary's picture album are not my real self. The true life I am becoming is "hid with Christ in God" and known to me only dimly in glimpses through the personal encounter with God which elicits repentance over of my failure to love as Christ loves. The one I truly am becoming in God's own likeness happens through the grace of personal encounter with Christ in such a way that I am gradually invited to lay down my life and pick up my cross, as He does, for the life of the world. The so-called 'right hand' of conscious awareness of my motivations is never fully comprehending of what the 'left-hand' of the Holy Spirit's mysterious presence is doing within me as He draws me through love to repentance crying out to God from the depths of the heart, 'Abba.' This is the Way of love that the saints tell us, along which gradually comes the discovery that it is no longer 'I' alone, but Christ who lives in me who is present in the "hidden person of the heart" (I Peter 3:4) in such a way that by God's Grace the sinner that I am begins to burn with the pure gift of the Uncreated Life of the ONE I AM who loves the world as Christ loves the world and gives His life for it. Through this process, we are all sifted, and our hearts weighed existentially in the form of our actions and choices in a way that mere words and reflections alone can never declare. It is why Martin Luther can say what seems otherwise incomprehensible. "Living, or rather dying and being damned make a theologian, not understanding, reading or speculating"[22] and the

---

[22] D. Martin, *Luthers Werke. Kritische Gesamtausgabe* (Weimarer Ausgaber). Weimar: Herman Bohlaus Nachfolger. 1883– (Series is not yet complete) (LW 42:11) quote trans. Ben Moravitz.

Spanish Philosopher Miguel de Unamuno can say, "Those who believe that they believe in God, but without any passion in the heart, without anguish of mind, without uncertainty, without doubt, without an element of despair even in there consolation, believe only in the God-idea, not in God Himself.[23]

There is an apophatic aspect to all human persons and to the world itself, which must be understood, just as there is with God whose essence remains unknowable and remains forever beyond science, beyond reason and beyond words to express as the philosopher Wittgenstein recognized. "It is not how things are in the world that is mystical, but *that* it exists."[24] This mystical element is what remains beyond the grasp of experience, yet is essential to it and which gives rise to all experience. What we yearn for and are privileged by the Grace of God to encounter and know through relationship, we may later find it difficult or impossible to articulate. As St. Paul recognized after his encounter with God in what he called "the third heaven" (II Cor. 12:1), for which he refused to take credit as part of his ordinary self identity. Wittgenstein, perhaps unwittingly echoing St. Paul and pointing to the same epistemological azimuth writes, "There are indeed, things that cannot be put into words. They make themselves manifest. They are what is mystical,[25] and "whereof one cannot speak, thereof one must be silent."[26] Such silence is the language of prayer and worship out of which all words arise, shimmering with the glory that issues from and points to a truth which cannot be fully spoken, except to the degree that it can be lived and shared with an other.

---

[23] M. de Unamuno, *Tragic Sense of Life* (New York: J. E. Crawford Flitch, Trans. Cosimo Inc., 2005), 193.

[24] L. Wittgenstein, *Tractatus Logico-Philosophicus* (United States: Seven Treasures Publications, 2010), (6.44).

[25] Ibid., (6.522).

[26] Ibid., (7).

CHAPTER FOUR

Pondering the Swish of Therapeutic Encounter: Reflections of a Spiritual Medic

> *I never think of myself as an icon. What is in other people's minds is not in my mind. I just do my thing.*
> Audrey Hepburn

Those priests, physicians and mental health professionals who have the privilege of encountering hurting, wounded souls in their pilgrimage through this world in search of the One who is searching for them, do well to heed Audrey Hepburn's humble and unwittingly wise counsel as far as not confusing oneself with any exalted imagination based on the collection of snapshots our inner press-secretary has taken of being a responsive co-partner with the Spirit's work of healing the people that consult with us. In a conversation about the priesthood, Metropolitan Alexios of Atlanta made a helpful observation along the same lines when we were discussing the outward forms of ordination as distinct from its spiritual core. "The black *riassa* is a tool used for a purpose. It is important not to get the ego tied up with it." This simple observation gets at the core of realizing that we have an objective duty in the world, whether as priests or as helping professionals, to fulfill our role conscientiously and dispassionately so that our genuine human responsiveness accepts the ascetical restraints of professional boundaries, ethics and the special purposes of our respective disciplines, while inwardly standing vigilant so that egotism does not get mixed up in the process by confusing our personal identities with the sometimes marvelous events and revelations that take place through these forms of service. Like Jesus who did not even consider being God a thing to be grasped for Himself (Phil. 2:6), and the Apostle Paul who did not permit himself to identify his own personal ego with the revelations he experienced when lifted up into the third heaven (2 Cor. 12:2–5), the priest, pastoral counselor and physician all serve as junior partners with the Holy Spirit, who as the Good Physician remains the source of revelation and healing operating by condescension through our co-creative partnerships.

In the same way, pastoral counselors and psychotherapists, who are privileged to be guests in the depths of the soul of another human being, do not consider it a thing to be 'grasped' for one's own elevation. More often than not, such encounters are humbling because of the impact of being witness to the vulnerability, courage and tenacity of suffering persons finding their way back to life from the hells they have endured or if not, finding the faith and love to convert the suffering into an offering by accepting what they cannot change, as Paul did with the "thorn in his flesh." In this way,

> good psychotherapy, like good religion, helps people suffer for the right reasons and stop suffering for the wrong reasons. When psychotherapy occurs in the context of shared Christian faith between client and therapist, all other things being equal, I believe the conditions are ripe for the highest quality therapeutic alliance. Nevertheless, whatever the therapist may say or do, it is essentially the grace of God working through the client's growing faith that is at work. Put another way, we can say that the therapeutic alliance is a temporary relationship designed to clear away obstacles to a person's permanent therapeutic journey in faith and good pastoral psychotherapy occurs when we are least intrusive in people's lives while at the same time being most interested, caring, and careful as we help them recognize the conscious and unconscious obstacles to the grace of God working in them through the presence of our Lord Jesus Christ and the power of the Holy Spirit.[1]

---

[1] S. Muse, "Your Faith Is Making You Well," in J. Chirban (ed.), *Sickness or Sin?:*

The plain truth is that God is attentive to the cries of His children and pours Grace into us through any and every vehicle, whether through a person or a jackass, as in the case of the prophet Balaam (Num. 22:28), whose donkey was able to sense the presence of the angel to which the prophet himself was blind because of his stubbornness. But if the donkey that prophesies begins to think it is the source of the revelation coming through it or begins to feel special and/or superior to others who have not been so privy to the miraculous, then it becomes delusional, which leads to a bad state. Elder Paisios of Souroti remarked somewhere that he did not know how he knows the prophecies the Holy Spirit frequently offered to his receptive heart. The same was true of Elder Porphyrios and other wonderworking elders.

A SCETICALLY-ACQUIRED PRACTICAL WISDOM AND ILLUMI-NATION BY GRACE. Along these lines, an Athonite monk, who had first-hand experience with some of the holy elders on Mount Athos, showed some interest in this modern discipline called *pastoral* counseling offered outside the context of the confessional and the ordained priesthood. With sincere interest, he asked, "What does a pastoral psychotherapist know that an enlightened spiritual elder does not know?" Aside from complete trust in his own elder, the monk was also an impartial scientist of human psychology, and his question was a legitimate and humbly offered one which interested me and invited me to begin to clarify something for myself. I think the question could be paraphrased as, "What does an experienced medic know about dealing with combat wounds that a well-trained surgeon does not?" Father Philotheos Faros reminded me once in this regard[2] of the Lord's saying in Luke 16:8: "The children of this world are in their generation wiser than the children of light." There is, indeed, something to be learned in the foxholes, trenches and struggle with the passions in daily life and through scientific research that may not

Spiritual Discernment and Differential Diagnosis (Brookline, MA: Holy Cross Orthodox Press, 2001).
[2] Personal correspondence with the author.

be available to one who has lived most of their life in a monastery. Elder Paisios of Mount Athos notes,

> If monks and nuns aren't careful, their hearts can become very hard. Laypeople see accidents, the suffering of others, and are pained. We don't see this suffering and may pray only for ourselves… We may reach the point of wanting to make ourselves comfortable and having a heart stony from indifference, a condition that is contrary to the Gospel. The monk must care for, be pained over, and in general pray for people. This is not a distraction, but, on the contrary, he himself is helped by the prayer and so are the others.[3]

Of course, the reverse is also true, even though both are dealing with the same stuff of the human psyche. When combined with faith in Christ and rootedness in Orthodox Christian worship and life, such acquaintance with the world's sin and pain and the intimate details of a person's struggles to overcome their tragedies, teaches the therapist and becomes a wealth of practical wisdom. Because of the relative paucity of holy wonderworking elders, the need for 'spiritual medics' experienced in the ways of the world is great, and God does not abandon His people, but even helps these medics care for them. If there are no medics, then surely even donkeys will offer encouragement and the rocks and stones themselves will start to speak, for the Lord does not abandon humankind, but assures us, "I will be with you until the close of the age" (Mt. 28:20).

In response to the monk's question, first of all I want to affirm the distinction similar to that which Metropolitan Hierotheos Vlachos makes[4] between ascetically acquired natural intuitive wisdom learned "in the foxholes of life" by wrestling with the passions versus charis-

---

[3] Elder Paisios, *Spiritual Counsels, Vol. II* (Souroti, Thessaloniki, Greece: Holy Monastery of St. John the Theologian, 2008), 349–350.
[4] Cf. H. Vlachos, *Orthodox Psychotherapy* (Levadia, Greece: Birth of the Theotokos Monastery, 2005).

matically offered Divine Grace that is supernatural in origin and given through a purified *nous* from beyond the wisdom and experience of the one through whom it is offered, for the sake of the suffering soul to whom it is offered. Sometimes this is done with the knowledge of the one through whom it is offered, and sometimes, like Balaam's donkey, it happens without the one through whom it comes even comprehending that he or she is prophesying at the time. For those whose hearts have begun to undergo cleansing of the passions and relative freedom from phantasia through prayer, repentance and ascetical struggle, as Archimandrite Sophrony pointed out, and begin to develop discernment of spirits, the distinction between ascetically-acquired experience from struggling with the passions coming to know oneself gradually through repentance in contrast to the supernatural charism of the Holy Spirit that is active through the prayer of the holy elder as a gift of Grace are closely related and hard to distinguish. It is, of course, difficult or impossible to learn from experience without the counterpoint of Grace shedding light on the situation. Where the uncreated energies of God end and the natural energies of the created world begin remains a mystery that eludes both scientist and theologian as an object of knowledge, yet by God's grace may be personally encountered, noetically recognized through the Holy Spirit's witness through the therapeutic trialogue between self, other and God.

Perhaps this is why the Eastern Orthodox Church describes the theologian as "one who prays," that is, one who is in perpetual call and response dialogue of encounter with the persons of Christ and the Holy Spirit. Though recognizing many saints who have evidenced this in their lives, the Eastern Orthodox Church has reserved the title of 'theologian' for only three figures in its history: St. John the Apostle, St. Gregory the Theologian and St. Symeon the New Theologian. As for elders who are regarded as spiritual physicians, those wonderworkers whose intimate dialogue with God causes them to be recognized as possessing the charisma of Grace in hearts given to constant prayer and protected by ascetical restraint, though few in number, these have existed throughout Christian history. From the wonderworking Apostles to the Unmercenary physicians, Sts. Cosmas and Damian, all the way to the nineteenth century Sts. Seraphim[5] of Sarov and Makarios and Ambrose of Optina Monastery to the twentieth century figures like Elder Porphyrios, the chaplain of Polyclinic Hospital in Athens, whose clairvoyant "TV" showed surgeons how to operate on tumors;[6] Brother Joseph the Hesychast,[7] whose clairvoyant vision is recorded on numerous occasions and whose five disciples all became remarkable elders themselves, helping to rebuild monasteries on Mount Athos and offering consolation and guidance to many Christian pilgrims in search of the true wisdom and life in Christ; St. Silouan of Mount Athos[8] and his disciple Elder Sophrony of Essex, each of whom are very different as personalities, all witness to the same faith and continuing presence of the Holy Spirit that made the fisherman wise and able to travel the world witnessing to the events that had once confused and shattered them, eventually undergoing martyrdom themselves.

Fr. Zacharias, one of Elder Sophrony's monks, described[9] how he and his brothers witnessed persons with paralyzed faces instantly straighten out in response to the Holy Spirit answering the elder's prayers as well as other miracles of physical healing and they were amazed. By contrast, Elder Sophrony never made a fuss over these things. Then one day after the elder prayed for the healing of a man and nothing happened, he prayed again and still nothing, so he lifted up the *epitrachelion* covering the man's head and said, "Well, we're not miracle

---

[5] A. Moore, *An Extraordinary Peace: St. Seraphim Flame of Sarov* (Washington: Anaphora Press, 2009).

[6] Cf. C. Yiannitsiotis, *With Elder Porphyrios: A Spiritual Child Remembers* (Greece: Holy Convent of the Transfiguration, 1991).

[7] Cf. Joseph of Vatopaidi, *Elder Joseph the Hesychast: Struggles, Experiences, Teachings (1898–1959)* (Greece: Vatopaidi Monastery, 1999).

[8] A. Sophrony, *St. Silouan the Athonite* (Essex, England: Stavropegic Monastery of St. John the Baptist: Essex, England, 1991).

[9] Cf. Z. Zacharias, "The Ascetical & Pastoral Theology of St. Silouan the Athonite and Archimandrite Sophrony." From audiocassette lectures recorded by Orthodox Christian Cassettes, Inc. Springdale, Arkansas.

workers after all!" But when he did so, the elder noticed the man's face visibly changed into an expression of joy which was so evident that he asked him what had happened. The man told him it was true, he was not healed physically as he had hoped, but he had received a transformative experience of coming to faith which he valued even more. He had been inwardly healed. The monks were all thoughtful about this incident because their elder was overjoyed at this, while with all the amazing physical miracles they had witnessed right in front of them with their own eyes from the elder's prayers, he had never showed any reaction, perhaps in itself a testimony that of the spiritual gifts, faith that brings inner healing leading to salvation is a greater gift than physical healing itself. The dispassion that prevents the ego from taking the slightest credit for the miracle is also vitally important.

These remarkable spiritual physicians, though relatively rare, continue to reveal the power of Divine Grace operating in our lives just as in Jesus' time so that the Lord's words are abundantly fulfilled, "Truly, truly, I say to you, whosoever believes in Me, the works that I do shall he do also; and greater works than these shall he do; because I go to My Father" (John 14:12). These theologians and physicians of soul and body, by their lives of intercessory prayer and love for others suffering in the world, set the bar for the rest of us by pointing us constantly toward Christ who is active in our midst and testifying to a quality and depth of relationship with God that is possible through faith, neptic vigilance, continual prayer and ascetical struggle that bears the fruit of eternal life in our midst, transfiguring the created order with the uncreated divine energies of Grace. Their existence also points us toward an essential formational context for becoming pastoral counselors who serve the truth of Christ, which remains primarily one of entering into relationship with others in the world and with Christ through the Holy Spirit.

THE USEFULNESS OF SPIRITUAL MEDICS. In light of these examples, as a layperson tonsured as a reader and set apart by Metropolitan Alexios for ministry as a pastoral counselor, I do not lay claim to being either a theologian or a physician, spiritually or otherwise. But after serving in the trenches of daily life with people as pastor of a small rural church for over a decade and later after my entrance into Orthodoxy serving in the *diakonia* of pastoral psychotherapy, teaching and training pastoral counselors and assisting clergy in crisis for some twenty years, like others in my field, I have become, by experience, necessity and the Grace of God, something of a "spiritual medic." I have seen things I cannot explain and witnessed lives and marriages come alive in ways that moves me to tears and at times starts the Jesus Prayer going within me so that I come away grateful and blessed from the encounter. At other times, tired and numb, full of vicarious trauma from hearing the stories of pain, abuse and suffering that seems resistant to change, I find myself contending with the same old demons that seek to use suffering — my own and others — to twist my intention off center from relationship with Christ and the mystery of the Grace-filled *thatness* of our gifted lives toward the functional atheism of seeking some kind of control on my own. At the end of a good day, sometimes I stand before the icon of Christ, the Panagia and St. John the Baptist and weep as the faces of suffering persons pass before my heart turned toward God. On bad days, overly tired, I eat chocolate, devour potato chips and watch distracting movies with my attention roaming about "as through waterless places" seeking some form of stimulation because I do not realize I am trying to escape from the pain and the questions absorbed in me through the intense engagement with suffering persons over the course of the day and the weeks before, residues of which remain just below the surface of my awareness, begging to be brought to God's attention and released in prayer so that joy can return once more. This is why care for the caregiver in the form of regular confession, fasting, exercise, friendship, worship, play and intimacy with my family and periodic retreats are so vital to renewing and growing the heart that can genuinely care for others.

THE WISE COUNSEL OF STARETS ILIA OF THE OPTINA MONASTERY IN RUSSIA. Once when I had the opportunity to talk through an interpreter to Starets Ilia of the Optina Pustyn Monastery in Russia, I asked him about vicarious trauma stemming from hearing confessions and intimate details of people's suffering and sins. Starets Ilia is a remarkable man of the quality of the wonderworking line of 19th century Optina elders before him, whom Dostoevsky visited in grief after the death of his child. The Holy Theotokos appeared to the elder when he was only three years old, and by the time he was fifteen, he was already drawn into seclusion as a hermit on Mount Athos. Matushka Evgenia told us that, like the elders of Optina, "St. Ambrose, St. Makarios and others before him, Starets Ilia is known to be gifted by the Holy Spirit with clairvoyant discernment, and people wait for weeks to be able to see him for confession and guidance in their lives. The quality of his presence had already caught my attention during the five and a half hour long worship service earlier that day. Unlike the dozens of other monks and priests taking part in the service, he alone among them seemed penetrated by the effects of ascetical labors, neptic watchfulness, humbled by long and deep repentance and full of Grace, which was evident in the very way his body moved. I had found myself wondering about him at the time and was not surprised when Matushka told us later about him and suggested we go to get his blessing.

Much to our delighted surprise, he asked to meet us in the church, and we sat together in a small group on benches in a corner. Our friend Lisa was translating from the Russian to English. He began the dialogue by asking us, "What questions do you have?" I found myself suddenly immensely grateful with tears rising up from deep within my chest coming out of nowhere as my heart was moved in a way I have come to associate with Grace's touch, as to Christ Himself. I managed to say, "My questions have all vanished because it is enough just to see you elder." To see a man raised up and to be offered the gift of presence is a living *Eucharist*. His response was a simple, "Thank you." He then spoke at length in Russian. When he had finished, Lisa, who struggled to keep up with some of the theological terms, said, "It was theologically dense and I can't remember everything because he said so much." She summarized the gist she recalled as, "Something about physical distance, that though we are apart, spiritually we are close and can pray anywhere just as much as here." This was very important to me, as it was a clear reminder that though my wife Claudia and I had traveled four thousand miles and I was moved in the depths by being in the presence of this holy elder who iconically represented Christ for me, it is also true that whenever and wherever this occurs, it is *always* simply Christ and the power of the Holy Spirit at work among us creating the possibility for renewal.

We are not tied to the person of any one holy man or woman through whom we discover the wellspring of this living fountain of Grace pouring up within us in "sighs too deep for words." He was in effect telling us what Jesus Himself told the woman He looked for who touched Him in the midst of the thronging crowd when He noticed "power was going out from Him." He had looked for her who had touched Him in such a way as to draw the Divine Energy of love from Him, and He found her and said to her, "Go in peace. Your faith has healed you" (Luke 7:50). In this way, Jesus unbound her from Himself, freeing her to realize that the bond she had with Him through faith would be with her everywhere she went. Rather than bind her to Him, He restored her to the community with the awareness that faith had opened a door within her that had access to Him in any place at any time. She could draw power from God through love that is constantly seeking to save and heal God's children wherever she was. This kind of love and humility is always the sign of a true spirit-filled elder. Whatever obedience is given to such persons out of humility and love is not received as to them personally for egoistic needs, but rather as a freely offered response of love to Christ for whom they are midwives of the Spirit's witness in the heart. Any elder, priest or counselor, who makes a claim of control over a person of any kind or who cultivates, consciously or not, admiration and acclamation from his spiritual children or clients, is self-deceived and deceiving and creates an oppressive relationship that injures both.

At this point, I described how "in my heart of faith, sometimes I just cry, while my mind doesn't seem to feel."

Starets Ilia answered, "The heart is like the sun. It warms us. The mind (*nous*) is more for discernment."

"How is it possible to integrate the two?" I asked. "To have the mind in the heart?" Lisa had trouble translating his response, so I continued, "Attention is something I am responsible for. Grace and faith are God's gifts. The will is moved to loving actions. Should I try to bring my attention within me to unite these three?"

Starets Ilia said, "God does not save us without our participation. It is good that you struggle and strive. The gifts of God are different for different people and not all are given at the same time." Then he said something about "sorrow being important."

I told him, "I am a pastoral psychotherapist. I hear many terrible things that create sorrow for me. How do I avoid being hurt by the accumulated residue of these things?" Starets Ilia said simply and quietly, "The way you keep the heart pure is through prayer and repentance." Nothing more. Fr. Georgios of Philotheou Monastery told me the same on Mount Athos some years later. Nothing new in his words, but I was grateful for the reaffirmation from this living struggler's experienced offering, arising out of having lived what he speaks and struggled in prayer with his own demons, confirming what others I have read about have said, and what I have repeatedly experienced through the cycle of sin, prayer and confession that plays like a record over and over in my own life. His words and presence had a calming effect in my inner being, perhaps as much because it had been offered personally to me from the elder as for the content of what was said. Words reach the heart only when they are personal. The problem in my life is not that I have not heard the words of life before, but that they have not been spoken and received into my heart from the Holy Spirit who alone can give them life and make them catch fire within me. When such words issue from one who has lived what he or she knows and through whose open heart the Holy Spirit speaks, they are powerful indeed, especially if they find soil in the heart of the listener also prepared by the Holy Spirit to receive the fruitful seed of the word. This is why St. Seraphim of Sarov could speak of evangelism from an entirely different and deeper sense than the modern Western notion of handing out tracks and preaching when he observed, "Find inner peace, and thousands around you will achieve their salvation." It is similar to St. Francis's often quoted exhortation to his monks, "Preach always, but only as a last result if you must, use words." And Ghandi's famous dictum, which adorns my computer as a scrolling marquee in my counseling office, "You must be the change you wish to see in the world."

The question of vicarious trauma experienced through hearing the confessions and intimate details of sins and struggles of clients and parishioners over decades which end up catching hold at times in places of the therapist or priest's own psyche where one is vulnerable to the same sins or could be under certain conditions, is an important area of self care that demands a fruitful spiritual life both inwardly and outwardly in healthy human relationships. Clearly, the root of the issue of sustainment in the work of pastoral care and counseling is to be found in the trialogue of prayer, repentance, confession, worship and acts of love that are part of the call and response between oneself, Christ and the world. "Cut off from Me, you can do nothing." Not only that, we should not attempt to do anything apart from prayer, for Christ is the Good physician and the Holy Spirit is the theologian and those do the work of God who act as midwives in response to these three in the work of pastoral care and counseling. Approaching the mystery of another person's soul apart from relationship with Christ, there is always the danger of violating the cardinal rule of psychotherapy taken from the Hippocratic Oath, which is *primum non nocere* — "first do no harm." From the Eastern Orthodox perspective, while this means avoiding approaching persons reductionistically, "seeing spiritual life from within psychological interpretations or contemporary anthropocentric psychological systems,"[10] it does not negate partnership with

---

[10] H. Vlachos, *The Illness and Cure of the Soul in the Orthodox Tradition* (Leva-

science in service of loving care guided by the Holy Spirit, but includes science as a partner. God and science only become antagonists when they are seen to be on the same level as competing paradigms, which is an epistemological error.

There have been in the history of the Church many elders whose prayers and intimacy with God opened up gifts of healing and discernment. Metropolitan Hierotheos Vlachos has written extensively from a theoretical perspective on the subject of spiritual healing and its roots in the patristic science of hesychasm. Drawing on the theological emphases of Fr. John Romanides, he characterizes these Holy Spirit-filled persons as "priests who can heal" in contrast to those who cannot because they have not undergone the ascetical and charismatic transformation that is part of the process of sanctification known in the Eastern Orthodox Church as deification or *theosis*.[11] This is a critical but subtle distinction which can be misunderstood if it is not clearly recognized that God is always the healer whether through the prayers of the elder, or the prayers at the Divine Altar during the Liturgy and the mysteries of the Church offered over the course of a lifetime, including Eucharist, marriage, confession, anointing, etc. Still, there is a co-creative partnership with God as Starets Ilia pointed out, whereby as Jesus says, "If you ask anything in My name, it shall be done for you" (John 15:7).

This raises the question of how pastoral counselors and priests are trained. Apart from the life of prayer, confession, worship, repentance, and experience in the ascetical struggle to be faithful to God in the world, psychological theories in and of themselves cannot create an elder or starets "who can heal." So what makes a person a better

---

dia, Greece: Birth of the Theotokos Monastery, 1993), 59.

[11] Cf. H. Vlachos, *Orthodox Psychotherapy* (2005); Archbishop Chrysostomos, *Themes in Orthodox Patristic Psychology: Humility, Obedience, Repentance, and Love* (Etna, CA: Center for Traditionalist Orthodox Studies, 2010); I. M. Kontzevitch, *The Acquisition of the Holy Spirit in Ancient Russia* (Platina, CA: St. Herman of Alaska Brotherhood), for a discussion of *theosis* which is too extensive to summarize here.

'transmitter' of the Spirit? What does it mean to 'abide in Christ' so that when we call on the Lord, He responds?

A critical distinction in this regard was clarified between the perspectives and approaches of the Western and Eastern Christian churches in the 14th century in the controversy that came to a head between the two respective spokespersons Barlaam of Calabria and St. Gregory Palamas of Thessalonica, over the nature of the human relationship with God. "St. Symeon the New Theologian whose daring claim to have seen God as Light set off a furor which culminated in the theology of St. Gregory Palamas. The crucial question which Palamite theology tried to resolve was 'Does (humankind) really encounter God in this present life on earth?'"[12]

Barlaam offered the Western, post-enlightenment, scholastic approach, which contended that God can only be known about as an object logically and philosophically, whereas St. Gregory Palamas pointed out that St. Symeon's experience was, indeed, representative of the Eastern Church's experience from the beginning, that God could be encountered personally and that the training of the attention to be present to this encounter through continual mindfulness (*nepsis*), repentance and prayer was an essential ingredient to being able to receive and metabolize the Divine Energies of Grace, which are freely given to all. These uncreated energies are one with the Divine Essence, which is unknowable, yet whose life is communicated through the energies that indwell a person and confront them as 'other' at the same time.

St. Gregory Palamas' summing up the Eastern Church's perspective in the hesychastic tradition of inner prayer leading to *theosis*, or deification by Grace, insisted on the possibility of personal encounter with God, with body, mind and heart, through the Divine Uncreated Energies of Grace. Metropolitan Hierotheos (Vlachos) draws on the implications of these differing points of view with regard to cure of

[12] J. Dunlop, *Staretz Amvrosy* (Europe; Belmont, MA: Buchervertriebsanstalt: Distributed by Notable & Academic Books, 1988), 21.

the soul in the Orthodox tradition, which is the heart of the pastoral counseling methodology from the Eastern perspective:

> Our method is ... to try to keep the commandments of Christ in our life. Whilst attempting to keep the commandments, our old self with its passions is disclosed, subsequently we struggle to be healed of our passions. In parallel, we attempt to keep our *nous* clear from malice and arrogance and it then distinguishes the good thought from the demonic one. We exercise ourselves in watchfulness and thus the *nous* can discern thoughts, as St. Diadochos of Photiki says; it stores the divine thoughts in the treasury of memory, while it rejects the "dark and demonic ones" from memory. And in this way true repentance is activated.[13]

From this perspective, the psychological sciences and theories of counseling are rightly used when they serve to clear away obstacles to Grace which invite repentance, which is seen as the primary path of healing and growth toward fullness of human potential. Of course, God loves all people equally, but not all people who are loved respond to God or one another equally. Still, any grasping of this difference in elevation of oneself is a misappropriation of God's gifts and leads to a form of elitism that is both delusional and dangerous insofar as it denigrates the mystery of Grace given through the Mysteries,[14] which remain effective, even if the priest who serves at the altar, is himself in a sinful state and "cannot heal" through his prayers. Nevertheless, not realizing this difference between the content of belief and the existential process of assimilating Grace in our lives through repentance and continual prayer is to fail to see the deepest mystery of the co-creative partnership of human and divine. As Elder Paisios colorfully puts it somewhere, "Human beings are two-winged creatures. One wing is

---

[13] H. Vlachos, *op. cit.* (1993), 51.
[14] "Sacraments."

moved by will and the other by God's Grace." Missing either one, the bird of life cannot fly.

WONDERWORKING ELDERS AND MIRACLES OF UNCREATED GRACE. The phenomenon of spiritual growth of those people recognized as holy elders whose center of gravity has shifted over time from the anthropocentric personal ego more and more to a theocentric position of faith in Christ and who live in solidarity with the entire community of humankind, whose "self is hid with Christ in God" and whose intercessory prayers work miracles, is well summed up in simple fashion by John Dunlop, author of the biography of Optina *Staretz Amvrosy*, when he writes:

> The Christian must pursue perfection through self-renuncia-
> tion, through a "shifting of the center" in which the overween-
> ing human ego is removed to the periphery and God Himself
> is placed at the center of the human personality. This vital and
> life-giving shift occurs only through the greatest effort (*praxis*);
> the soul must die to this world so that it may pass into the next,
> which has already been initiated by Christ and will culminate in
> His Second Coming.[15]

In Russia, my wife Claudia and I visited Starets Ambrose's cell at Optina Monastery, a short distance off from the main monastery out in the forest. Tears flowed quietly from Matushka Evgenia's eyes as she opened the door to his cell and led us into the elder's tiny room, kept the same as when he had lived there, his small bed off to the side and his few, but well worn leather-bound volumes of patristic theology and Holy Scripture on the table. She shared with us a story of one of the many miracles worked through the elder's intercessory prayers, about which I later read.[16] She said there was a man who suffered from

---

[15] J. Dunlop, *op. cit.* (1988), 17.
[16] Ibid. p. 93.

severe alcoholism to the point that he had attempted suicide several times and had not found help anywhere. He had come to see the *starets* but was unable to speak in his presence. So the elder spoke first telling him what he had discerned clairvoyantly through the Spirit: "When you were 13 years old, you stole money from your grandfather who was the treasurer of the church in order to buy wine. That is the origin and source of your problems." At that very moment, the man came to faith and was instantly healed of his long-standing 'incurable' alcoholism on the spot, entering into a living experience of faith in the truth of Christ not as merely an idea of something that happened long ago, or an idea to live up to by one's own will, but as a living personal reality embracing him *here and now* through the elder's intercession.

Elder Porphyrios, who reposed in 1991, is one of the more well-known and beloved twentieth century elders known for his "spiritual television," who was consulted for all sorts of problems, both spiritual and physical, by people from several continents as well as physicians at the hospital in Athens, where he was chaplain for many years. George Demetriou, the Regional Manager for the Central and Southern Europe Cyprus Airways, who had a long relationship with Elder Porphyrios, tells the story of their first meeting. Elder Porphyrios suffered from intense pain of shingles, kidney problems and a host of other ailments. His prayers healed others, yet he insisted his own sometimes excruciating pain helped him to repent so he would not pray for God to relieve him of it. When George arrived, he was told by one of the nuns that the elder was very tired and could not see him, so he went and sat in his car parked some ways away under a tree with the others. After a time, a nun approached him and said, "Sir, the elder asked for the gentleman in the green car to come and see him." When he met with him, Elder Porphyrios asked him if he had children and then began to describe both of their personalities exactly as if he had known them all their lives, a common experience of those who have consulted the elder and left in amazement at his profoundly accurate and detailed knowledge of their lives which was clearly supernaturally revealed. Realizing he was in the presence of a Grace-filled "holy man," George began to visit the elder as often as he could. Years later, his first grandchild developed serious problems shortly after birth and was taken to the children's hospital in Athens, where he ended up in the intensive care unit. After six days of prayer, George decided to visit Elder Porphyrios and arrived at eleven o'clock at night. He describes his encounter:[17]

> He saw me, and with typical simplicity, he asked, "What are you doing here at this time of night?"
> "Elder, my daughter, the rebel, as you call her, has given birth to a little boy and now the baby is in danger of dying." I then heard him say to me, "Sit down and let me 'X-ray' the child, to see what the matter is with him." He then told me the following: "There is a foreign substance on the lower right side of his lung. It has almost dissolved and will soon disappear. Do not be afraid. The child will live. You will take him home on Monday … On the following day, Monday, the child was fine and we took him home.

There are countless stories like this from the life of Elder Porphyrios and other elders already mentioned, which offer empirical testimony to the love of God for humankind and the continuing activity of the Holy Spirit in our midst. It is also a testimony to the vital importance of the would-be therapist's rootedness in Christian faith, worship, prayer and ascetical struggle as the primary ground of formation and sustainment in the work of pastoral care and counseling. If the Holy Spirit can use Balaam's donkey to help its stubborn, self-pitying owner who is not listening to God to be healed, He can also use those of us who, though we are not spirit-filled physicians and theologians illumined to the degree that these remarkable elders evidence, yet God still can and does use us when there is a need.

---

[17] K. Ioannidis, *Elder Porphyrios: Testimonies and Experiences* (Athens: Holy Convent of the Transfiguration of the Savior, 1997), 211–214.

REFLECTIONS OF A SPIRITUAL MEDIC. As pastor of a small church for eleven years, I have watched the Holy Spirit take ten years to bring about reconciliation in situations that seemed at the time hopelessly impossible. I have driven 50 miles prompted by a gentle nudge within, no more than a familiar flicker, and found myself walking into the empty hospital room of an old woman alone with her death rattle, then feeling my own breathing stop in wonder as the words of the Lord's Prayer I was praying aloud ended just as her last breath ferried her into God's everlasting arms. Had I not listened to that "still small voice within," she would have died alone without a prayer, or perhaps God would have found another servant to help.

Sitting with the survivor of the sudden rampage of a sister's ex-boyfriend who killed the rest of his family in a moment of delusional, vengeful grief over the break-up, burying dozens of people I had come to love deeply, holding their hands as they lay dying, visiting them in the hospital and celebrating their marriages, comforting another anticipating having her excruciatingly painful gangrenous legs amputated, responding to a frightened wife's appeal for me to go and talk with her estranged husband holed up in the house with his shotgun threatening to shoot anyone who approached, or comforting the fears of a reclusive woman who saw three-fingered demons crawling on her walls while enduring the suspicion and gossip of the small rural countryside as being a witch, along with twenty years and tens of thousands of hours living in the trenches of psychotherapy daily wrestling with the intimate details of people's lives hearing their stories of heartache, perversion, rape, incest and combat trauma; the dissociated numb pain of a woman dragged by her hair through a cornfield by the man she loved; a young soldier tormented by recurring images of muzzle-fire from his rifle and the screams of the pregnant woman whose belly he saw ripped open by the bullets he fired into the crowd; and pierced myself by the abject, forlorn anguish of a man whose sexual compulsivity was so out of control he could not stop himself from picking up any homeless vagrants he passed by on the street to have sex with him, while aching with the terror and guilt he lived with wondering constantly if he was giving his wife HIV without realizing it, doubling over in sobs in my office pleading for help, are representative of the encounters which have changed me and remain in some place in my mind that has been touched by the ravages of human suffering.

But by the Grace of God, even more powerful is the hope that arises in Christ who is present in all the places of our brokenness and shows forth in the courage, vulnerability and resilience of people who trust another human being enough to tell their stories and lay down the burdens that result from being alone with them. Sitting with people as a pastoral counselor makes it a necessity for me to turn to God for help, seeking with whatever scraps of wisdom and compassion are mine to offer while listening with as much attention and stillness as I am capable in order to discern what God is doing with these people, rather than what I want to do. Through this experiential process, I have in spite of myself, like many others who do this work of pastoral counseling, become something of a spiritual medic — someone who ties off the stream of cognitive invectives tormenting the person within and clears out the obtrusions to the airways of faith and hope so that the person survives long enough to get them to the hospital of the Church where the Good Physician and the community of the Beloved can help sustain and guide them further. Where this is not yet possible, I look for the invisible God who is at work in their lives in ways they do not yet acknowledge, the One whose presence is revealed through the extraordinary humility, hope, courage and love that are found at the place where the self-protections devised by the mind give way to the naked heart's truth and the body confirms the truth of their words.

While I am neither physician nor theologian in the Orthodox sense of the word, God has not abandoned me or the suffering souls He has sent my way. I have been taught lessons by the courage, vulnerability, hope and faith of those who have sought to heal their hearts in my office; couples whose love and intimacy are strengthened even more deeply after they bare their souls to one another in the aftermath of an affair, discovering in that first tenuous vulnerability a depth of mercy and Grace that awakens their sense of God's presence; a father whose daughter put a gun in her mouth and shattered her whole family's life in a few seconds. Talking with him over the course of two years on the way to Emmaus, I went with him as he entered Job's whirlwind of rage, numbness and self-flagellation, angry with God, angry with himself, intellectualizing in order to survive as he had done as a child in the harsh circumstances of his early life and ultimately finding himself alive in a way he has never known before, awakened to his body and to God, not as an idea, a mere Paschalian wager, but as *personal.*

Like Balaam's donkey, I have prophesied without knowing how it was happening and witnessed God using one of my supervisees to prophesy to me, without him realizing it, giving me a word so exact and timely that it stopped me in my tracks with wonder at God's mercy for sending an arrow with my name on it straight to my heart. I have been offered countless pearls of wisdom from my clients. Most of all, the courage, humility, vulnerability and tenacity of the people I have known in this work has gifted me with chances to observe repeatedly the places in my own life where each of the things people have suffered are things I can find the possibility of within myself if given the right conditions. It is humbling.

It seems clear that we share one human nature, even though each of us have a uniquely personal self. Ontologically, there is no 'us and them.' Existentially, there is. We are one humanity with many persons. This makes for the possibility of extraordinary encounters as well as painful avoidance at times. I share these few anecdotes and reflections as an offering of thanksgiving to all those who have taught me about life, forgiveness, mercy, hope and redemption over all these years, who remain in my heart, as well as in praise and wonder before God who is the Healer and Physician of our souls and bodies, whoever we may be and whatever we may suffer. And I offer them to stimulate further reflection on the training and formation of pastoral counselors and Christian psychotherapists who are increasingly called upon to help the suffering souls who seek us out when a true 'physician of soul and body' is either unavailable or they are unaware that such persons even exist in this world.

These experiences, of course, raise all sorts of questions for the
'scientist' and theoretician in me wanting to understand the difference between natural intuition born of experience and ascetical
struggle with the passions as contrasted with illumination by the
Holy Spirit, which is related to the question of how uncreated divine
energies of Grace are related to the created energies of the natural
world. What makes the mysteries of the Church effective as agents
of Grace? Why is it that a particular person's prayers are consistently
more effective than those of others?[18] It is clear there are finer and
finer vibratory states that interpenetrate one another and the phenomenon of 'distance healing'[19] and medical intuition has begun to
be of interest to physicians exploring the boundaries of conventional
medicine and the untapped world beyond this for which we do not
currently have inclusive paradigms. The more science probes, the
deeper is the mystery surrounding the relationship between these
two worlds of creation and the uncreated Kingdom of the Father, Son
and Holy Spirit. It is my hope that Orthodox Christians will increasingly recognize and support the value of interdisciplinary dialogue
begun by OCAMPR[20] and now in the field of pastoral care of hospital
chaplaincy through the initiative of the Ecumenical Patriarch who
convened the first worldwide Orthodox summit in Rhodes, Greece,

[18] From the Eastern Orthodox perspective, the great mystery of the Lord's words
in John 15:7 — "If you abide in Me and My words abide in you, you can ask for
anything you want, and you will receive it" — relates to the mystery of *theosis*
which is at the heart of διά-Λογος. The more God's grace affects and transforms
the heart, the greater the repentance. The greater the repentance, the more the
soul finds Christ in and through love for all persons, "in all places and filling all
things." As in the case of St. Paul, one discovers "it is no longer I but Christ who
lives in me" and recalling the words of St. Silouan to Fr. Stratonicus regarding
"perfect speech" and "perfect obedience" asks in prayer only for what the Holy
Spirit already wishes to give.
[19] Cf. L. Dossey, *Healing Words* (New York: Harper Collins, 1997) and *Reinventing Medicine: Beyond Mind-Body to a New Era of Healing* (New York: Harper-
Collins, 2000).
[20] Orthodox Christian Association of Medicine, Psychology and Religion holds
annual conferences for this purpose.

in 2008, for this purpose, bringing together monastics, hospital chaplains, pastoral counselors, theologians, physicians and priests for several days of talks, sharing experiences and exploring how best to alleviate human suffering and support spiritual and psychological well-being and growth in the hospital setting. These initiatives are part of what is becoming a worldwide growth in understanding what affirms the partnership between faith and science.

PONDERING THE SWISH OF THERAPEUTIC ENCOUNTER: THE IMPORTANCE OF MIND-BODY UNITY. After lifting weights at the local YMCA, I wandered into the gym, which was empty. My hands had not touched a basketball for nearly thirty years and even then I was a less than mediocre player. I threw the worn leather ball at the goal and missed it entirely, noticing the potential embarrassment and humiliation offered to me by my vainglorious inner press secretary, always hard at work taking pictures of my every action, ready to provide spins and commentary for public consumption aimed at enhancing my public image. Most of all, I felt the uncoordination of my body, arms swollen and rubbery from lifting weights, and an unfamiliar strangeness in the exercise of trying to throw a rough leather ball into a small rim after all these years.

Then I wondered, *What if I sensed my body and extended ki toward the goal as I learned to do in Tai Chi, Aikido and sensing awareness exercises I have practiced for decades?* Becoming familiar with inner silence and attentiveness to qualities of sensation, feeling and the postures with which they are linked and to which they give rise, increases the ability to listen to the sound of another person's voice and watch the subtle movements of a person's body while remaining still within and attentive to the sensation of my own presence, in order to gain a felt sense of the person's unspoken pain and characterological defenses. Stillness and mind-body-feeling connection serve as a kind of eardrum picking up otherwise inaudible messages. It is as though the human body in motion is a kind of hologram upon and through which the entire history of the person's life as well as current conscious and unconscious motivations is written. To know one's own self opens up access to know others in ways that are not possible without this, particularly as it serves as a foundation for being present to God, self and other.

Mind-body unity. The center of gravity of my inner state changed in seconds. I took the ball and went to the sideline out beyond the stripe that defines three-point goals. There was no backboard to bounce off in case I over shot the distance. This makes it a more difficult shot requiring a very accurate feel and sense of distance with only the distant round wire hoop as the bulls eye. Even an inch or two off and it will be a miss. Yet there is a subtle sense of almost being able to 'touch' the rim of the basket even from that distance.

Without hesitation, I glanced up at the goal, my eyes and inner sense felt now an extension of the proprioceptive[21] sensation of my whole body saturated with consciousness as I lofted the ball in the air ... swish! I retrieved it and returned to the corner lofting a second shot ... swish! My mind is calmly concentrated now, feelings quiet except for the subtle peripheral sense of wonder and puzzlement elicited by the impartial witness of what is occurring. From somewhere arises the feint echo of a voice that seems destined to get the attention of the inner press secretary; maybe it *is* the press secretary posing as a scientist, I do not know. "Probability suggests that it cannot happen three times in a row." I lofted it a third time ... swish!

At this point, my attention was hijacked. A young boy had come into the gym and was serving as the backdrop for my inner press secretary's concerns and enthusiasm. I became split as part of my attention was taken by emotional reactivity and mental energy involuntarily reacting to projections onto him from my egoistic picture-taking sidekick, as a false 'I' began to surface, stealing credit for the three amazing shots — seeking to apply the success in some way to my vainglorious self who is always looking at events like this and

---

[21] The interior sensations of the body that indicate the level of autonomic nervous system arousal and give an indication of the quality of tension levels and feelings that are present.

making a photo album of still shots to stare at later and use for publicity purposes as some sort of narcissistic defense against the deeper recognition of my own nothingness.

This all happened in less than a second or two, but it was enough to throw off my entire equilibrium, and the fourth shot missed. The magic of mind-body unity and purity of motive which allowed inner stillness had dispersed as quickly as it had come. I had fallen from the glory of simple surrender to I-Thou dialogue with the basketball hoop to the vainglorious willful striving of monological self-aggrandizement in order to burnish my addictive starving need for more pictures to build my self-image photo album. Willfulness and willingness are miles apart.

Outwardly, little appeared to have changed. I was still trying to shoot a basketball, but inwardly, I was now very 'different' and it showed up in uncoordinated movement stemming from mixed inner motivations. I was divided — less an impartial dispassionate scientist now, no longer committed to the dance of presence and the wonder of encounter with my whole being. The press secretary was giving orders to continue, for the sake of vainglorious posturing for the boy, but the rest of me was dispersed. Where had my relatively collected inner peace gone? What happened to my inner unity? Wonder had flown out the window. Calmness of feeling and the relaxed tautness of one-pointed *ki* in harmony with my surroundings was replaced with the passions of acquisitive greed and vainglory. Willingness was superseded by willfulness. Unity of mind, body and soul had given way to hypocrisy — a self divided. As Jesus observed, "When your eye be single, your whole body will be full of light, but when your eye is darkened (divided) then great is the darkness" (Mt. 6:23).

There are all manner of stories in religious traditions from Eugen Herrigel's *Zen and the Art of Archery* and Karlfried Durckheim's *Hara* to the Bible and Desert Fathers, in which the disciple accomplishes all sorts of seemingly impossible feats by the power of the Spirit and then in a single moment of hubris, succumbing to the deception that he or she alone is the author of such events rather than a kind of flute that the Divine Spirit plays, falls from grace creating great suffering for self and others in the process. As Jesus is recorded by the Apostles as saying, "Cut off from Me, you can *do* nothing." These all point to a kind of central plumb line for the work of pastoral counseling, showing us at once, both the deep moral foundations rooted in the relationship between the person and the Holy Spirit as well as the potential sacredness of the material world and the power of the human person to enter the place of dialogue reconciling the apparent dissonance between the two.

What is happening when that 'swish' takes place with a client as contrasted to a willfully imposed model-led approach which interferes with the shot? It is easy to determine with a simple experiment that the body's speed and intelligence exceeds the mechanical thinking and associative reasoning of the more superficial reasoning mind (*dianoia*). Take typing, for example. Anyone who can type more than 40 words a minute has observed that as soon as you try to think about moving the fingers across the keyboard to each letter, you slow down, mistakes are made and you realize that in order to think of the letters and the pattern of typing them, you sacrifice the ability to type fast as well. This is a misplacing of trust in the deeper mind-body coordination of the soul in favor of the willful, over-controlled oppression of the personality-driven mechanical mind.

Feeling is even faster than the body and combines with non-verbal intuitive processes to speak quietly to the attentive mind in the moment. In essence, we know through our being before we realize we know with our minds. When there is stillness and a fine quality of feeling that matches a certain kind of intentionality, the message gets through. But do we trust it enough to *act* on it, to let it into our bodies, to make it *flesh* through *deed*? Martin Buber suggests that the "Spirit seeks a body through speech." By the time speech or verbalizing has occurred, the Spirit has already moved us and we are translating its meaning.

Once with a woman in crisis whom I had seen only a couple times, I made a statement about something missing in her life and then felt the quietest nudge within me that led me to add one more thing. I do not believe in twenty years of counseling I had ever before used the word I was about to say in therapy. Following this subtle nudge I added, "...and be sure that what I'm saying reaches the little *caboose*." The woman was moved instantaneously and responded with surprise, "*Caboose* is the nickname that I was called as a small child!" God can make Balaam's jackass a prophet if necessary, but the donkey must never afterwards think of himself any differently as though he had *done it himself*. Neither should the therapist! The *swish* of meeting between I, other and Spirit is made possible by the receptive loving presence and intention to be *available*. One seeks to be *vulnerable* — receptive to an intelligence far greater than one's own mechanical associative mind and emotionality. We can think of this vulnerability to the actual conditions here and now on the ground as a prerequisite of what Dr. Jamie Moran calls "situated action."[22] Metropolitan Anthony of Sourozh suggests that asceticism in religion has as its goal this *vulnerability* to the Spirit. In a similar way, the most important training ground for counseling is, I believe, purifying the intentionality of the heart and the quality of attention of the mind and soul tuned in dialogue to the wavelength of the mystery of the other person in the presence of God. God is the healer. As a therapist, I am trusting God, the client and my own being to be engaged in a single action of listening together until there is a kind of epiphany or theophany of 'Christ in our midst' who appears always at that mysterious intersection between I and other, so that there is a perfect 'fit' that proves transformative in linking our ordinary world with an invisible one that witnesses the Holy Spirit's activity in our heart.

Once near the end of an interpersonal group, when all the group members had spoken of the courage of a special forces soldier whose silent presence in the group over the course of the year had intimidated most so they would not confront him, with some mild trepidation I responded differently. I did not want to wound him, but neither did

---

[22] Dr. Jamie Moran has developed this concept of "situated action" extensively as it contrasts with model-driven therapies in his book *The Intelligence of Love* currently in process at the time of this writing.

I want to miss naming the wound that was keeping him from being fully alive. He had admirably served his men in several deployments, suffering wounds in his emotional heart that were basically grief. I affirmed his courage and strength and his desire always to be a man for others, which was true, but I suggested that his quietness in the group was not evidence of that strength. Rather it was his avoidance of a different kind of courage that has to do with risking entering into dialogue with others in a real way because he was trying to avoid the intense feelings of dialogue within himself that would inevitably be elicited if he risked a real encounter where he would speak so his body confirmed the truth of his words. He was dissociating and experiencing some psychic numbing characteristic of PTSD. He had grown up as a mixed blood on an Indian reservation, and I suggested to him, "If I were to give you a name, I would call you *He who walks alone* and encourage you to share your heart not only for your own healing, but for the strengthening of your brothers." He was stunned. This was the name he had been given by the tribe he had lived with decades earlier, which he had not told to anyone.

Where do these nudges come from? How often do they come, and I am too 'busy' inside with the small plans of my inner press secretary or my own agenda of what needs to happen, to be able to hear them? Or if I do, do I lack the wisdom, courage or *love* to respond? How often is this 'still small voice' of the Spirit ignored in favor of more visible and seemingly 'safer' routes of not risking a real encounter with the other in favor of stereotypical empathic responses that pose little risk of disturbing the peace from emotional shrapnel in a confrontation gone sideways when the inner press secretary goes to war doing damage control over an intervention that has hit the mark of the heart like an arrow? Such is a moment of truth. Either the recipient is seeking the truth and grateful or against it and so turns to attack or reject the one who offers it. Speaking so that your body confirms the truth of your words is risky business, for client and for therapist.

Once a brilliant, deeply troubled man, who had been chronically depressed for years, anxious to the edge of psychosis and fighting suicidal ideation on a daily basis, was telling me how he had spoken to his adult children, who felt responsible for him, about his suicidal desire. He had seen many psychiatrists and therapists over a decade, trying all sorts of psychoactive medicines without relief and was desperate. I was the latest in a long line and had seen him enough to have a solid therapeutic relationship of trust with him. He was some years older than me in age, but there was a mutual respect between us. One day, as he was telling me what he had recently said to his adult son about how he was going to kill himself, I experienced within me an intimation of the pain that a child feels in such a situation combined with what seemed a clear sense that his talk of suicide was manipulative in some way — drawing his son in through coercion rather than authentic relationship. He had done this for many years, and his children had slowly grown weary of talking to him always on these terms. Within seconds of noticing all this as I was sitting with him, I made the choice to allow the anger I felt over what he was doing to his children to enter my body. It was a clear choice. The anger was united with love for this man and for his children. I made the decision to tell him, knowing that my body would confirm the truth of my words: "Stop doing that to your children." I said quietly with conviction. "Don't ever tell them you are going to kill yourself again!" I knew it was a highly directive response, which I rarely do, and charged with the force of anger, which is even rarer in therapy. It could be misinterpreted. My words were a *deed*, but I could not guarantee the outcome. He was taken aback; stopped in his tracks, puzzled even, and also relieved. He explained to me that it was one of the most loving actions he had ever experienced from a therapist in all his years. He felt *cared* for. He said he felt like I was at that moment the father he had needed to help him find his way. To my knowledge, he never burdened his children with talk of suicide in that way again. I also believe that his neediness had never come up against anyone who believed in his greater health enough to challenge him. Because of his superior intelligence and giftedness, he was able to outmaneuver therapists intellectually. He had needed the existential challenge of a personal confrontation to find and trust something greater in himself.

Once at the end of our last session together, I anointed a woman with oil from the grave of St. John of Kronstadt. She wrote me later and said that she had felt fire course through her and the problem we had discussed in her therapy related to sexual abuse as a child, the effects of which she had suffered for years and had created a situation of not being able to touch people or let them touch her that was interfering with her ability to do her job, had vanished, changing her life in a way for which she was so grateful, poetry of wonder and praise had spontaneously begun to flow through her. She sent me a framed version of her initial wonder and surprise at what had happened to her at the moment of encounter between me and her and the Holy Spirit through the intercession of the saints.

T HERAPY AS IMPROVISATIONAL DIALOGUE. In many ways, such moments in therapy are very much like improvisational music. How does one know when and what to play when there are no predetermined notes? The creative urge to risk moving into the dialogical expression of improvisational jazz, where the musicians become the music, requires a special kind of listening and acting together. It is fundamentally dialogical. Like fire inhabiting iron until it is red hot, it is not clear where one ends and the other begins and yet there is a clear distinction between voices that make for the unique creations that arise. Furthermore, it is the improvisational call and response of co-creating the between which is shared by client and therapist (as in the case of child and parent, and the human person and God) that is of paramount importance. "Process leads content in this conception, so that no particular content needs to be pursued; rather the enlarging of the domain and fluency of the dialogue is primary and will lead to increasingly integrated and complex content."[23]

Stephen Spielberg, in his popular film "Close Encounters of the Third Kind," illustrated this transition by staging a climactic scene on

---

[23] Lyons-Ruth & Boston Change Process Study Group (2001), 15, cited in D. Wallin, *Attachment in Psychotherapy* (New York: Guilford Press, 2007), 125.

the top of Devil's Peak where the calculations of government scientists are used to produce a series of tones in a combination that is designed to communicate with an alien spacecraft that has descended from the stars, using similar simple musical tones to communicate. The 'conversation' begins in a very measured way as a kind of mathematical operation with a wall of supercomputers, but as it continues, the alien life form begins to speed up until it is playing a symphony at a rhythm and with joyful abandon in such a way that, in order to remain in the dialogue the scientists, must leave their purely mathematical model-driven calculations and risk moving into the artful intuitive play of dance and jazz and pure feeling. Now they are caught up in the new rhythm of creation that is emerging between them.

This kind of improvisational dialogue is not possible by following a theoretical model every step of the way with the mechanical attention of the ego and reasoning mind in the lead and certainly not with the interference of emotionality and anxiety that are rooted in preserving the *status quo* of self image. The co-creativity of call and response in jazz is not compatible with selfishness. Yet counseling, like jazz, and like the creative process itself, is not without a mathematical architecture that guides it. The music of I-Thou dialogue is both science and art, mathematics and soul, materiality and uncreated Spirit. The deeper processes of body, mind and intuition must be trusted to respond to the Spirit of the dialogue without over-controlling the process or having assurance where it will lead and end. One inevitably proceeds mindfully in faith, guided by love into mysterious and unknown territory, unique for each person and for each moment in time, which is laden with possibilities never before realized, and if missed, never again approached in precisely the same way. As the ancient Greek philosopher Heraclites observed, "You can't step into the same river twice."

So what exactly is the therapist's equivalent of this musicality? Over the years, I have learned to listen to the story a person's breathing tells and the tilt of their head, the quickness and direction of their eyes at just that point when they have met mine in such a way as to become aware, for just a second, that they exist, to gain a sense of the suffering of soul that each is carrying in the world. Attunement to these seemingly small, non-verbal movements are pathways into much deeper places than the content of the spoken words are able to convey. People know more than they can say until their attention has begun to notice this forgotten, "undiscovered country," which appears somatically to consciousness before it has been captured in words. It is an area of pre-conscious, inner somatic and visceral awareness that is constantly in motion and evident in the person's body, tone of voice and actions in response to changing meanings, both internally and in the experience of the relationship. These meanings and associated somatic responses are constantly influencing the relationship with the therapist in subtle ways which are not recognized when the focus is only on the verbal content. In order to be aware of this and use it therapeutically, the therapist must cultivate an inner stillness and a well-honed capacity for oscillating between observation of his/her own inner state and the non-verbal somatic presence of the client.

> The therapist must find ways to connect with what Christopher Bollas (1987) has called the patient's "unthought known." Grasping the unspoken (or unthinkable) subtext of the therapeutic conversation requires what several writers (Bateson, 1979, Bion, 1959) have referred to as the clinician's "binocular vision" that tracks the subjectivity of both the patient and the therapist. The underlying assumption here is that the patient who cannot (or will not) articulate his/her own dissociated or disavowed experience will evoke it in others, enact it with others, or embody it.[24]

In less than a second, it is possible to know what musical composition is being played just by the special timbre of the sound of a musical instrument or a particular band. The same is true for the instrument of the human voice, which conveys all kinds of information. Each person's

---

[24] D. Wallin, *Attachment in Psychotherapy* (New York: Guilford Press, 2007), 3–4

vocal chords, cadence of speech and pronunciation expresses itself in a special timbre all its own as unique as a fingerprint conveying the spontaneous arising of feelings as well as the calculated nuances of contrived appearances, distinguishing conscious and unconscious motivations.

In a similar way, the movement of the body — its rhythm and form — is a visible timbre equally unique. The peculiar gate and sway of a person's body, the way she sits down and the slight hesitation that appears before she changes position in the chair, reveals with just a glance hidden traits of fearfulness, poise or vainglory. Habitual postures assumed over and over tell a story of strengths and weaknesses and characterological defenses that have been etched deeply into the psyche like the iron chariot wheels carved ruts in the Roman stones in the streets of the city of Pompeii. Hard-wired feelings that are not under central nervous system control show in the flicker of the muscles around the lips, the flushing of the skin, and the tightening of the throat as the breath shifts up into the upper quadrant of the chest as anxiety rises in response to the split awareness of seeking to conceal oneself as one becomes aware of experiencing oneself and being experienced by the other simultaneously.

I orient my clients to the work of pastoral counseling by saying simply, "Speak so that your body will confirm the truth of your words." It is going to happen to some extent regardless, but there is a difference between the simplicity and integrity of speaking the truth in this way versus the various game playing, diversions and subterfuges that are set in motion by our characterological default programs and defensive fronts. These 'skins and fig leaves' acquired to protect us from the shame of having lost genuine authentic dialogue with others and the world around us impede the kind of self-examination that is the essence of repentance. The difference between health and disease, virtue and vice both come down to the task of becoming as vulnerable and transparent as children while having reason in tact and being as willing and interested as St. Augustine observed, "to become a question for myself." When this is set in motion by Grace, repentance is the doorway into a new life. But for this to occur, there must be a secure relationship that is non-threatening, highly attuned to the client's inner world and safe in such a way that the person feels free to experience, explore and name aspects of their experience that are frightening, painful and/or even feel forbidden, based on their internalization of the conditions of their family of origin, culture and past traumatic experiences. Much of this operates outside of conscious awareness and is brought to light through the body itself and through the pattern that develops in the relationship between the client and the therapist over time.

Practically speaking, the pastoral counselor's work has to do with developing a capacity to be as fully present and available as possible, using one's whole body as a kind of eardrum rendered sensitive through mindful attention, in order to discern the subtle changes in feeling from moment to moment arising from the encounter with the other person. It means being mindful of the larger context of one shared life together in which the dialogue is taking place with the expectation of discovery, of meeting in the presence of God. "A mindful and present-centered stance fosters an experience of being inside, and aware of, the body. The resulting attunement to our own somatic response amplifies the signals that allows us to tune in to the non-verbal expression of the patient's internal state."[25]

Drawing on the spiritual anthropology of St. Maximus the Confessor, there is definitely a synergy of *nous* (deep intuitive mind), *thymos* (incensive power) and *epithymos* (feeling) involved. When only mind is involved, the therapist is too removed from somatic experience. If only incensive power to influence is involved, the process is too behavioral, skills-based, top down, expert-oriented rather than mutually co-creative, and, therefore, potentially more therapeutically aggressive. Where there is only feeling and a sincere desire to help, the therapist is potentially over-identified with the client, not likely to bring the necessary 'salt' of awareness of one's own self as distinct from the 'other,' which is a necessary catalyst for the change that real meeting makes possible.

---

[25] Ibid., 7.

An Eastern Orthodox spiritual anthropology consistently points out that the proper place of the mind is *in the heart*. Where this occurs, the somatic body participates in the fineness of feeling and direct intuitive perception that is made even more keenly perceptive by the activity of Grace. This is in contrast to the mind operating outside of the heart purely by logic and reasoning and without mind-body unity. A mind dissociated from a body and using reason alone is hard, cold and cannot 'meet' the other person as co-pilgrim with compassion and mercy for the one life that each shares, though as separate persons. Without mind-body unity and mind in the heart, there can be no authentic meeting.

Martin Buber's idea of "imagining the real" expresses this well. It is more than what is generally referred to as empathy. The whole person has to be involved and rooted within himself or herself yet simultaneously attending to the other, *feeling* the other, *sensing* the other through one's own feeling-saturated sensation, and noticing the other, as I did the basketball hoop, intentionally being open to the recreation of the other's world as it is in itself situated in the ground of current experience, while remaining in touch with one's own situated world at the same time. This is experienced more as a fine oscillation, a kind of breathing, rather than a static simultaneity. It is an ongoing dialogue. The actual process is much more multilayered with human beings and moves in and out of presence and attention over the course of a counseling session in a variety of ways that go unnoticed and unverbalized opening up to subtle intimations that would not even register in consciousness dominated by willful or emotionally reactive agendas.

Contextually, pastoral counseling is always a triadic encounter between Self-Other and God, who is in the 'between' of the encounter. As Jesus said, "Where two or more are gathered, there I am in their midst." The Holy Spirit is active in both persons, and as C. G. Jung found carved into the stone mantel of his home at Bollingen, "Whether invited or not, God is present." Both counselor and client are co-pilgrims in the presence of the deep mystery of the unseen God. The therapist is not attending simply to the other, but also to the experiencing-self who is attending to the other and to God, whose presence changes both. In this way, as the Australian aboriginal elder Lila Watson has observed, it remains true for all healers that "if you have come to help me, you're wasting your time, but if you have come realizing your liberation is bound up with mine, then let us work together." Every authentic dialogue moves into uncharted territory beyond the previous maps of the universe and, therefore, changes both persons in the process. I tell my counseling students, "If you have not been changed by the relationship, then you have not *met* the person yet."

CHAPTER FIVE

Encountering the Person of the Therapist: Supervision as Trialogue[1]

Alone I yearn for someone other than myself.
Approaching the other,
I notice differences that disturb me.
In denying differences between us,
I fail to reach beyond myself.
Failing to reach beyond myself,
I deny God's love for the world through me.
Choosing God's love over self-love,
I discover the world and become myself.
In becoming myself,
I find common ground with all who are not myself.
Walking common ground,
I recognize that each and every other is my neighbor.
In loving neighbors,
I discover each one is hid with Christ in God.
Alone again,
it is no longer "I" but Christ who lives in me
And Christ has become all in all.

With thanks to my wife and children, students, friends and colleagues and all others who are responsible for my education and formation toward the ultimate goal of some day, by the sheer Grace of God becoming a human being.

May 13, 2004

---

[1] Expanded and revised from article first published as "Chaplain, Soldier, Counselor, Pilgrim," *Journal of Pastoral Care & Counseling* Vol 58(4): 307–318.

The Church is more than a hospital, as St. Basil suggested in the 4th century. It is a developmental proving ground, an arena where we struggle to become beings capable of loving as we are loved by Christ. To the extent that pastoral counseling is an intention initiated by the action of the Holy Spirit motivated by love to encounter the authentic 'other' for the purpose of discovering the exact 'fit' which heals, liberates and transforms persons, it involves much more than simply rendering psychological first aid according to even the best of methodologies. Similarly, supervision and training of pastoral counselors in an Orthodox Christian context is more than teaching theories and methods. Each involve an encounter with the person of the therapist that occurs within the larger context of attending to the presence of God which helps establish conditions that 'privilege the between' of the relationship with the supervisor so that the therapist gets a living experience of what is involved in doing the same with one's client. Therapy and supervision are both a spiritual formation process in which therapist and supervisor continue to be confronted by Christ in and through the process of self-examination for the purpose of learning to love.

By accepting the relationship with God, living contact with one's own self and openness to encountering the other as an equally beloved and unique being as the primary context for counseling and supervision, the process of supervision becomes one of learning and discovery through the confrontation of authentic meeting. This trialogical encounter always has a primary dimension of gift and discovery connected to it, in contrast to being something that can be orchestrated in a manualized or technique-driven approach that seeks to guarantee outcome. To paraphrase Jesus, "Wherever two or more are gathered so as to privilege the life shared *between* for the purpose of discovering truth in love, there I AM in their midst." We can be open to love, but we cannot force it or guarantee it. One need only look to the life and Passion of Christ to see this demonstrated in action and to stand in awe before the cost involved in this kind of servant relationship that empowers the other by being vulnerable to full encounter with them which necessitates openness to being changed oneself.

Whether in the church or the consulting room, humility begins for the pastoral counselor with recognition that God is already active and involved in the process, whether acknowledged or not. The pastoral counselor is not the lead therapist, but a kind of midwife who facilitates the birthing of new life that God is always working to create. Since both client and pastoral counselor share the same world, partaking from the one body of life and are beloved to the same Creator, what eventually emerges will also affect the counselor as well as the client, the supervisor as well as the supervisee. Love leaves no one untouched. I remind my pastoral counseling trainees, "If you have not been changed by your encounter with your client, then you haven't met the person yet." Imagine God attempting a pastoral care relationship with humanity without willingness to be affected deeply enough to become fully human in the process. Heresy. Disaster. Bad theology and ineffective pastoral care.

Among the core dogmas which Eastern Orthodox Christianity hold to be foundational for Christian faith are the Holy Trinity and the Theanthropos. These both point us toward an existential engagement that seeks to live the truth of the faith through simultaneous relationship with both the created world and Uncreated Divine Energies. Intellectual apprehension and consent to these verbally formulated doctrines themselves do not constitute faith. Faith is expressed in and through the call and response of relationship. Truth is something that must be lived in order to be understood, something that emerges from personal encounter and is known in 'sighs too deep for words' emerging from living encounter before it ever becomes formulated into words and concepts. By the time theory has been developed, the lived encounters which gave rise to it have already been converted into experience.

THE DANGER OF RELIGION AND SCIENCE AS IDEOLOGY. Faith is not entered into by 'knowing about' God, nor do pastoral counseling and supervision occur by responding to the other as an object of knowledge existing as a projection of the counselor or supervisor's subjective experience or worse, as a diagnosis or disease to be treated or merely as a subject to be educated according to a certain theory and methodology. The pastoral counselor approaches the full humanity of each person, including the mystery of the "life which is hid with Christ in God" (Col. 3:3), with recognition that the doctrines of the faith and all scientific theories, both of which generate a multitude of helpful ways of looking at people, can also be burdens that blind us to the very reality they describe when they become ideological tools. It was the best educated of the day who were most blind to the reality of Jesus, whose life could not be contained by ideological forms. Religious faith, tradition, asceticism and liturgical worship, when they are reified or ideologically absolutized, inevitably serve egoistic and political ends as they did in Jesus' day, which led to His rejection and execution. How was it that all it took to render the Jewish people of Nazi Germany vulnerable to abuse and 'legal' extermination by the German state was to revoke their passports? Because, from the standpoint of the law of the land, if they had no legal status, they did not come under protection afforded by the law. Since they were not recognized as citizens, those citizens who 'abided by the law,' rather than their conscience, no longer could see them. The leaders of Germany and its people, with the stroke of a pen on a piece of paper, did a sleight of hand that rendered a whole group of human beings *invisible*[2] with disastrous results. This willingness to hold abstract law above the law of conscience that is born of love, which recognizes all beings as sharing one life, ultimately leads to the murder of Christ wherever it occurs. Scientific theories and reason also can be co-opted similarly for egoistic ends, creating resistance to a new way of seeing the person and the world because of attachment to previous paradigms[3] which have become part of the safe and familiar that keeps the *status quo* in place.

---

[2] R. L. Rubenstein, *The Cunning of History: The Holocaust and the American Future* (New York: Harper & Row, 1975).
[3] Cf. T. Kuhn, *The Structure of Scientific Revolutions* (Chicago: University of Chicago Press, 1962).

When Nicodemus approached Jesus cautiously and surreptitiously by night from the perspective of his well-educated religious training and said, "Rabbi, *we know* that You are a teacher come from God *because of...*" (John 3:2), he was operating out of a familiar paradigm. Jesus immediately confronted him with a different one, an epistemology of personal encounter between human and Divine, between created and Uncreated. Nicodemus was assuming he and the Sanhedrin could determine what is true about Jesus through diagnostic lenses with which they were already familiar, based on reason, the valued tradition and world view of the privileged religious ruling class. Instead, Nicodemus was invited by Jesus beyond himself to a trialogical meeting with Him through the Holy Spirit proceeding 'from above.' It was a threshold that must be crossed by the humility of interested *not-knowing.* "No one can see the kingdom of God unless they are *born from above*" (John 3:3). Jesus is involved in trialogue and those who would know Him must themselves enter into engagement with God, while being in the world with each other. This is a Theocentric orientation in which humankind depends on God for a revelation that cannot be attained apart from personal relationship, rather than an anthropocentric position in which we try to define and adjudicate God's reality from the limited powers of human intellect, apart from such a relationship.

Pastoral counselors have our assumptions continually challenged as well as our foundations inspected and re-inspected in order to ensure that we are not functioning as spiritual Lone Rangers, colonializing imperialists, functional atheists or therapeutically aggressive fundamentalist propagandists taking responsibility for being the agents of change all by ourselves based on what we already know and are sure is right. I remember the words of the professor of philosophy from a university in Athens who was present at the first international meeting of the Ecumenical Patriarchate on Pastoral Healthcare in Rhodes, Greece. Eminent theologians, priests, professors, physicians and a couple of counselors were on hand to discuss common issues related to the ministry of hospital chaplaincy, uniting medicine and pastoral care for suffering persons. Discussion of relationships between the Sacraments and medical illness, the partnership between Divine Grace and human responsibility were lifted up with great intricacy and passion, at times in ways that seemed to defy resolution. At one point, this professor stood up and offered a word that parted the theological mists among us in one sentence: "The surer you are of something, the more sure you can be that it is psychological and not spiritual." Later, walking back to our hotel rooms, I had a brief conversation with Prof. Christos Yannaras, who also agreed with the statement, and he added as an aside, "and you can be sure it is also ideological."

Good theology, like good pastoral care, holds all theory, canon law, doctrine and the rituals of faith and worship gently, like Kierkegaard's famous thistle, which cannot be grasped too tightly and made absolute, or it can only lead to injury and a failure to comprehend its significance. If we are to avoid re-crucifixion of the Living One in our midst among those we seek to serve in counseling and supervision, we must be on guard against the ideological and psychological appropriation of our religious and scientific learning so that these do not ever efface the mystery and absolute freedom of the person. Fr. Vasileios Thermos, MD, PhD, a psychiatrist in Greece, captures this elegantly in a line from one of his poems: "Every word we say is a translation from an original manuscript that has been lost."[4] Scripture itself has only the life that the Holy Spirit, whose comings and goings we cannot fathom or control, breathes into it through our encounter with the one who is written about. Otherwise, we make the hermeneutical mistake that Jesus Himself pointed out. "You search the Scriptures, because you think that in them you have eternal life; and it is these that bear witness of Me; and you are unwilling to come to Me, that you may have life" (John 5:39–40).

Like being unable to see the Jews in Nazi Germany because attachment to the law had rendered them invisible, Jesus' Divinity re-

---

[4] Personal correspondence with the author, July 2010.

mains invisible to anyone who is not moved by his humanity right in front of our eyes. "For whoever does not love brother or sister who can be seen, cannot love God who cannot be seen" (John 4:20) Or as Ghandi rephrased the same thing, "If you haven't found God in the faces of those around you, don't bother looking for Him anywhere else." This is the dilemma each one of us faces every day — whether to make it our aim to encounter others beyond our concepts and experience, or to refuse the continual repentance that reveals my own mind as being the "log in my own eye." The path of love that arises from and leads toward theophany leads through constant self-examination. Whoever would conduct therapy must but undergoing it as well.

The pastoral counselor can no more presume to comprehend the uniqueness of a person based on abstract theories and diagnoses then one can be enlightened by the words of Holy Scripture apart from the witness of the Holy Spirit working through the communal relationships of the Church living through particular circumstances and events. Pastoral counseling always requires an invocation before the altar of one's client or supervisee, in the same way as the priest who stands and prays before the altar in the Divine Liturgy intercessing for himself and for the people before God. Both these διά-Λογος encounters are trialogues wherein a high quality attention is called for, a form of neptic wakefulness evidenced by the intention to stand responsively before the deep and invisible eternal presence of God with one's whole self: body, mind, and feeling, and *listen*. There is a Hasidic saying, "The Spirit seeks a body through words." Pastoral counseling is concerned precisely with this encounter with the other in order to hear the person into the speech confirmed by the body which conveys what the Spirit is saying from moment to moment in a given particular situation unlike any others, however similar it may seem on the surface.

The pastoral counselor works with the paradox that every personal experience, just as every theoretical model which helps reveal persons, also inevitably distorts and objectifies the other, deconstructing her/him from the uniquely real being living through a specific one-of-a-kind concrete situation, always threatening to reduce the person to a kind of Procrustean embedded abstraction by virtue of whatever theory is informing the inevitable not-fully-unexamined proverbial 'log' in the pastoral counselor's own eye. Experience always stands between me and the other, waiting to be reformulated by an authentic encounter with the other.

CHRISTIAN **F**ORMATION AS THE **P**RIMARY **T**RAINING **G**ROUND **FOR P**ASTORAL **C**OUNSELORS. Orthodox writers have typically addressed the formational focus of Christians from within the context of the deification process of *theosis*[5] by lifting up obedience, repentance, prayer, fasting and the other aspects of ascetically supported worship and prayer life, which are integral to salvation, but more than these, the most important factor of all is love, which draws us beyond what is possible by ascetical endeavor alone. This is the realm of existential relationship between beings that in its essence is most clearly seen in the offering of Christ's own life for the world. Because in Orthodox tradition, pastoral care and counseling have traditionally been regarded as the province of the priest, there lingers an unfamiliarity with the role of the lay person as a pastoral counselor as well as, in some instances, vestiges of suspicion and ignorance in some circles of the Orthodox world regarding whether the mental health professional is a servant of the Church or kind of Trojan horse introducing 'strange doctrines' going back to Freudian atheism or forward toward New Age amalgams. It is also not entirely clear for some Orthodox how *pastoral* counseling can be provided by a lay person, albeit there are examples of holy elders who were not ordained, such as Brother Joseph the Hesychast and the beloved Elder Paisios of recent years, whose practical wisdom and clairvoyant gifts have brought each of them wide recognition throughout the Orthodox world. Nevertheless, it is only recently that there has been an effort among a growing

---

[5] *Theosis* is the Orthodox word for deification, becoming in the likeness of God through the synergy between human person and Divine Grace.

number of Orthodox psychotherapists and lay theologians to draw from patristic sources and the richness of Orthodox anthropology and soteriology to offer perspectives that contribute to the emerging dialogue between the field of modern psychotherapy and pastoral theology in order to begin to articulate the theological foundations for an Orthodox Christian approach to pastoral counseling.[6]

From the Orthodox perspective which is deeply influenced by the hesychastic Patristic Tradition contained in the extensive writings of the *Philokalia*,[7] people are said to be truly free only to the degree that there is progress toward *theosis*.[8] This places an Eastern Orthodox approach to pastoral care and counseling firmly within the realm of formation of personhood in Christ through coming to love, rather than a pathology focused approach, which merely stabilizes and normalizes persons according to prevailing cultural norms of health and well being without taking into consideration more hidden passions of egotism that block the heart's receptivity to Grace and, therefore, to love, even though the person may seem a paragon of health and

---

[6] Archbishop Chrysostomos, *A Guide to Orthodox Psychotherapy: The Science, Theology, and Spiritual Practice Behind It and Its Clinical Application* (Lanham, MD: University Press of America, 2006); B. Chrysostomos, "Towards a Spiritual Psychology: Synthesis of the Desert Fathers," *Pastoral Psychology* Vol. 37 (4) (1989): 255–274; Jean-Claude Larchet, *The Theology of Illness* (New York: St. Vladimir's Seminary Press, 2002); J. Chirban, *Sickness or Sin: Spiritual Discernment and Differential Diagnosis* (Brookline, MA: Holy Cross Orthodox Press); J. Chirban (ed.), *Personhood: Orthodox Christianity and the Connection Between Body, Mind, and Soul* (London: Bergin & Garvey, 1996); S. Muse (ed.), *Raising Lazarus: Integral Healing in Orthodox Christianity* (Brookline, MA: Holy Cross Press, 2004); V. Thermos, *In Search of the Person: True and False Self According to Donald Winnicott and St. Gregory Palamas* (Montreal: Alexander Press, 2002); V. Thermos, *Thirst For Love and Truth: Encounters off Orthodox Theology and Psychological Science* (Montreal: Alexander Press, 2010).

[7] Cf. E. Kadloubovsky and G. E. H. Palmer (trans. and eds.), *Writings from the Philokalia On Prayer of the Heart* (London: Faber and Faber, 1975); and G. E. H. Palmer, P. Sherrard, K. Ware (trans. and eds.), *The Philokalia: The Complete Text*: Vol. I–IV (London: Faber and Faber, 1995).

[8] H. Vlachos, *Orthodox Psychotherapy* (Levadia, Greece: Birth of the Theotokos Monastery, 1994).

success. Archbishop Chrysostomos, a priest-monk, Princeton-trained psychologist and an exceptional patristic scholar rightly points toward the greater life to which Orthodoxy turns its attention:

> A theology which ignores the ineluctable nexus between the spiritual aspects of (persons) and (their) psychological nature and needs fails to be a *real* theology. It renders essentially ineffective the therapeutic milieu of Christianity, which seeks to restore the human being, through the Mysteries of the Church, to a state in which the soul brings human action and thought into perfect harmony with the higher, noetic aspects of spiritual vision.[9]

In the same way, I believe, it holds true that a psychology that fails to include the larger therapeutic and soteriological milieu of Christianity with *theosis* as the potential ideal for human well-being and development fails to be a *real* psychology. This, of course, is not possible apart from help from God to lift humankind up beyond where we can go on our own power. It requires a co-creative partnership or, as Elder Paisios colorfully puts it, humankind is a bird with two wings. One wing the person is responsible for moving. The other, God alone can move. But without both wings, the bird cannot fly.

The importance of this for the training of pastoral counselors is captured by the simple question St. Silouan asked the widely respected and learned ascetic Fr. Stratonicus in their remarkable encounter recorded by Archimandrite Sophrony.[10] St. Silouan had noticed earlier that Fr. Stratonicus "spoke from his own mind," and now he asked him "How do the perfect speak?" The older man uncharacteristically fell silent, humbled in the presence of the younger monk whose Grace-filled understanding he recognized was beyond his own. He realized

---

[9] Archbishop Chrysostomos, *Orthodoxy and Psychology* (Etna, CA: Center for Traditionalist Orthodox Studies, 2004), 16–17.
[10] Elder Sophrony, *St. Silouan the Athonite* (Essex: Holy Stavropegic Monastery of St. John the Baptist, 1999).

he had something to learn from him and said, "I do not know, you tell me." Silouan then answered quietly, "The perfect never say anything of themselves, they only say what the Spirit bids them to say." In his extremely valuable account of the life of this true theologian and pastoral care-giver *par excellence*, formed by the Orthodox Way, who was entirely without academic education, Archimandrite Sophrony has offered the twenty-first century evidence of the living continuing prophetic tradition of Orthodox spirituality. Above all, it is concerned with dialogue with God, and the ascetical struggle needed to say "no" to whatever impedes this dialogue. One grows in maturity of discernment, practical wisdom that emerge with self-observation and increasing repentance, mindfulness,[11] self-awareness, compassion and mercy that are the fruits of spiritual struggle, but most of all, with an increased yearning for and attentiveness to God's presence, which is the source of our true yearning. As St. Gregory of Nyssa observes, "To find God is to seek him incessantly."[12]

Taken together, St. Silouan and others like him[13] constitute a kind of divinely wrought, 2,000-year, replicating, longitudinal research design of how charismatic clairvoyant elders have repeatedly been formed in the Christian tradition through trialogue with God and the community. These abbas and ammas are pre-eminent pastoral counselors with an ability to stand in the presence of God with and for others, maintaining ascetical boundaries while bringing compassionate, childlike hearts, impartial dispassion, and discernment of spirits along with bringing to bear the accumulated wisdom of natural intuition in clearing away obstacles for encountering and comprehending the other. Such persons can read others in part because they know themselves through observation and experiential struggle with

[11] For a good operationalized definition of the qualities of mindfulness common to most practices, cf. D. Siegel, *The Mindful Brain: Reflection and Attunement in the Cultivation of Well-Being* (New York: W. W. Norton & Company, 2007), 12.
[12] Cited in E. Cardenal, *Abide in Love* (New York: Orbis Books, 1995), 64.
[13] H. Middleton, *Precious Vessels of the Holy Spirit* (Thessaloniki: Protecting Veil Press, 2003).

their passions that is the mark of long ongoing repentance and in part because God shows them charismatically what they cannot see with their own natural intuition and powers.

In just this way, Elder Porphyrios noetically found the right 'fit' for people, because it was a response to the trialogue of the Spirit speaking to him in prayer specifically for this person and no other. What makes this all the more fascinating and important is that some of the most remarkable elders of the twentieth century, like Porphyrios, Cleopas, Paisius, Joseph and St. Silouan, had no formal academic education and training whatsoever,[14] knew no modern counseling theories and yet they were theologians and pastoral counselors of the highest caliber, taught in the 'university of the ascetical desert' by the professors of the Holy Trinity.

This underscores one of the most significant contributions of Eastern Orthodox Tradition to the contemporary discussion of pastoral counseling, and that is the central place of formation of the *person* in the training of pastoral caregivers born of the διά-Λογος of worship, prayer and the ascetical life that serves the aim of learning to love through acquisition of the Holy Spirit. This is because the theologian, from the Orthodox perspective, is one who is in direct contact with God; the one who prays, not simply one who 'says prayers,' but rather as St. Silouan notes, the theologian is one who has become prayer itself by loving as Christ loves, who Himself acknowledges that He can do nothing on His own human power and initiative, but only does what God the Father shows Him to do through intimate dialogue (John 5:30).

Recognizing the need for deep self-examination and awareness, but lacking moorings in the hesychast tradition of examination of conscience, Protestant voices in the pastoral care field, which was birthed under the auspices of the American Association of Pastoral

---

[14] Cf. Elder Joseph, *Elder Joseph the Hesychast: Struggles, Experience, Teaching.* (Mount Athos: Holy Monastery of Vatopaidi) and C. Yiannitsiotis, *With Elder Porphyrios: A Spiritual Child Remembers* (Athens: Holy Convent of the Transfiguration of the Savior, 2001).

Counselors in the United States in the 1960's, drew heavily from both humanistic, client-centered and psychoanalytic models of therapy, placing emphasis on extensive psychodynamic examination of the unconscious of the therapist as a preparation for conducting therapy along with ongoing supervision. One of the founding fathers of the Pastoral Counseling movement, Dr. Charles Gerkin, referred to persons as "living human documents"[15] requiring a pastoral hermeneutic to interpret accurately. As the field has developed over the last half century, it has incorporated the systemic emphasis of marriage and family therapy and been influenced by liberation theological perspectives as well as feminist, womanist and social justice critiques. In recent years, there has been a growing variety of post-modern approaches aimed at shaping the pastoral counseling process at the theoretical level in order to safeguard against unconscious isogesis by creating the other in one's own ethnocentric image[16] or delimiting them according to the unexamined assumptions of power and privilege that accrue to members of a dominant culture.[17] This is a valuable tool in exposing abuses

---

[15] Contributions to Pastoral Counseling literature generated over the past 50 years by members of the American Association of Pastoral Counselors (largely Protestant with some Roman Catholic representation) are too numerous to mention, but representative volumes that have proven helpful to me in this regard include C. Doehring, *The Practice of Pastoral Care: A Postmodern Approach* (Louisville, KY: Westminster John Knox, 2006); E. Lartey, *Pastoral Theology in an Intercultural World* (New York: Guilford Press, 2006); *In Living Color: An Intercultural Approach to Pastoral Care and Counseling* (London: Jessica Kingsley Publishers, 2003); P. Cooper-White, *Shared Wisdom: Use of the Self in Pastoral Care and Counseling* (Minneapolis: Fortress, 2003); B. Grant, *A Theology for Pastoral Psychotherapy* (2001); C. Neuger, *Counseling Women* (Minneapolis: Fortress Press, 2001).

[16] J. E. Hinkle & G. A. Hinkle, "Surrendering the Self: Pastoral Counseling at the Limits of Culture and Psychotherapy," *The Journal of Pastoral Care* Vol. 46, No. 2 (Summer 1992): 103–116; B. Hooks, "Reworking History," *The Other Side Magazine* March-April (1993): 20–26; L. Dyche, L. Zayas, "The Value of Curiosity and Naiveté for the Cross-Cultural Psychotherapist," *Family Process* Vol 34. (1995): 389–399. D. Augsburger, *Pastoral Counseling Across Cultures* (Philadelphia: The Westminster Press, 1986).

[17] Cf. J. Poling, *Deliver Us From Evil: Resisting Racial and Gender Oppression*

of power that stem from institutional religion and unexamined privilege masquerading as pastoral care but lacking the power that stems from authentic spiritual life of humility and love.

Countertransferential interference happens on many levels, so the hermeneutic for approaching persons involves identifying unexamined power and privilege accruing to racial, gender and cultural biases as well as context of the counseling relationship itself which Martin Buber pointed out always contains a contextual power differential that cannot be fully overcome, regardless of the authentic mutuality that occurs.[18] The pastoral counselor must try and take all these into account so as not to create hidden iatrogenic damage in the counseling relationship resulting from unconscious biases of the proverbial "log in one's own eye." Repentance, born of the willingness to have the press-secretary's version of the self repeatedly challenged, is an essential for offering pastoral care.

Finding the right 'fit' that is liberating for a person requires that pastoral counselors and supervisors approach the dialogical encounter as one does prayer — with all the ascetical boundaries, repentance-engendered humility and interest that are evoked by anticipating meeting the Lord Himself, which Metropolitan Anthony Bloom likens to "entering the lions den."[19] For this reason, pastoral counseling is usefully seen as a spiritual formation process for the counselor who is continually being confronted through empathic engagement with the reality of the 'other,' whose differences from her/himself cannot be grasped accurately apart from privileging the reality of the other as being on the same level as that of the counselor. In this way, the counselor is 'vulnerable' to being affected by the client just as God,

(Minneapolis: Fortress Press, 1996); James Poling, *Render Unto God: Economic Vulnerability, Family Violence and Pastoral Theology* (St. Louis, MO: Chalice Press, 2002).

[18] Cf. the famous 1957 videotaped dialogue between Martin Buber, then almost 80, and Carl Rogers, who was in his 50's. R. Anderson and K. Cissna, *The Martin Buber-Carl Rogers Dialogue: A New Transcript With Commentary* (New York: SUNY Press, 1997).

[19] A. Bloom, *Beginning to Pray* (New Jersey: Paulist Press, 1970).

who seeks to have διά-Λογος meeting with humankind, is vulnerable to being affected by humanity. Laying aside the privilege and power that are part of God's essential nature in order to create and preserve conditions for humankind's freedom to respond to God's love and become like God, constitutes the ground for the possibility of becoming a *person* as God is person. This goes beyond conventional therapy to the formation process of deification, which is the ultimate goal which pastoral care and counseling serve.

Toward a Theory of Training and Supervision: I Am Loved and so I Learn to Love. Both my theoretical approach to pastoral psychotherapy and supervision have their philosophical moorings in the existentialism of Eastern Orthodox Christianity. I also draw on the philosophical anthropology of Martin Buber[20] and his approach to dialogue as a valuable epistemological framework which I find complementary with Orthodox approaches. Buber's philosophy of dialogue, which has both ontological and existential dimensions, has been developed by others for its significant hermeneutical value to the field of psychotherapy.[21] In contrast to the mind-body dualism and subject-object split represented by Descartes' famous dictum "I think; therefore, I am," the Eastern Orthodox approach is one in which the willingness to be loved and the capacity to love in return are paramount. "I am loved into learning to love; therefore, I am." is central and reflects both the existential as well as the wholistic anthropology of the Eastern Church. Quality of consciousness, freedom of choice and responsibility for one's thoughts, feelings, behavior and personal values with and for others in the pres-

---

[20] M. Buber, trans. R. G. Smith, *I and Thou* (New York: Charles Scribners & Sons, 1958); M. Buber, *The Way of Man According to the Teaching of Hasidism* (New York: Kensington Publishing Corp., 1994); M. Buber, *Meetings: Autobiographical Fragments, 3rd edition* (London & New York: Routledge, 2002).

[21] M. Friedman, *Martin Buber: The Life of Dialogue, 4th Edition* (New York: Routledge, Kegan Paul, 2002); J. B. Agassi (ed.), *Martin Buber on Psychology and Psychotherapy* (Syracuse, NY: Syracuse University Press, 1999); P. Kramer, *Martin Buber's I and Thou: Practicing Living Dialogue* (New York: Paulist Press, 2003).

ence of God are all aspects for which supervisory attention proves valuable. As my friend Dr. Jamie Moran rightly observes, "Projection is a failure of repentance." Only God is without projection. The rest of us, as we move in and out of our experiences, continually need to identify the unconscious enactments that we co-create with our clients, supervisees and others around us, in order to become better able to see clearly with dispassionate interest. No strings attached passionate loving interest is what God has for each of us. The more we encounter this, the more desire there is to release others from any requirements to be how we need them to be. Rather we become interested in who they actually are in the light of God's love.

From a practical standpoint, all behavior can be viewed as a function of a combination of intrapsychic and intersubjective factors, which include conscious, intentional choices as well as unconscious, automatic, reactive behaviors. These stem from family-of-origin-derived internal object relationships as they are shaped by interpersonal, biological, spiritual, circumstantial, developmental and socio-systemic (culture, gender, race, powers and principalities) interactions within the various sub-systems that make up the human community. While all these make up the stuff of our experience, I agree with the late C. G. Jung's observation, which points to a much larger context than psychology and behavior *per se*, casting all these in a new light.

> Among all my patients in the second half of life, that is over 35, there has not been one whose problem in the last resort was not that of finding a religious outlook on life ... Every one of them fell ill because of losing that which the living religions of every age have given to their followers. None of them has been really healed who did not regain their religious outlook.[22]

---

[22] C. G. Jung, *Modern Man in Search of a Soul* (New York: Harcourt, 1934), 264. Though Jung's view of religion is very different than Orthodox Christianity, he rightly recognizes that psychology without a transcendent dimension is incapable of healing human suffering. Just as importantly from the Eastern Orthodox perspective, Christianity reduced to a 'religion' on par with other faiths or 'de-

PRIVILEGING THE 'BETWEEN' OF RELATIONSHIP. Modern studies of the plasticity of brain functions which grow toward ac-
commodation of repeated thought patterns[23] and how attention is
repeatedly used, is congruent with the perspective that change and
transformation in therapy and supervision are the result of *experiencing and owning one's experience in the presence of the other and
choosing.* Mindfulness, or what the Orthodox call *nepsis,* is a critical
field of action for all pastoral counseling and supervision. Consciousness of one's *self*—body, mind, thoughts and feelings activated and
continually refined by the momentary breaking into consciousness
that *I AM and Thou Art* is a mystery related to trialogue with God
which must occur again and again over a lifetime for growth to occur,
e.g. "If you *continue* in My word, you are truly My disciples; and you
will know the truth and the truth shall set you free" (John 8:32). The
pastoral supervisor recognizes, whether stated explicitly or not, that
relationship with God situated in the eternal present of each moment
is the primary context for all psychotherapy and supervision. To facilitate personal and professional growth of the supervisee in accordance with his/her religious faith and values and immense potential
for aliveness in Christ involves assisting persons in discovering how
one's way of 'doing therapy' is uniquely one's own, which is related
primarily to 'becoming authentically oneself.'

The supervisor helps people find a connection between their immediate experience of life (mental, emotional, intuitive, proprioceptive and interpersonal) and consciousness itself[24] through encourag-

---

mythologized' by a rationalistic epistemology and leveled to a worldly accom-
modation both suffer the same fate as Timothy observed, which is to "have the
form of religion but deny its power" (2 Tim. 3:5).

[23] J. LeDoux, *The Emotional Brain: The Mysterious Underpinnings of Emotional
Life* (New York: Touchstone, 1996); A. Damasio, *The Feeling of What Happens:
Body and Brain in the Making of Emotion* (New York: Mariner Books, 2000); R.
Ruden, *The Craving Brain* (New York: HarperCollins, 1997).

[24] There is more of an interest in facilitating a person becoming aware of being
aware than in examining the contents of awareness itself. The great mystery is,
as Meister Eckhart observed, "The eye with which I see God is the same eye

ing a highly active quality of attention toward self-observation as well as observation of the client and of the process of the shared relationship between client and therapist and therapist and supervisor. This parallel process invites becoming familiar with the uniquely personal inner representations of self and of the other that make up the person's inner psychic theater as they are linked with the proprioceptive resonances experienced in the body which accompany dialogue. These will inevitably be related to the sequences of interpersonal behavior and responses that constitute the process of interpersonal transactions. Unless a decision or cognition is confirmed by the body in some way by a change in behavior(s) and/or a change in quality of sensations accompanying a thought, however subtle, no real change can be said to have occurred.

Naturally, the kind of vulnerability and honesty in the face of one's true experience that makes for healing and growth requires a significant amount of trust which is part of the crucible that protects the vulnerability of exploration into sensitive areas beyond the client or supervisee's current awareness. Various defenses, both intrapsychic and/or interpersonal, function to keep intimacy with self, others and God at tolerable levels. The more disturbed a person is, the more ways will be employed to avoid being present and responsible for oneself, placing a greater strain on the supervisor. Persons who do not feel safe to *become a question for themselves* repeatedly will experience little or no growth and can prove a danger to their clients in the future. In this sense, belovedness to God is the condition for undergoing such questioning and constitutes the ground for the possibility of all human relationships that are conducive to growth — therapeutic or otherwise. This faith and capacity to trust is first born through the attachment with the mother or primary caregiver of the children. As psychoanalyst Dr. Anna Maria Rizzuto has

with which God sees me." Orthodox Christian pastoral approaches focus on freeing consciousness from attachment to content that darkens and impedes this connection which is experienced in the heart where mind and body, Uncreated and created, meet in Christ through the Holy Spirit's intervention.

pointed out, this holding environment becomes the foundational theological experience of the child before words are ever used.[25] A secure attachment provides the infant with the ability to move beyond the comfort of the familiar to explore the larger world. In the same way, by extension, the more secure the attachment of faith in God, the greater the capacity to become a question for oneself in reaching out to understand another.

The supervisor seeks to facilitate and encourage this process by privileging the 'between' of meeting with the supervisee over the demand that he or she conforms to a theory or model or to the supervisor's way of doing things. The stuff of life is always new and beyond an abstract theory to describe fully, and the supervisor uses his or her experience as a way of coming to understand the supervisee through the differences that emerge along the way. Cultivating a trusting supervisory alliance that conveys an appreciation for the uniqueness and belovedness of the supervisee by privileging the 'between' of encounter is the primary prerequisite and ongoing supervisory task, whether for beginning therapists or advanced. It is a well established fact that growth occurs most readily and without harm in the context of a supportive supervisory alliance where respect, encouragement and empathic support[26] are established and maintained. This requires that the supervisor is motivated for the work of supervision as far as possible by a co-suffering compassionate interest with the supervisee in which there is a clear co-pilgrimage wherein the supervisor is present in such a way as to learn her/himself from the supervisee's originality and uniqueness. Accurate empathic intuition, faith in people's ability to solve their own problems

---

[25] Cf. A. Rizzuto, *The Birth of the Living God* (Chicago: University of Chicago Press, 1981).

[26] G. W. Brock and S. Sibbald, "Supervision in AAMFT Accredited Programs: Supervisee Perceptions and Preferences," *The American Journal of Family Therapy* 16 (1988): 256–261; P. D. Guest & L. E. Beutler, "Impact of Psychotherapy Supervision on Therapist Orientation and Values," *Journal of Consulting and Clinical Psychology* 56 (1988): 653–658.

in the presence of God and concrete experiences that afford reason
to be hopeful that the supervisory relationship will be conducive to
this are all necessary for this.

The supervisor needs a solid, integrated personal and professional
identity with clear boundaries between self and other which permits
enough interpersonal flexibility to maintain empathic openness to all
levels of the clients' experiences, presence and choices while protecting the supervisee's freedom of self-determination in all areas. This
requires sufficient personal psychotherapy on the supervisor's part
to make one's own issues well known. This includes a comprehensive
understanding of the impact of one's own family of origin, gender,
culture, faith, sexual orientation and value system in creating certain
inevitable biases in one's way of experiencing the world. Equally, if
not more important, the supervisor needs a deeply rooted capacity
for mindfulness that allows for a fluid kind of flexibility. While the
trialogue of meeting provides the central dynamic of supervision, it
is also true that, within this context, roles change and the supervisor
may at times serve as consultant, teacher, counselor,[27] coach, pastor
as well as co-pilgrim[28] in order to invite the supervisees to be intentionally aware of and responsible for their experience and choices.
Attending to voice tone, body posture, behavior and the movement
and quality of the supervisee's attention is equally, if not more important, than how they conceptualize what they are doing. Therapeutic
dialogue is most meaningful when it is not dominated by the linear
logical processes of the *dianoia*, but draws from the deeper encounters mediated by direct intuitional perceptions of the *nous*, which are
seeking words to describe what is newly emerging.

---

[27] L. D. Borders and G. R. Leddick, *Handbook of Counseling Supervision* (Alex-
andria, VA: Association for Counselor Education and Supervision, 1987); A. K.
Hess, "Training Models and the Nature of Psychotherapy Supervision," in A. K.
Hess (ed.), *Psychotherapy supervision: Theory, Research and Practice* (New York:
John Wiley & Sons, 1980), 15–28.

[28] B. Estadt, J. Compton, M. Blanchette, *Pastoral Counseling* (New Jersey: Prentice Hall, 1983); B. Estadt, J. Compton, M. Blanchette, *The Art of Clinical Supervision: A Pastoral Counseling Perspective* (New York: Integration Books, 1987).

For this to happen, the supervisor, like the therapist, must be able to utilize his/her subjectivity objectively for diagnostic purposes. This is done by noting the soundings of one's own heart, mind and body as a kind of resonance[29] in order to identify underlying feelings that may be indicators of unconscious empathic processes of projective identification[30] at work. These can then be verified by observing similar transactions within the family, gathering and verifying history of similar patterns among friends and in the family-of-origin dynamics.

Finally, cultivating belovedness has to do with the supervisor's capacity to elicit and clarify the deepest existential values and religious faith in the person's life which are seen to be the primary motivations for growth and the *raison d'être* for enduring the necessary suffering of moving beyond the kinds of homeostasis that leads persons into therapy in the first place. Such a holding environment allows for a constant engaging of the supervisor's own self. For this reason, pastoral supervision always focuses a great deal on the person of the therapist and the journey toward personal and professional integration. It as a basic maxim that one cannot be open toward areas of other people's lives which one cannot respond to in oneself.[31] To the degree that the supervisor or therapist is blocked in facing his/her own issues, some form of empathic arrest will occur, which opens the door to therapeutic aggression with one's client in some form. Supervision focuses on identifying empathic blocks and enabling persons

---

[29] J. S. Scharff, *Projective and Introjective Identification and the Use of the Therapist's Self* (New Jersey: Jason Aronson, 1992).

[30] W. Burke & M. Tansey, "Projective Identification and Counter-transference Turmoil and Projective Identification and the Empathic Process," *Contemporary Psychoanalysis* 21 (1985): 372–402 and 42–69. S. Cashdon, *Object Relations Therapy* (New York: Norton & Co., 1988).

[31] R. C. Cushing, *Opening to Empathy: The Experience of Opening to Understanding What Has Been Preventing or Blocking a Supervisee from Opening to Empathy with a Client.* Ph.D. dissertation. California Institute of Integral Studies (1989). UMI order number 8926006; J. Welwood, *Awakening the Heart: East/West Approaches to Psychotherapy and the Healing Relationship* (Boston: New Science Library, 1985).

to experience the truth for themselves and those they work with in a seamless way.

Liddle and others have pointed out the isomorphic nature[32] of supervision. Emotional differentiation of the therapist is a key variable in therapeutic competence, allowing the therapist effectively to interrupt negative feedback loops, change homeostasis and facilitate second order change[33] in individuals, families and couples,[34] and it is the same in supervision.[35] In one way or another, I am always seeking to facilitate greater awareness of what the trainee is experiencing; what she/he is observing, feeling, and consequently how and why she/he chooses to intervene or is automatically reacting with persons (or with me) in a particular way. This invites greater mindfulness in the therapist which enhances freedom to respond by opening up more choices in order to help them reach their goals and facilitate differentiation. To paraphrase and adapt Catholic theologian Karl Rahner's perspective, the task of supervision (theology) is not so much to fill supervisees with theory (religion) as it is to draw out of them the richness of their own particular way of understanding and doing things. My supervisory approach is consequently both inwardly attentive as well as outwardly observing and interpersonally active in order to facilitate this process. I am attempting fulfill my golden rule of supervision, which is to give to the trainee the kind of

---

[32] H. A. Liddle, "Systemic Supervision: Conceptual Overlays and Pragmatic Guidelines," in H. A. Liddle, D. C. Breunlin, and R. C. Schwartz (eds.), *Handbook of Family Therapy Training and Supervision* (New York: Guilford Press, 1988), 153–171.

[33] Second order change refers to a fundamental change in the complexity and differentiation of a living system, in contrast to first order change which merely lessens the tension in the system while leaving it structurally the same as before.

[34] D. Schnarch, *Constructing the Sexual Crucible: An Integration of Sexual and Marital Therapy* (London: W. W. Norton & Co., 1991); D. Schnarch, *Passionate Marriage* (London: W. W. Norton & Co., 1997); F. Shapiro, *Eye Movement Desensitization and Reprocessing* (New York: Guilford, 1995), Vol. 14, 142–160.

[35] D. V. Papero, "Training in Bowen Theory," in H. A. Liddle, D. C. Breunlin, and R. C. Schwartz (eds.), *Handbook of Family Therapy Training and Supervision* (New York: Guilford Press, 1988), 62–77.

high quality attention, empathy and pastoral responsiveness of my full personhood on their behalf, that I hope they will give to their clients and that I myself want. This, of course, must be congruent with what the supervisee is able and desiring to learn, and it is necessary to 'check in' frequently with the supervisee's experience of the process as to whether it is congruent with what is wanted. At the same time, the supervisor has an ethical responsibility not only to the supervisee but also to the clients whom the supervisee will engage in the future.

Training and supervision of pastoral counselors are built on a foundation of attending carefully to the deep and ongoing uncovering of the motivations and capacities of the person's primary vocation of 'becoming a person,' which is the *axis mundi* for integration of all these theoretical lens and approaches. In Orthodoxy, the person is primary; the ontological foundation of creation is not created substance but the *person* created in God's image who comes into full likeness through remaining in dialogue with both God and the world simultaneously over a lifetime.

H OLY TRINITY AS ANALOGUE FOR HOW POWER IS DISTRIB-UTED IN THE SUPERVISORY RELATIONSHIP. The Holy Trinity represents three distinct relationships of persons who exist in a harmony without Bowenian triangulation and provides the prototypical participatory model for supervision insofar as it is evidences hierarchical order and differentiation of persons, while still being equal among all its members. In pastoral counseling supervision, as in pastoral counseling, the supervisor's relationship with the supervisee ethically and professionally is illumined by the relationships among the Holy Trinity. As an iconic representation of Christ, the supervisor is a servant leader. She/he stands *below* the supervisee in terms of placing the supervisee's welfare above her/his own. She/he stands *above* the supervisee hierarchically in terms of the power inherent in the evaluative relationship as well as unconsciously engendering family of origin transferences. She/he stands *beside* the supervisee, as sister or brother and friend in co-pilgrimage on the road to Emmaus. Through transparency and the use of appropriate self-disclosure, the supervisor helps confirm the supervisee's own strengths, normalize her/his growing edges and celebrate the shared mystery of God's activity in our midst. Ultimately, we are all part of one Body and in process together, sharing one common ground, while experiencing it from the unique vantage points of our respective personhood so that the I-Thou encounter with the other is the nexus in which Christ emerges afresh. To the extent that there is a genuine διά-Λογος encounter, a third 'Emmaus' dimension always appears in the between which is holy ground.

The Holy Trinity also provides a prototypical relational model that unites systems orientation with intrapsychic and transpersonal modalities. The Word must be made flesh (Incarnation) through existential engagement that includes both mind and body in order for the heart to appear. I often tell my clients, "Speak so that your body can confirm the truth of your words." This is the direction for healing, renewal and growth. Re-membering is the cure for being dis-membered by lies or injustice, which separate mind and body and numb the heart. Re-membering includes both the dimension of telling the truth as well as living it. Just as Jesus Christ, the Theanthropos and only begotten Son, pays a price existentially in the flesh to link God and Creation in a seamless embrace, while preserving creation's freedom from being dominated, so the heart is the link between mind and body, even down to the cellular level of neuroreceptor sites, which regulate affective states and convey information across all biological systems.[36] The heart is the arena where through struggle marriage between heaven and earth is born and grows or where it is rejected. Consequently, in supervision, I focus a great deal on helping supervisees increase mindfulness of being present, calling their attention to the linkage between mind and proprioceptive sensations of body and how they are responding to their clients and to me in the moment, what they are choosing consciously and what is 'happening,' so that they begin to be able to attend to this dimension in their clients.

---

[36] C. Pert, *The Molecules of Emotion* (New York: Simon & Schuster, 1998).

THE IMPORTANCE OF CO-PILGRIMAGE. In my work at the Pastoral Institute, Inc., an interdenominational not-for-profit counseling, education and consultation agency, along with providing pastoral care and psychotherapy for a general population for nearly twenty years, I serve as the Director of Counselor Training and have been involved in the specialized task of training clergy, military chaplains and clinical post-graduate residents in the art and science of pastoral counseling and psychotherapy. One part of my work is to help therapists, loaded down with counseling theories, diagnoses and HMO requirements for demonstrating evidence-based therapeutic approaches and behaviorally based treatment plans, reawaken to the mystery of human persons by encountering others in the presence of the Living God. Humility is the foundation for utilization of all theory and clinical skills so that they remain in the service of empathic *not knowing* in a compassionate way that invites people to self-confront, rather than serving to distance people from the other behind the role of expert and 'sick one.' Balancing these two initiatives of assuming less as we learn more is a difficult and ongoing task, just as is repentance before the gifts of Grace that are offered along the way of the spiritual journey. Six years after graduation from the program, one of the members of the first group of chaplains I worked with came back for a reunion. He laughed as he said, "You guys were easy with us. I can see it now. It is amazing what we didn't know!" Along with pleasure in his enthusiasm, I took solace that his remark indicated he had matured over those intervening years and was appreciating the kind of 'not knowing' we hope for, which grows out of the experience of encountering human suffering that defies all attempts to 'manage' illness apart from the invitation of Grace and respect for human freedom even with the best of tools.

The more pain we have experienced vicariously through the eyes of our clients and parishioners and the more joys and heartbreak we have known in our own lives from confronting the gap between the eternal God and the seemingly infinite ways of evasion of love that we discover in our lives, the more mercy and wisdom emerge along with vicarious trauma, which the therapist and supervisor must constantly metabolize through prayer, therapeutic support and a healthy life-style and relationships. Facing what cannot be changed by our own power, the intractable resistant sins of our personal lives that pierce our illusions of perfection; hearing the stories of perversions and the scarring of abuse and violence, combat trauma and addiction, either activate our own issues or lead us deeper into intercessory prayer. In a similar way, witnessing the immense capacity for vulnerability, courage and tenacity of persons to reclaim their lives through the dialogue of psychotherapy inspires and humbles, drawing the thera-pist into thanksgiving, gratefulness and prayer.

Only one who receives love and care, partnering with God in tending to the wounds of others, can remain present with and for others, to wield the tools of the counseling profession without hid-ing behind them in order to avoid the challenge of human suffering as Job's counselors began to do after their first seven days of silent empathy. To confront another human being's suffering and the ques-tions raised by it means being open to being confronted oneself by the questions. St. John Chrysostom says, "who loves acquires a new self." Counseling is a long pilgrimage to many small Theophanies. God is love and is always 'between' the priest-counselor and client who are co-pilgrims regardless of the difference in experience be-tween them and the professional context. It is the humility and hon-esty of the trainee as pilgrim that elicits in the supervisor a similar humility, which opens up a conduit for God's activity. As it is said among the Omaha people, "If you speak from the heart, you will be answered from the heart." In this sense, the counselor, as well as the supervisor, is largely 'created' by the courage and depth of search of the one seeking assistance. I have witnessed how God can cause even Balaam's donkey to prophesy if the need is great enough and there is no one else who can respond.

I see supervision of pastoral counselors as a trialogical, relational process in which the supervisor encounters the supervisee with an intentional awareness of being in the presence of God, just as the counselor in training is encouraged to do with his/her clients. Until the pilgrim in me has surfaced from beneath the mass of 'the already known' as I begin to recognize the uniqueness of the person before me in the presence of God, I have not yet had a real encounter with myself, the other or Christ who is always at the nexus between me and the other waiting to be visible through relationship. From this perspective, pastoral psychotherapy and supervision are best approached with the same quality of ascetical sobriety, self-confrontation, vulnerability and openness to the Beloved that accompany worship and prayer. Counseling is the activity of prayer which is love. Love is what enables truth to be discovered, and it is truth which sets us free.

A ND THE GREATEST OF THESE IS LOVE. Some years ago, Hans Strupp, a noted early researcher into therapeutic clinical outcomes, summed up a decade's findings in words that intimate what I am talking about when he observed,

> techniques seemed to matter less than the therapist's personal qualities. I felt that Albert Schweitzer's idea of reverence for life captured the distinction I was struggling with. Some therapists, regardless of their theoretical orientation, length of experience, professional affiliation, etc., appeared to have this quality, and I came to surmise (although I could not prove it) that they were better therapists. Others appeared to be notably deficient in this regard. They seemed to be technicians who plied a trade; they might have shrewd insights into the patient's dynamics; they might be clever in confronting the patient with his conflicts and neurotic patterns, but they lacked a human quality I came to regard as the supreme qualification of the good psychotherapist ... Perhaps the principal ingredient is compassion. It is the deeply felt understanding of another human being's suffering, coupled with gentleness and tenderness. It is empathic in the sense of understanding another per-

son's inner world — notably his loneliness, anguish, suffering, and basic helplessness.[37]

To stand in relationship with God in the present moment over a lifetime of choices as the primary means of becoming *fully human* is beautifully captured by Martin Buber in his Hasidic explanation of the story of Adam and Eve's encounter with God following their disobedience in eating of the tree of knowledge of good and evil.

G-d's question to Adam and Eve, 'Where are you?' is G-d's intimate I-Thou loving question to each of us at every moment of our lives. It is a pastoral intervention offering the opportunity to become truthful at a simple and deep level, to *reveal* oneself and the choices made in the secret place of the heart that has born the fruit of dislocating us from the Creator, each other and our own souls to the extent that *knowing-about and controlling* has supplanted *knowing through intimate relationship*.

As a substitute for Divine intimacy, we are provisioned with *skins:* family of origin scripts, personal self-defining narratives, unconscious intrapsychic object-relations and systemic patterns of behavior, all of which shape and are reshaped over time by each other and the larger communities of meaning and relationship in which we live. Much effort is spent preserving these acquired skins in order to feel like *somebody* in the wake of loss of intimate relationship with God and alienation from the self-in-loving-relationship. The rest of the time we are trying to lay these skins aside and draw from the mysterious reviving depths in order to relate to one another and God with honesty, intimacy and immediacy just as *I am-with-You.* As the proverbial rusty knight found out, armor is good under certain conditions, but becomes a virtual prison, destroying capacity for life, when you get stuck in it!

In the realm of pastoral psychotherapy, there really is no short-term therapy. Just as with supervision, training and learning are

---

[37] H. Strupp, "The Therapist's Theoretical Orientation: An Overrated Variable," *Psychotherapy: Theory, Research and Practice* (1978): 315.

never finished, regardless of theoretical models employed, because we are always growing and discovering in our relationship with God and others, places in the heart that resist life. Both psychotherapy and supervision endeavors entail a lifetime of becoming and remaining a question for oneself as we encounter God and others along the way. God's question to each of us is *always personal* and straight to the heart. "Where are you?" is a question that invites us to be *real* at increasingly deeper levels and for an eternity. It invites us, from a position of trusting faith in our belovedness to God, to look upon and be responsible for how we have become adulterated, a *legion* of competing desires and reactivity. With our divided selves, we constantly project onto others and scapegoat them, consciously and unconsciously, as a means of avoiding awareness of the truth which we cannot bear to experience within ourselves.

For this reason, in supervision, I frequently ask counselors two questions, upon which much of supervision hangs: "Who is in the room?" and "What question is your client(s) asking Jesus?" Both the supervisee and the client's body movements, pauses, tone and tempo of speech, the types of questions asked and the observations made, all help answer these questions along with exploration of their subjective experiences. What is being-with-the-client-in-the-presence-of-God eliciting from the counselor? This question relates to gender, power, culture, race, rank, family of origin, faith and unconscious defenses. Facing the Thou of God as we are face to face with one another and self διά-Λογος, we are all co-pilgrims in a great embrace, learning from the impact such inter-subjectivity[38] has on us. From these questions flow several foundational learning areas that are critical to ongoing clinical and theological integration in pastoral care and

---

[38] Διά-Λογος is situated beyond intersubjectivity to the extent that the latter involves mutual projections of two subjectivities onto the other, but without a third I-Thou which makes possible standing existentially in relation to the other so as to be affected by the reality of the being who confronts one as 'other' beyond the projection of one's subjectivity, which involves what Buber calls authentic meeting. I interpret this always to involve the third person of Christ.

counseling by way of the motivations and quality of attention of the person of the therapist:

1) developing the capacity for compassionate, interested, empathic, 'not knowing,' which is a *sine qua non* for authentic meeting;
2) identifying the presence of 'therapeutic aggression'[39] and taking steps to reduce anxiety in order to establish a deeper and freer willingness to accompany the client into his/her unique situation and pain;
3) uncovering the presence and degree of 'functional atheism,' which tends to surface in relation to fluctuations in 1 and 2 above, taking on responsibility for making something happen oneself rather than serving as witness to what God is already doing before we arrived on the scene.

WHAT IS YOUR QUESTION TO JESUS? A CASE EXAMPLE. An experienced male chaplain had been working with a woman who was very angry with her husband. He feels he is getting nowhere with her and is considering termination; however, it is evident that progress in therapy is occurring. We reviewed a portion of tape from the 8th session after the client had burst into the room and said, "Y'all have to get me through five more years until my son is old enough to leave and then we're gone." She talks with pressure of speech, powerfully, loudly and continuously as is typical of her. "At this point he's fair game! He's bothered me so much over the years that I think to myself 'F-- you! I'll say whatever I want! And I do!'" (After a few minutes, the supervisor asks him to pause the tape in order to discuss.)

S   What's her question to Jesus?
T   Why — when are You going to make me normal?

---

[39] R. C. Cushing, *Opening to Empathy: The Experience of Opening to Understanding What Has Been Preventing or Blocking a Supervisee From Opening to Empathy with a Client*. Ph.D. Dissertation California Institute of Integral Studies. UMI order number 8926006. 1989.

S   Okay, but that's — let's say that's a victim response. That's not yet a question to Jesus, because it would require Jesus to first do an intervention with her to get her to be responsible for herself. Until we get to that, we don't have the question of that soul to Jesus yet. What is the suffering behind "Why don't You make me normal?" Has she found where she's blind? Does she know how she has been bleeding for 16 years or is she just saying, "Why me Lord?" which isn't a real question?

T   I don't know… she's got the nightmare family background. The whole family has got some type of mental problem. I'm not diagnosing *per se*, but just by her descriptions. She's probably the most healthy one in her family.

S   What does she elicit in you?

T   Her histrionics.

S   Tell me how that works. What are you aware of?

T   I'm aware that I feel — well I started out feeling um — just inadequate, blown away. Lost. When she would start into her monologues, because I mean it would — I just can't… can't bring too much back to a thread. It's not a conversation…

S   What's the inadequacy connected to?

T   I can't bring it back to a thread to connect it.

S   So she's causing you to be incompetent by controlling your normal ways of relating?

T   Yeah.

S   Okay. What does that tell you? If you're getting that kind of reaction… How do you use that counter-transference diagnostically?

T   Yeah. I'm not surprised that it comes up in me simply because of the language and the loudness and the — everything. Um… Trying to make connections with what I wonder about her (*anxious laugh*) Um… I want to say guarded. Through the noise and the curse words and the rate and volume. Just the — all over the place — and listen for that question — I hadn't thought of it in that way… listen for that question, listen for what she is asking for. Because she'll let it — I mean — she has let it down. The last session was the least amount of that stuff and it was almost more ... she was just shattered. I mean, I've never met anyone like her ... in the counseling I mean. You know, outside I can walk away from her outside, but she'll tell us, "I have ya'll trapped for an hour and you have to listen to me."

S   So she actually confirms what she's saying — part of how you're experiencing things. So this lets you — you can use the fact that she is taking up a lot of space in that room just to be passive and observe.

T   Um-hmm.

S   This lets you look and see, "Now what conditions is she creating? You look at what's going on in you ..."

T   Um-hmm.

S   Then ask, "Why would she create these conditions? How do they help her? What are they telling us and how does it serve her?"

T   Well, it seems to keep the other things a little bit more at bay.

S   Okay. So it could be protection. When it's not there, what happens for her?

T   She looks pretty normal. I mean it's like somebody who is actually saying, "This is why I hurt."

S   That sounds better.

T   Yeah. It sounds better than this!

S   So why does she do what isn't productive for her?

T   I don't know. (*anxious laugh*) I mean — part of my assumption is ... part of the way I'm thinking is it allows her to maintain the "not normal" in relationship to the husband and then everybody else. You asked about themes? "I don't — I like to work, but there is not a job I enjoy." "I want friends, but I don't care to have people around." I mean just all these.

S   You have to break those down. I don't know what they mean.

T   (*talking over supervisor*) I know. They're almost like complete opposites. I'll be tracking on one and I'll be going, "Okay. We've talked about jobs she's had, but 'I can't hold a job because there's none I like.'"

S   Then I don't know what "I like to work" means.

T (*laughter*) I know.

S So my point to you is that if you let those go by at face value —

T (*laughter*) So I'm trying (*laughter*) to get a definition and we end up with — Dang! It's five till ten and we have to leave the room. It's very — I mean its almost gotten to — started out it was just painful. It was easy to be passive because I didn't know what the hell to say. It was almost like watching someone on display...

S Can you tenderly structure it?

T Well I tried in this session. I mean somebody comes in and they close the door and say "I'm cured!" loud enough to raise the Hallelujah chorus. For about five seconds, I thought she was serious and then I realized what she was doing.

S She was sarcastic.

T Yeah.

S And you tried to work with her gestures a little bit to try to get her to explore what might be a sense of power for her like almost a solution focused frame to catch her doing what she needs to do sort of thing.

T Yeah. I fell into that later on, and someone pointed out I actually did Solution Focused Therapy! I brought up in supervision (on Post) the most interesting thing as far as the dynamics I've seen was you know somebody said, "Have you drawn boundaries with her cursing and stuff?" So much of that for her doing it right now —

S (*interrupting*) This is almost style rather than saying anything destructive.

T Yeah, it's a filler word to connect between something or other. But in the 2nd or 3rd session, I almost felt like it was beyond control and she was getting into some story and I tried to do like a time-out thing (*holds hands in time-out formation*) taking some suggestions and doing some structuring. She blew right by "Time-out" and later on said "I don't play football!"

S She had noticed it and overruled it.

T Yeah. And said, "I don't play football..."

S What did you do with that?

T   Well, at that point, I was sitting there thinking, What would be a word that would stop her cold in her tracks? Without yelling. Because I can't match her for voice. So I said "her name" (softly, like a whisper). In the middle of her tirade: "her name." She stopped for a moment and looked up. I knew I was at a yellow light and I knew if I didn't go through...

S   You asked for her softly by her name as opposed to — and aren't you the one that noticed (several months earlier in a group meeting in another room) and remarked on that quotation of Virginia Satir ("Allow yourself to go to that sacred place within yourself that is called by your name.") on the wall in the room where we had our first group meeting?

T   Um-hmm.

S   That was you wasn't it?

T   Yeah.

S   Um... I'm just wondering if there is a connection here for you?

(Here I am looking for something that is precious and important to the chaplain's own personal pilgrimage and "question to Jesus" that may be an important link with the woman's pain which allowed him to empathically connect with her. This particular chaplain works extremely hard to meet inner self-imposed demands, and he skips over affirmation easily, as I believe he did in this moment. Rather than take it in and ponder it, he remains focused on seeking to understand his client as if it can occur apart from depth encounter with his own journey. This could also be that it is difficult for him to allow himself the kind of vulnerability that is entailed in becoming a question for himself, yet this kind of interested, non-judgmental 'not knowing' is exactly what can help his client. I believe that supervision involves inviting the supervisee to experience for him/herself what it is he/she wishes to invite the client into. It seems important that he speaks the client's name in this way in so far as it was he alone among the group that noticed and commented on the Virginia Satir quotation about the sacredness of the name. Who speaks his name in this way?)

T   I mean she responds to that. I was thinking of Jesus with Mary when I literally—I was thinking, "How can I get her attention?"

S   I wonder where that came from and what that means, because it's on target?

(Supervisor is trying once more to invite the therapist's wonderment of his own inner processes related to the importance of his personal name that might be related to his question as pilgrim to Jesus and thus a means of listening from his pastoral and human heart for the woman's core question, i.e. heart listening for heart.)

T   Yeah. Well. You know part of it going back to the genogram and things she's said and repeated use of *normal*. I mean, every session is "normal, normal, normal." So I'm thinking over the weekend before we had a session, "What of this woman is normal?" And I knew if I asked her, I'd get, "I don't know! You tell me!" It seemed to go back to—you know the husband—she's his sex toy. Um … It's always a—everything in her life is a role that she fulfills. For him it's sex. For mom it's—you know, a dopey daughter. For her daughter, who's now a stripper, it's money. And who else calls her by her name? I didn't think it'd be that powerful, but it's the only thing in seven sessions I've seen that slowed her down.

S   Well, that's real interesting. We have to stop, but from what you started out with, I wonder what intuitive process allowed you to find something out of all the impressions coming in that was right on target and what implications that has for what she would ask Jesus? Does she want to be called by her name? Does she want to be known truly, but it's so scary that she puts up a popsicle stick person that's real entertaining and controlling at the same time? She so dominates the space that she doesn't have to worry about any input coming in that could further hurt her, but yet she starves because since there's no input coming in, she can't ever know if she's really known? If she could ever get conscious of that and own it, she'd have power in her life. Someone has to be with her, enter

into it, identify the process and then help her out of kind of disinterested love – by disinterested I mean non-coercive love —

T   Sure.

S   Help her see what she's doing, not TEACH her about it, but
    say —

T   Yeah

S   Like "My experience is this with you. I'm really curious about
    why you could ignore the 'time out' but you heard your name
    whispered. 'Cause you're so alert. You know everything that's go-
    ing on in this room even when it looks like you might not! How
    did you learn that?" Then you could get fascinated with her and
    she might respond to your interest.

T   Instead of piquing in us the same response she gets from most
    everybody else.

S   Yes. Yes.

T   Which is finally they will have enough of me and either fire
    me —

S   Yes.

T   Or just tell me we can stop making appointments or something.

S   Yes.

T   Lord, to even mention the word terminate now, you know, I'm
    wondering what that would — It would sound like rejection ...

S   Yeah. And now you're into an object relations perspective. You
    don't act it out, but you begin to draw it out of her in terms of
    her awareness of it. You're helping her inwardly connect with the
    process she creates all the time and see why she's doing it, which
    in my mind I would say is analogous to going to the Lord and you
    bring the Lord your process and He enters it and doesn't give it
    back to you, doesn't act it out with you but finds a way to bring
    you to consciousness about it and then you have a choice about it,
    like the rich young ruler, about what you're going to do about it.
    And those existential choices are where our freedom is as people.
    Do I choose God or not? I have a hard time when I've got this
    stuff in the way and I don't know what it is. Someone's got to help

me see that. That's where the wise abbas and ammas come in. They help us see that. (*end of verbatim*)

INCARNATION AS AN EXISTENTIAL ANALOGUE FOR PSYCHO-THERAPY. The Incarnation and seamless natures of the Theanthropos provide helpful prototype and analogy for what is needed in therapeutic encounter. God's activity in Christ enters into the homeostasis of human life while yet remaining separate. Jesus is both human and Divine. Thus, God's activity in Christ is from the most differentiated position in the universe, effecting a transformation in the world through His incarnational life, Passion and Resurrection which link the deepest brokenness and lostness of human suffering and predicament with heaven and the everlasting love of the Creator. Christian doctrine is instructive for us at this point. A Jesus who is only human and not Divine, the Pelagian or Arian perspective, would be analogous to the technical error of the therapist lacking root in him/herself, not being sufficient and identifying with the client's projective identification, acting it out, so that no healing takes place and perhaps even contributes to the ruin of all. This is evident in cases where the therapist's own unacknowledged needs and depression lead to boundary violations and professional ethics violations resulting from losing perspective of dialogue and fusing with projections.

On the other hand, there is the docetic solution, e.g., Christ did not really suffer, but was dancing above the cross, only 'appearing' to be compassionately incarnated. In this scenario, the therapist is too far removed from being affected by the projective identification process of the client to either comprehend or 'feel' it. So the therapist is blind to the person's question to Jesus at the process level. The therapist loses his/her own capacity for being transformed by the encounter. If the therapist has not been changed in some way by the encounter, then there has not been a real meeting with the person. He or she was operating from a sealed-off expert status. This is the docetic version of therapy, and priests and counselors who fall into this trap not only fail their parishioners and clients but begin to starve themselves, for the heart is cold. Those are loved, who risk loving begin to suffer a loss of the sense of being beloved in a kind of "fall" from Grace, for the gift of love which is not given away in re-turn, is eventually lost.

So the doctrines of the Trinity and the Incarnation of God in Christ both have existential analogues in pastoral psychotherapy. Relationship is the healing element stemming from both. From an object relations theory perspective, as Cashdon notes,

> the therapist does more than just help the patient deal with inner objects. In the course of treatment, *he becomes one of these objects.* By allowing himself to become part of the patient's projective fantasy and rearranging the outcome of the relationship scenario that ensues, the therapist becomes a powerful new presence in the patient's inner world ... The therapist thus functions as an internal counterforce that enables the patient to combat — and ultimately let go of — the destructive object relations that existed beforehand ... What does it mean to "let go"? It means to forgive ... The final necessary step in therapy is *forgiveness*: forgiveness of what happened, forgiveness for what is happening, forgiveness of what may still happen.[40]

THERAPEUTIC AGGRESSION. Addressing identity issues, such as personal and professional integration and self-other representations related to the intersection between pastoral vocation and self-worth, is a vital part of pastoral and clinical integration. The basic idea is that therapeutic aggression is an empathic block resulting from identification with various projections, and projection is a failure of repentance. There is no being who is without therapeutic aggression but God, because the rest of us are tied up to some extent by identification with our reactions to our projections onto each other, which are in fact subtle judgments that scapegoat others and disallow

---

[40] S. Cashdon, *Object Relations Therapy: Using the Relationship* (New York: W. W. Norton & Co., 1985), 139.

persons from being just as they are. Lowering therapeutic aggression requires both repentance and the mercy and compassion that flow from humility engendered by receiving our value not from our own hand, but from the gift of God's love. Jesus' supervisory instruction is clear: "Get to know the log in your own eye..." and then you will see your neighbor more clearly. Ghandi captured the significance of ignoring this, when he observed, "I like Christianity, but I don't like Christians," and "You must become the change you wish to see in the world." This frees other people from being my scapegoats and me from being a victim who cannot change until those around me stop reacting to my projections!

Supervision focuses on three areas: deep self-confrontation effects a change in relationship with God and others; experience of a change in relationship with God involves a change in experience of self and others. There cannot ever be a change in one of these three without the other two relationships being affected as well. So, we say that working with supervisees and clients is a triune spiritual formation process rooted in the supervisor/therapist's own self-examination, prayer and continual repentance, which are catalyzed and informed by carefully attending to the effects of empathic encounters with others in the presence of God. As St. Isaac the Syrian reminds, "One who knows himself (in this way), is greater than one who raises the dead." Or again, St. Anthony, "Who does not know himself cannot know God." Continual repentance purifies the heart and opens the door to Grace-inspired humility, empathy, kindness, guilelessness, clarity, simplicity, joy and valuing the *thatness* of all beings and creation. Without this kind of ongoing training, pastoral counselors at best offer psychological counseling couched in religious words and symbols "having the appearance of religion but without its power" and at worst, an unwitting substitution of other gods. Similarly, without serious attention to Christian formation, pastoral supervision easily degenerates into a process that subtly reinforces functional atheism and cultural fads by underestimating the role of purity of heart and peace of conscience in making space for prayerful attentiveness to

God and humble reverencing of God in other souls, which has been
a cornerstone of Christian experience for two thousand years. Cut off
from the root of Christ, too much emphasis is placed on psychological theory and technique, labels and 'expertise' that can subtly disem-
power persons by lulling them into unawareness of the inextricable
link between theory and practice in Christian life. Spiritual realities
are always present, even when unrecognized. As Don Browning observed twenty-five years ago, every practice and the theories that give
rise to them have an implicit religious dimension which influences
persons and sets their course.

> Psychoanalysis, Jungian psychotherapy, Bernean, Rogerian, and
> gestalt psychotherapy clearly have taken on for certain segments
> of the public a quasi-religious meaning. When this happens, the
> theories and techniques of these therapies become inflated into
> encompassing orientations to life that function very much as do
> religious myths. They offer highly generalized interpretations
> about the purpose of life, the origin of human difficulties, and
> the secret for human change and betterment.[41]

'NOT KNOWING' AND FUNCTIONAL ATHEISM. 'Not knowing'
is closely akin to repentance, inner sobriety and attending to
the presence of God. It is a willingness to be present without relying
on one's knowledge to protect us from the unknown. Or as D. W.
Winnicott observed from his perspective, "When the therapist is
reacting, there is no room for the client's mind." The most important preparation for pastoral counselors in training as well as one
of the most important sustaining factors in avoiding therapeutic
aggression, eventual therapist burnout and ethical boundary violations is whether or not the therapist is in continual repentance and
regular confession, prayer and worship as the foundation for any

---

[41] D. Browning, *The Moral Context of Pastoral Care* (Philadelphia: Westminster
Press, 1976), 13.

and all supervision and consultation that one receives regarding one's pastoral work.

One trainee wondered about his client, "Did she say I was helping her because it's real or because she thought I needed to hear that?" He was excited by the insight (from a previous supervision session) into his family of origin dynamics of feeling missed by his mother and not visible as he needed to be to her. It had freed him from disliking his client whom he felt, was not paying enough attention to him. He said, "I have reflected on this every day since." Realization of his unconscious tendency to expect this attention from the women he was working with had helped him become more responsible for himself and lower his therapeutic aggression which was causing him to distance from his clients as a means of soothing his own anxiety rather than being able to remain present to God's unfolding purposes in the midst of two pilgrims genuinely encountering one another along the road to Emmaus.

I asked the chaplain if the tape he had brought was connected to any of his discoveries in a prior session. He could see none initially. Then on tape the woman described her relationship with her mother who "needed me to need her to an extent that it stifled me," and I wondered with him whether he was concerned that she might fall into that kind of relationship with him, particularly if she sensed that he needed her to be needed by him. We both laughed at this as he saw the parallel process with his own history and long-standing need which was still a bit unconscious for him. Nevertheless, his growing awareness of himself had begun helping him raise questions about how he might be subtly influencing the client. At the end of session, we touched on a third parallel system, that of the supervisor-supervisee. Aware of my own need to be of help and tendency to give very much when the supervisee is open and interested, I wondered, "Did I give you enough space in the session? Was I attentive to your unfolding or did I create a situation of needing you to need me by being the guru?"

Functional Atheism is closely akin to therapeutic aggression. It is the "unconscious unexamined conviction that if anything decent is going to happen here, we are the ones who must make it happen — a conviction held even by people who talk a good game about God."[42] Driven by unconscious attempts at self-preservation and self-regulation, or to complete unfinished childhood agendas, functional atheism crowds out empathic presence and the patience of waiting on God. Structurally, it is a function of poor quality of attention dominated by ego rather than trusting God in faith and entering totally into the moment.

> Ego is the systematic affirmation of emotional reaction. This system is fueled by the energy of attention. Therefore as long as a man has no control over his attention, his possibilities remain imprisoned in the ego no matter what ideals he espouses and no matter what efforts he expends.[43]

By contrast, as St. Mark the Ascetic observes, "Remembrance of God is suffering of heart endured with devotion to God. Who forgets God is self-indulgent and insensitive." The asceticism involved in pastoral care and counseling (and supervision), of not turning away from others and our own experience or interfering with their freedom in order to meet our needs, while simultaneously relying on God in prayerful attention, prepares the heart to see and bear our responses to other people's pain as well as to hope in other people's possibilities. It trains and refines the attention to perceive depth and breadth and height beyond superficial content and our attempts to manage it according to unconscious needs.

RELIGIOUS GROUNDING. Effectiveness in pastoral psychotherapy, as the American Association of Pastoral Counselors has long emphasized, is in direct proportion to how *humanly available* we are at any given moment and consistently over time. Availability is

---

[42] P. Palmer, *Let Your Life Speak: Listening to the Voice of Vocation* (California: Jossey-Bass, Inc., 2000), 88.

[43] J. Needleman, *Lost Christianity* (New York: Doubleday, 1988).

a function of the counselor's groundedness in his/her own religious tradition in an integrated existential whole that is greater than the sum of the intellectual, emotional and behavioral parts. Consensus among the Eastern Orthodox Christian tradition is that full human development requires continual repentance and striving in prayer to "bring the mind down into the heart." We might say, "When the therapist is present from the heart, the client is more likely to respond from the heart." Depth calls to depth. I do not see this occurring apart from seeking to be continually present to God with all that this entails in our daily lives outside the consulting room.

Over the years, I have noticed repeatedly that availability to others and treasuring their *thatness* with joy and hope is functionally related to feeling known, forgiven and loved by God. By contrast, reflexive attempts to protect the "self-made self" and the associated passions rooted in self-will and self-indulgence are in direct proportion to loss of belovedness to God. I always seem to do my best work immediately after having gone to confession and found my heart's joy and gentleness renewed. Remorse of conscience, confession, worship, internal sobriety and constant prayerfulness are not only medicines for the fallen human condition, but the primary training ground for good pastoral counselors. After eleven years as a parish minister and twenty-five years in the field of pastoral counseling as both psychotherapist, supervisor, and educator, I am of the view that 90% of the work of pastoral counseling is done before the therapist ever enters the consulting room. This is because it has to do with being who we are in terms of the faith, hope and love engendered by cultivating a relationship with the Holy Spirit. *Working the program of Christianity as "Way and Truth and Life" on a daily basis over a lifetime is the ground out of which the living plant of integration of clinical theory and religious faith grows and is sustained. It occurs exactly at that point of intersection where God, Self and Other meet and at no other place. The work of supervision of pastoral counselors is the work of facilitating genuine human encounters in the presence of God.* Growth in this dimension is always διά-Λογος given by God through the activity of loving actual human beings. It is not and can never be a 'technique' or something we 'do' to another person.

Pope Paul VI observed, "When you can see the face of Jesus Christ behind the face of every person you meet and behind Jesus Christ, you see the face of God then your humanism becomes Christianity." Pastoral counseling is a walk together with burning hearts toward an Emmaus encounter. It takes place when there is a real meeting of souls beyond the habitual mutual projections, regardless of the clinical theory or approach which may be used to conceptualize it. Apart from a truly *personal* encounter, I would submit, no real *pastoral* counseling is occurring, for '*pastoral*' by definition emerges from triune God-self-other inter-relatedness. God is made visible not through our expert attempts at managing and fixing people's problems but through being vulnerable and present to and with them as priest, midwife, gardener and fellow pilgrim while people rage and weep, celebrate, give thanks, birth new meaning, learn to compost painful experiences and find the courage and inspiration to move out of the prison of self-esteem-seeking into pilgrimage through uncharted territory. It is in moving out beyond the already known, over and over that God slowly becomes all in all and the true 'self' which is hidden with Christ in God grows not according to human will and design, but by God's Grace in the midst of loving relationship in ways that we cannot see. This is the Emmaus journey in which hearts become flame together through dialogue of meeting wherein the presence of the stranger confronting us becomes a source of revelation of the deepest mystery of the person of Christ himself in our midst. In this mystery, the guest becomes the host.

Finally, I would submit that assisting clients in drawing nourishment and new meaning from the deep well of religious faith and life is clinically necessary if they are to find solutions to presenting concerns that are more than short-term 'solution forced' interventions that fail to encounter the depths of brokenness and sin that invade human life from behind the scenes or to encourage the fullness of potential growth in Christ. Had Jesus failed to encounter the full depth and breadth of human depravity, the gift of our createdness in the Divine Image and the hope of attaining God's *likeness,* which is the only real solution to the human problem, would not be possible. As we encounter those we seek to serve in pastoral counseling, can we expect of ourselves to succeed in pastoral work by doing less? This moves in the direction of merely helping persons comfortably adjust to prevailing cultural and psychological norms, further obscuring their hunger for intimacy with God and the yearning to be obedient to the pristine values that emerge in the mysterious liminal space of the deep heart encountering-the-personal-God-here-and-now-with-you-just-as-I-am. It is truly holy ground.

CHAPTER SIX

Clergy in Crisis:
When Human Power Isn't Enough[1]

All life is meeting.

Martin Buber

The self is hid with Christ in God.

Apostle Paul

The Chinese character representing 'crisis' means both danger and opportunity. Conflict in ministry is inevitable, but burnout does not have to be. Jesus endured and used conflict to bring redemption through it. He predicted it for all those who followed His path. Without a mindful and reflective approach to conflict, stemming from dialogue with Christ that affords an opportunity to remain faithful while engaging the resistance in the world and in one's self, there is no growth. For many clergy, conflict exposes the attempt to succeed in ministry on human power alone, fueled by unconscious attempts to carve out a self in the process which threatens the development of both and, if undiscovered, leads to burnout. Finding the path that leads through conflict rather than avoiding it or caving in to it and losing the integrity of your ministry in the process, is one of the key issues facing clergy today and central to an authentic response to the Gospel, which like the Divine Liturgy and the dialogue of pastoral counseling, is always a continuing call and

---

[1] First published in *Journal of Pastoral Care & Counseling* Vol 61:3 (Fall 2007), and in Russian for *The Moscow Journal of Psychotherapy* Vol. 54(3) (2007): 146–166.

response between the priest/counselor, the church/clients and the Holy Spirit.

EPIDEMIOLOGICAL CONSIDERATIONS RELATED TO PERSONS LEAVING PASTORAL MINISTRY. Among Protestant evangelical churches, research suggests that more than 1,500 pastors leave their positions in ministry every month. Half of these leave ministry altogether within their first five years.[2] While the reasons given are varied, conflict of one sort or another is always central, which often leads clergy to question the validity of their call to ministry and takes a toll on their personal sense of self-worth and family well-being. Conflicts contributing to clergy leaving ministry include lack of support and/or conflict with their denomination officials (26%); conflict with conflicting demands leading to burnout (12%); conflict between church demands and the needs of family and children (11%); conflict with church members (9%); conflict with senior pastors (8%) and conflict among church staff.[3]

The term 'burnout syndrome' was first used in the early 1970's by psychoanalyst Herbert Freudenberger[4] to refer to a cluster of symptoms indicative of mental and physical exhaustion essentially caused by long-term overwork. Significantly, it occurs most often in the persons who are highly motivated and extremely competent and who tend to identify their value and their life increasingly with their work, to the

---

[2] M.E. Foss, "A Renewed Call to Discipleship," *Changing Church Perspectives* Vol. 34, No. 4 (2000).

[3] D.R. Hoge & J.E. Wenger, *Pastors in Transition: Why Clergy Leave Local Church Ministry* (Michigan/UK: Eerdmans Publishing Co., 2005).

[4] U. Kraft, "Burned Out," *Scientific American Mind* June/July (2006): 29–33. See also W. Tomic, D.M. Tomic and W.J.G. Evers, "A Question of Burnout among Reformed Church Ministers in the Netherlands," *Mental Health, Religion and Culture* Vol. 7 (2004): 225–247; C.R. Figley, *Compassion Fatigue: Coping with Secondary Traumatic Stress Disorder in Those Who Treat the Traumatized* (New York: Brunner/Mazel, 1995); Van der Kolk, McFarlane & Weisaeth (eds.), *Traumatic Stress: The Effects of Overwhelming Experience on Mind, Body and Society* (New York: Guilford Press, 1996).

neglect of meeting legitimate human needs for relaxation, intimacy and play. Gradually becoming exhausted, cynical, losing joy and fulfillment in the work itself, they begin to question their self-worth, all the while attempting to work even longer hours as a way of compensating.

Research conducted by the Pastoral Institute, Inc. in partnership with Florida State University (n = 427 clergy families) found that the well-being and long-term viability of clergy in parish ministry is related primarily to what might be considered the two main resources for sustainment of persons in ministry. For clergy, the quality of spiritual resources was identified as most significant, while for clergy spouses, the key predictor of wellbeing was the quality of family life.[5] This is particularly significant in that ninety-four percent of clergy say they feel pressure to have an 'ideal' family, while eighty percent say their ministries have actually had a *negative* impact on their families.[6]

A large-scale study (n = 324,000) of clergy and 6,900 congregations in Australia from both Protestant and Roman Catholic denominations suggests levels of burnout[7] among clergy are much higher. Nineteen percent of clergy in this study were in the severe range, and another 56% identified themselves as being at 'borderline burnout.' Only 21% indicated burnout was not an issue for them. Analysis of these findings revealed vulnerability to burnout was significantly related to three variables: personhood, parish environment and leadership style. Among the protective values for clergy was the quality of marriage and family life, physical health, friendships preventing social isolation, a strong sense of call to ministry and relative freedom from financial problems.

[5] C. Darling & W. Hill, *Understanding Stress and Quality of Life for Clergy and Clergy Spouses: Summary of Quantitative Research Data* (Tallahassee, FL: Florida State University College of Human Science, Dept. of Family and Child Sciences, 2000).

[6] S. Rabey, "Ministering to the Ministers," *Colorado Gazette Telegraph.* 1993, Section E1.

[7] P. Kaldor & R. Bullpitt, *Burnout in Church Leaders* (Australia: Openbook Publishers, 2001).

In terms of parish environment, the factors preventative of burn-out included clergy being able to see some good in modern life teamed up with congregations who value active involvement with the broader community. The more insular self-absorbed parishes that feared out-side contact with the community are similar to clergy who inwardly split by inveighing against an 'evil' world while identifying only with the 'good' aspects of the conscious ego. This increases the likelihood of walled-off, denied parts of each being projected onto the world and other people creating a playground for the passions which gain power to the degree that there is a lack of mindfulness and prayer rooted not in dissociation from the body and the world, but a deeper involve-ment with both, based on love. Small churches were seen to be more stressful than large ones frequently because of concerns over viability and the overwork of a few persons. Pastors were less likely to burn out in churches where members were growing in their faith.

Pastoral leadership style analysis revealed that clergy who inspire and empower parishioners were less likely to burn out than those who suffer from a familiar syndrome which Parker Palmer insight-fully refers to as *functional atheism*.[8] This unwillingness and/or in-ability to delegate authority and empower laity is also a syndrome that is frequently tied to the clergy's unmet childhood needs which reappear in the form of unconscious posturing in the 'parish family' seeking to maintain a precarious equilibrium as the 'favorite child' who becomes exhausted and frequently loses both the joy and the prophetic integrity of the pastorate by striving to meet everyone's needs, legitimate or not, in the process.[9] Not surprisingly, the Aus-tralian study revealed that clergy who are able to delegate responsi-bilities fare better than those tending to 'do all the jobs themselves.' Clergy who are flexible and do not need to be 'kept on a pedestal' by parishioners and who are skillful in their ability to handle parish-

---

[8] P. Palmer, *Let Your Life Speak: Listening to the Voice of Vocation* (California: Jossey-Bass, Inc., 2000), 88.
[9] S. Muse, "Keeping the Wellsprings of Ministry Clear," *Journal of Pastoral Care* Vol. 54, No. 3 (2000): 253–262.

ioners suffering from personality disorders[10] (which includes about ten percent of the average congregation) also had greater longevity in their parishes.

One study conducted among Orthodox Christian priests (n = 49) found a strong link between measures of burnout, overwork and emotional isolation. Twenty percent of priests in this study indicated a high degree of burnout (emotional exhaustion, depersonalization, lack of sense of personal accomplishment) and another 18% experienced moderate levels. Fifty percent of these priests indicated they consistently worked 50–99 hours a week. Fifteen percent of those surveyed indicated that they were isolated and had no one with whom to share their emotional life. Particularly significant was the finding that priests with spiritual confessors and mentors were a full standard deviation above the others in protection against burnout and satisfaction in ministry.[11]

These trends take on increased urgency considering that, among the population at large, research consistently indicates that persons who are emotionally isolated have a two- to three-fold increased risk of death from both heart disease and other causes as compared to persons who experience greater emotional connection to others.[12] Significantly, such results appear to be independent of other cardiac risks factors such as cholesterol level, blood pressure, genetics and so on.[13] Failure to confide emotionally in others is stressful and associated with long-term health problems by putting chronic stress on the heart and on the immune system.[14] Clergy, though surrounded by persons socially, are frequently extremely emotionally isolated. Sev-

---

[10] S. Chase, "Coping With Radical Evil in the Community of Faith," in S. Muse (ed.), *Beside Still Waters: Resources for Shepherds in the Marketplace* (Georgia: Smyth & Helwys, 2000): 129–144.

[11] J. Caparisos, *Burnout in Greek Orthodox Priests of the Southeastern States* (Walden University Ph.D. Dissertation. UMI International, 1999).

[12] Cf. D. Ornish, *Dr. Dean Ornish's Program for Reversing Heart Disease* (New York: Random House, 1990), 89.

[13] Ibid., 90.

[14] Ibid., 91.

enty percent of the clergy surveyed at one gathering (n = 30) said that they did not have a single close friend.[15]

While the spiritual importance of the mentoring relationship may be seen as primary, the secondary benefits of emotional empathy and understanding in human relationships should not be underestimated or devalued. Obviously, such studies have implications for clergy health insurers, judicatories and poorly served parishes that end up paying the price of poor health and frequent illness among clergy. These studies suggest that greater attention needs to be given to clergy wellness programs as well as the need to include thorough assessments and follow-up plans for physical health and well-being in crisis intervention.

HISTORY OF THE PROGRAM AND TYPOLOGY OF INTERVEN-TION. Taken as a whole, these findings are confirmed by the trends found in working with hundreds of clergy through the D. A. and Elizabeth Turner Ministry Resource Center's national Clergy in Kairos program. Ministers travel to the Pastoral Institute, Inc. in Columbus, Georgia, for a week of intensive dialogue with a team of pastoral psychotherapists and ministry coaches. Suggested readings are provided between sessions, along with ample time for rest and recreation and therapeutic massage if desired. Participants stay free of charge[16] in an upscale hotel along Columbus's beautiful riverfront with 16 miles of hiking and historical attractions.

Initially begun as a crisis intervention program, the week has come to be used not only as a resource for judicatories when clergy are at conflict points with their congregations or in their personal lives, but also for those who are seeking a mini-sabbatical for purposes of spiritual discernment and spiritual refreshment. Three main

---

[15] S. Muse and E. Chase, "Healing the Wounded Healers: Soul Food For Clergy," *Journal of Psychology and Christianity* Vol. 12, No. 2 (1993): 146.

[16] This is made possible by the generosity of several hotels in the area who provide these services as a partner in ministry with the Pastoral Institute, Inc. to clergy who so often are the last to be recognized and cared for in the midst of caring for others. This makes the week extremely cost effective.

areas are addressed during the week by a team of pastoral counselors, each one meeting individually for dialogue with the pastor and in some cases his/her spouse. The basic areas addressed are those which have been consistently identified by research and found by our team as most significantly bearing on clergy wellness and effectiveness in ministry. Following the categories noted above, three important dimensions are addressed.

Personhood includes psyche (body/mind/soul) and spirit. It is inclusive of spiritual resources available to and used by the pastor as well as his/her physical and emotional well-being, personal and professional boundaries, relationship skills, and awareness of the impact of unfinished areas of growth stemming from trauma and family of origin issues. Not only have many pastors neglected having a pastor-mentor for themselves, but they have had little or no psychotherapy to understand their own issues better. Consequently, "the log in their own eyes," which Jesus insisted was critical to effective relationships with others, remains largely unexamined. Attempting to offer care and mentor others without receiving this for one's self is questionable to say the least, if not a kind of malpractice that puts both the clergy and parishioners at risk.

Environment includes both the type of ministry and/or the parish setting, its politics, socioeconomic, gender and class privilege, history and systemic configuration, as well as the smaller *oikonomia* of the clergy's home where the well-being and quality of his/her family life has been identified as a critical and often overlooked factor in successful ministry.

Leadership style has to do with the pastor's ability to draw on awareness of personal style, skills and growing edges in conjunction with motivations stemming from the sense of call in order to accomplish the tasks of ministry. This involves a delicate and often elusive, but crucial balance between meeting legitimate human needs while responding to the Divine Energies of Grace to serve others selflessly unencumbered, as much as possible, by compulsivity arising out unconscious dynamics stemming from unmet childhood agendas, which frequently lead to problems of burnout and/or professional and ethical violations.

M ETHODOLOGY. The core of the week consists of twelve hours of dialogue with three different pastoral counselors, each devoted to assessing aspects of the various issues identified above as they are constellated uniquely in each person and his/her particular context. Over a decade's experience with clergy, we have found a personalized approach that invites trust and intimacy and encourages I-Thou dialogical encounter[17] in a setting away from the circumstances and temporarily relieved of demands upon the clergy that are associated with the crisis, allows for significant breakthroughs in a very short time. Frequently, the downward spiral of emotional and psychological pain, if not arrested, is at least redirected with hope and new inspiration stemming from untwisting the sense of self-worth and the call to ministry that are almost universally found together in unconscious ways in clergy who are suffering this inner *folie à deux*. Recognizing the importance of the wisdom of St. Paul's observation that "the self is hid with Christ in God" in contrast with something self-made, one discerning bishop asks of each new candidate for ministry, "Is this a whole person seeking to express wholeness through ministry, or is this a person trying to find wholeness in the ministry?"[18]

Following Frederick Buechner's simple but profoundly useful definition of vocation *as the place where your deep gladness meets the world's great need*, these three main areas are assessed and addressed by the clinical team, each of whom approaches them from several different directions, which overlap in a variety of ways while paying careful attention to this tension between self-making and 'God-and-community-serving' ministries. The first clinician to see the clergy completes the primary clinical intake, addressing psychosocial aspects of the

---

[17] Cf. M. Buber, trans. R. G. Smith, *I and Thou* (New York: Charles Scribners & Sons, 1958) and M. Friedman, "Martin Buber and Dialogical Psychotherapy," *Journal of Humanistic Psychology* Vol. 42, No. 4 (2002): 7–36.

[18] T. Maeder, "Wounded Healers," *The Atlantic Monthly* (January, 1989): 42.

problem—both systemic and intrapsychic, while a second clinician is free to focus more on spiritual discernment and vocational issues as these relate to the current crisis. Although in practice these two may significantly overlap, it has never been the case in over a decade that they merely duplicate one another. When similar insights emerge, having dialogues with several persons at once intensifies the impact of what is discovered and often elicits important nuances in the same material that deepen its import. This concentrated and personalized attention in the context of pilgrimage within the larger arena of Christian faith and the presence of God in the process is one of the primary advantages of the Clergy in Crisis week in effecting breakthroughs.

Prior to arrival, clergy take psychological inventories that will be used in the third clinician's assessment, which focuses primarily on leadership style. Though these may change according to the particular need, the typical battery includes the Myers-Briggs Type Inventory in conjunction with the Fundamental Interpersonal Relations Orientation-Behavior (FIRO-B), which together yield a Leadership Profile, along with the 16 PF, which is used adjunctively to assess both the congruence of one's personal energies and interests with the tasks of ministry as well as the options of avocational recreation and/or in some cases, retooling for work outside the pastoral ministry. This member of the clinical team provides professional consultation to the clergy stemming from data assessed in the inventories and shares the results with other team members during the week.

THEORETICAL MODELS. The author has developed two heuristic models to conceptualize the various parameters of the assessment and dialogue. These can be used regardless of the clinical theoretical or theological orientation to help ensure that the full range of pressures confronting clergy in the areas discussed above will be addressed, along with assessing the degree to which there is confusion between self-making and ministry-making. They help provide a compass to orient both clinicians and clergy as these issues are identified, explored and a follow-up plan is developed.

CLERGY BURNOUT CYCLE

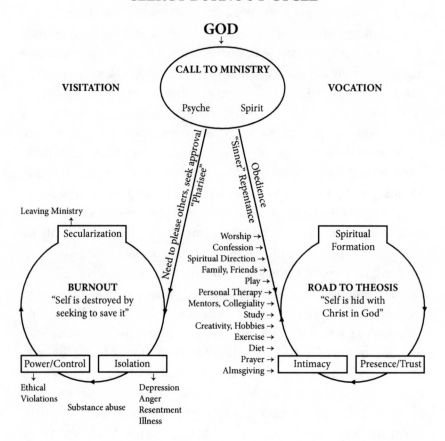

The first model is a developmental approach to the Clergy Burnout Cycle, which addresses the intersection of psychic and spiritual domains by focusing on the difference between self-making and Spirit-bearing ministry, which tend to be the areas most often in tension with clergy seeking treatment. The model draws on a four-fold heuristic schema called the "Hazards of VIPS,"[19] which is an anachronism signifying the tensions inherent to ministry throughout the lifespan.

---

[19] S. Muse, "Boundaries: The Hazards of VIPS," in S. Muse (ed.), *Beside Still Waters: Resources for Shepherds in the Marketplace* (Macon, GA: Smyth & Helwys, 2000), 109–128.

Values and choices are lived out in each of the areas of *vocation* versus *visitation*; *intimacy* versus *isolation*; *presence* versus *power and control*; *spirituality* versus *secularization*. Tensions within these antinomies help discriminate free and compulsive ways of functioning in ministry. The path of vocation represents the movement of responding authentically with awareness of legitimate human vulnerabilities while relying on faith and traditional spiritual disciplines in ministry. The path of visitation, by contrast, is the way of the 'wolf in sheep's clothing' who 'visits' ministry in appearance, but because of lack awareness of unconscious motives and tendencies toward functional atheism, falls prey to co-opting the work of ministry for the purpose of making and protecting the individual ego.

One very talented, charismatic and capable clergy at the midpoint of his week in the program, when this chart was first presented to him, studied it quietly and after a few seconds looked up and asked me, "Did you do this for me?" He was both serious and playful, and his words echoed similar statements by others. He found himself looking through the chart at years of ignoring his own legitimate human needs in compulsive efforts to meet the illegitimate needs established by his characterological armor. His real task was to live authentically present from moment to moment, risking real encounter with others, while trusting that his real self is ever "hid with Christ in God." This self is born in synergy with the Divine, "not born of the flesh or made by human will." From this perspective, it is not possible for any human being to know his or her own self or that of another which remains forever a mystery beyond all labels and images. In the process of trying to protect his picture of himself, he was actually rendering himself more vulnerable to powerful addictive cravings. These addictions seemingly functioned to 'protect' him from the anxieties stirred by awareness that he was not rooted in his real self and was in fact compromising his ministry in the process of working even longer hours in a never ending cycle to 'justify' himself. It is a pattern of many variations in which compulsive activity of one sort or another gradually replaces authentic life in a negative feedback loop that intensifies in direct proportion to the person's growing awareness of his/her inauthenticity, placing the clergy, their families and their congregations in jeopardy. The psychological, emotional and spiritual pain stemming from the forgotten places and people within and of those in the community at large will not be denied. They end up creating pressures and mischief that demand attention often in indirect and harmful ways. Discernment and diagnosis are both needed to find the denied roots in order to allow them to be consciously redirected toward healing and growth.

The developmental path of Christian formation is seen as one of increasing capacity for embracing vulnerability, particularly the seeming 'enemies' of grief, broken heartedness, and other conflicted places of walled off feelings stemming from division within and without. The fruit of this meeting between the known and the unknown, between that which is 'in control' and that which is not yet known and potentially 'out of control,' at least from the standpoint of the conscious self, is that God breaks freshly into our lives precisely at the meeting place of encounter between 'I' and 'Other.' This is Eucharist in the midst of Emmaus — the place where dialogue with brokenness is revealed as ultimately redemptive. Vulnerability is more valuable than security; 'not knowing' more revealing than having an answer. Wonder, awe, compassion and humility are more transformative than compulsive needs to preserve the heaven-bearing seed of the self which is fulfilled only by being planted in the soil of earthly life and in dying, giving birth to the miracle observed by St. Paul, that "it is no longer 'I' but Christ who lives in me."

A second heuristic tool for assessment of the multiple stressors in clergy's life is designed to stimulate a thorough consideration of mind, body, soul, Spirit, and systems in each person's circumstances from both the psychological and the spiritual discernment domains.

Quadrant I is the domain of spiritual discernment. Questions are raised concerning what in the Eastern Christian Tradition is called spiritual beguilement (*plane* in Greek, *prelest* in Russian) in the in-

```
┌─────────────────────────────────────────────────────────────┐
│                      DIVINE ENERGIES                          │
│        (Grace, eros of repentance, love, joy, humility)       │
│                                                               │
│       DEMONIC                    POWERS &                     │
│     PROVOCATIONS                PRINCIPALITIES                 │
│                                                               │
│         IV                          III                       │
│                                                               │
│ (spiritual forces outside psyche)  (systemic external forces) │
│      metaphysical evil          gender, race, class, economics,│
│                                  politics, family of origin,  │
│                   ╭──────────────╮    community               │
│                   │ EXISTENTIAL  │                            │
│                   │ CHOICE + ACT │                            │
│                   ╰──────────────╯                            │
│                                                               │
│      SPIRITUAL                 PSYCHOLOGICAL                   │
│     DISCERNMENT                  DIAGNOSIS                     │
│                                                               │
│          I                          II                        │
│                                                               │
│ (intrapsychic spiritual forces)  (intrapsychic patterns)      │
│ Fallen passions: pride, gluttony, lust, DSM, object relations, trauma, │
│ rancor, accidie, envy, despair, etc. developmental, personality │
│                                 disorders, psychological factors of │
│                                        addiction              │
│                                                               │
│                      BIOLOGICAL                               │
│          (genetics, nutrition, environmental)                 │
└─────────────────────────────────────────────────────────────┘
```

trapsychic realm.[20] This domain presumes an implicit spiritual anthropology, which sees persons through the lens of Christ as called to sanctification, or as it is referred to in Orthodox Christianity, *theosis.* From this perspective, each person is afflicted with unredeemed human passions because of misuse of our existential possibilities inherent to freedom of choice. This can be from self-deception related to

---

[20] Cf. G. E. H. Palmer, P. Sherrard, K. Ware (eds.), *The Philokalia: The Complete Text,* 4 vols. (London: Faber & Faber, 1997).

attraction to previous mistakes, or as in Quadrant IV, from falling prey to provocations from spiritual forces outside the psyche leading to idolatry. Our calling in Christ sets the azimuth for all these passions to be redeemed and integrated in the process. This is more than a lifetime's work and cannot be done by human power alone, nor is it a selfish process of 'individuation' for one's individual self alone as if this could take place apart from engagement with the suffering and life in the rest of the world. As clergy drift into the cycle of self-preserving activity which intensifies under the impact of interpersonal isolation and lack of consistency in confession, prayer, etc., these afflictive passions grow in strength, offering addictive compensations which have dimensions in each of the four quadrants, theological, psychological, biological, systemic evil along with values and choices reflected in existential actions.

Quadrant II is the area of intrapsychic issues recognized by various schools of psychology as well as the internalized forms of prevailing cultural norms, such as gender privilege and cultural, racial or economic imperialism. The clinician may utilize a variety of categories for purposes of assessment and psychological diagnosis, while always keeping in mind that these, as with any diagnostic schema, are merely theoretical lenses or descriptors and should never be reified to eclipse the mystery of the person who is "hid with Christ in God" and forever beyond reduction to any theoretical categories or limited to any one form of gender or cultural expression.

Quadrant III addresses the larger contextual systemic variables that are often hidden in the background and need to be identified and named in order to correct injurious self-attributions and avoid further victimization or disempowerment indirectly through the mental health system by focusing on pathological individual symptoms apart from their relationship to larger pathological environments that can elicit them. For example, women in ministry frequently experience conflict with male privilege among senior ministers and there remains a glass ceiling in larger congregations who tend to resist calling women to large staff positions as senior pastors, which may help account for why women leave ministry in greater numbers than their male counterparts.[21] These problems are sometimes subtle and may appear unrecognized in the etiology of the pastor's depression and/or questions about her sense of call. She may question herself instead of recognizing the effects of gender inequalities still embedded in the larger system which are placing added pressure on her.

After a decade of fruitful ministry, a highly talented female pastor serving as a new associate on a large staff found herself becoming worn down emotionally and beginning to distrust her inner intuition. She found that even some of her trusted female colleagues had found ways to rise in the male-dominated environment at the expense of connectedness and solidarity with other female clergy. A large part of her consultation focused on recovering the power and confidence inherent in her awareness of her inner world and being able to articulate the issues as she saw them, within a safe and personal context and getting some validation for her concerns. She found empowerment through a dialogue, which elicited her personal concerns and locating them in the larger narrative of her life which had been punctuated by many moments of a deep sense of God's abiding presence and a call to ministry, which superseded her treatment and disappointments within this one particular church.[22] Rather than assume that she was somehow inadequate or accept that she could no longer trust her own inner voice that had linked her with the divine summons to ministry in a way that had been central to the meaning of her life, she found encouragement to exercise her freedom to choose whether to stay in creative resistance in her current situation or to move forward to a new position.

Quadrant IV invites theological investigation of provocations and influences stemming from origins outside of the individual psyche and even the various systems that make up the larger social and political environment. This is the realm of 'evil' which is at work in subtle ways throughout all the quadrants just as are the

---

[21] D. R. Hoge & J. E. Wenger, 173–174.
[22] Cf. C. Neuger, *Counseling Women* (Minneapolis: Fortress Press, 2001).

Divine Energies of Grace and which, like the latter, has its ontological origins outside of human will. While this must not be used as an excuse for not being responsible for one's choices (i.e., "the devil made me do it"), neither is it to be overlooked by means of psychological reductionism. For example, the problem of self-medicating with alcohol or sexual stimulation via internet pornography, an increasing problem among clergy, may have not only a biological and psychological etiology related to childhood neglect and the human organism being out of balance, but from the perspective of spiritual beguilement evidences a theological meaning as a conflicted personal response to the Divine Energies of love which may involve *sin* and spiritual beguilement by evil forces which ultimately prove misogynistic and misanthropic.

The various emphases of these four quadrants are reminders not to collapse the theological dimension into the psychological, because this tends to preclude theological analysis that is part of finding deep healing and renewal of meaning. For example, the clergy mentioned earlier, whose drug and alcohol addiction was embedded in the larger theological context of idolatry, was able to see how his self-medicating with drugs and alcohol was related to his refusal to accept that his real self "was hid with Christ in God." He had always identified it with the one he had developed in his family of origin, replete with many negative self-attributions. Neither had he recognized that within this addiction, at its root, was the theological stance of being his own god and preferring his own self-judgment, i.e. *Until I am perfect, I am not worthy of relationship with God,* over embracing the grace of God's love for him. This is a stance which I refer to as having eaten 'devil's food,' which has the seeds of fear, misogyny and misanthropy hidden within the appearance of zeal for perfection. Thus, what might have been seen as a biological disease only and/or sequellae from childhood trauma takes on a multi-leveled 'thickness' that offers more possibilities for addressing it with all the powers of the soul in the faith-journey context of a renewed trust in God. One session after not sleeping well the previous night, I found this man sleeping in the waiting room. He turned and looked over his shoulder at me as he was leaving the session, smiled and said, "Thanks for waking me up." He made sure the next day that I understood it was a double-entendre and referred to his new awareness of the link between the psychological and theological dimensions of his pilgrimage.

This underscores why it is particularly important for counselors who work with clergy to be familiar with both the domains of classical spiritual discernment as well as medical and psychological diagnosis in order to elicit and give voice to the full picture of the struggle to remain faithful to their calling. They must be able to invite theological critique of the intrapsychic and systemic systems that constitute the environments in which development is occurring. Like a good optometrist, it is important to use all lenses available while keeping in mind that diagnosis always remains a tentative exploration in the larger context of dialogue into unknown territory of the 'other' toward the goal of clarity that provides a renewed sense of hope and meaning.

At the heart of the diagram is located Existential Choice and Act. This is the point of origin where 'spiritual pain'[23] related to the existential challenge of confronting the true givens of human existence emerges and is lived out. It is the core to which all four domains are related like spokes in a wheel, the place where existential choices and actions show forth the true treasure of the soul, which is being sacrificed for love[24] — "*Unless a seed die ...*" For this reason, I frequently lift up the prophetic utterance from Deuteronomy in which the Lord says what seems all too obvious and yet is not: *I place before*

---

[23] R. Burton, "Spiritual Pain: A Brief Overview and an Initial Response within the Christian Tradition," *Journal of Pastoral Care & Counseling* Vol. 57, No. 4 (2003): 437–446.

[24] Cf. J. Moran, "Spiritual War: The Relevance to Modern Therapy of the Ancient Eastern Orthodox Christian Path of Ascetical Practice," in S. Muse (ed.), *Raising Lazarus: Integral Healing in Orthodox Christianity* (Brookline, MA: Holy Cross Orthodox Press, 2004), 145–215.

you this day, life and death, blessing and curse; therefore, choose life so that you and your descendants may live. Freedom of choice is one of the ontological *sine qua non* conditions that give us the possibility of being human, the other being love. In the midst of the constraints of heaven and earth, and the struggle with powers and principalities both within and without, many questions arise: What exactly is the person choosing from moment to moment? What is he/she willing to act on? How does the person experience the Divine Energies and existential challenges of the Holy Spirit driving him/her into the wilderness as in the case of Jesus? What are the pastor's values and understanding of how the activity of God is present in the various tensions identified in each of these domains? How is the pastor drawing from the well of spiritual resources of the church, such as ongoing regular confession, continuous prayer, moment to moment mindfulness, *guarding the heart* and seeking to achieve *mental sobriety,* that have been the primary treatment of the Church's 'therapy' for two-thousand years? Is the clergy seeking to 'go to heaven by betraying earth?' or the reverse, heedlessly, cynically, angrily or despairingly falling into the world without attention to spiritual meaning calling 'from above.' Either of these postures avoids the primary paradox of the priesthood of humanity who stand in and with Christ at the place where the two roads of heaven and earth, spirit and matter, eternity and time, ontological and existential cross. Collapsing in either direction is a betrayal of both.

One pastor during his consultation identified how he did not believe that a man could be raised from the dead. For a variety of reasons, he had become thoroughly entranced by the post-enlightenment rationalism of modern science and echoed Bultmann in saying, "I do not believe anything could happen then, that cannot happen now." As we explored what his values were and what he actually believed, it became clear that although he was presenting himself as a traditional Christian pastor, he had in fact been offering his congregation the 'Gospel of Jungian psychology' in Christian disguise, and they were objecting strenuously, creating conflict and suffering for him. The question arose of whether it was honest to preach 'individuation' in the place of sanctification[25] and redemption, which have been the Christian kerygma for centuries based on the bodily resurrection of Christ. By clarifying and owning what he truly believed, the man ultimately chose to pursue a specialized ministry that was more congruent for him.

EMMAUS ENCOUNTERS: THE HEALING DIALOGUE. Regardless of the areas assessed and the cognitive categories used, I believe the power of the Clergy in Crisis week of consultation lies in the personal and time-limited quality of the extended dialogues of depth. Bonhoeffer has suggested that Christ always stands between me and the other. In this sense, I would submit that all authentic meetings are triadic — I, Other and God. Clergy come with great need, frequently with great fear of exposure and both temerity of trusting as well as a yearning to trust, and to be revealed to another in ways they have not allowed themselves, stemming from their enormous professional isolation. In many ways and in spite of using many words, clergy have often been living a kind of series of monologues that do not come from and fail to move the deep heart as a result. As Martin Buber notes, this kind of monologue is the sign of a deeper problem.

"The mark of contemporary man is that he really does not listen... I know people who are absorbed in 'social activity' and have never spoken from being to being with a fellow human being... Love without dialogue, without real outgoing to the other, reaching to the other, and companying with the other, the love remaining with itself — this is called Lucifer."[26]

---

[25] Buber pointed out, "Jung tries to divinize persons before they have been sanctified." Cf. M. Buber, trans. M. Friedman, et al., *The Eclipse of God; Studies in the Relation Between Religion and Philosophy* (New York: Harper Torchbooks, 1952).
[26] M. Buber, *Between Man and Man* (New York: Routledge and Kegan Paul, 1993) xiv. 24.

The chance to draw from the well of the heart in transparent dialogue is, like confession, always deeply refreshing for the soul, if tiring for the ego. Usually, by the second or third day, a breakthrough occurs as the clergy choose to trust and open up to this congruence. This is often the place where hope re-emerges and release from the straight-jacket of functional atheism begins to occur with the dawn of a re-newed sense of God's presence and commitment to the fundamental task of ministry.

One of the great discernments of ministry has to do with how clergy understand and navigate the demands of selfless service to others that is co-creative partnership with God rather than "all depending on me." This involves allowing legitimate care for themselves and their family's well-being. It means allowing themselves to be loved. There is no real contradiction between self-care and self-denial. They are more like breathing in and breathing out, which together make for life. It is when these are confused and out of balance that problems occur.

> For if self-realization means self-fulfillment in the narcissistic sense of satisfying one's every desire, then it must be rejected as not only anti-Christian but anti-human. Such fulfillment is an impossible illusion. If self-denial means denial or sacrifice of the true self and its radical exigencies, then it must be rejected as not only anti-human but anti-Christian. Such denial would sacrifice the possibility of love. But we must affirm self-realization as the fulfillment of the exigencies of our true selves, just as we must affirm self-denial as the rejection of any interest, desire or wish of the self that interferes with the realization of our true selves.
>
> Self-transcendence, incorporating both authentic self-realization and genuine self-denial, embodies the radical dynamics of the Christian spiritual life. Through self-transcendence, the self is not sacrificed, but realized in its paradoxical view that authentic self-realization results not from an attempt to fulfill one's

desires, but from a movement beyond oneself in an effort to bring about the good of others.[27]

Spiritual resources available to persons are as immense as the whole two thousand year rich history of Christianity, which take on renewed power as the person awakens in a real way to a new appreciation for Christ's saying, *cut off from Me you can do nothing.*[28] It is precisely when and to the extent that clergy gain a sense of acceptance of their legitimate human limits and longings that have gone unmet and unheard, that God becomes available to them in a new and vital way. It is from this place of freedom that they can re-enter ministry with "a faith unashamed and a love unfeigned."

Metropolitan Anthony of Sourozh captured this in a pithy remark he once made, "God can save the sinners we are but not the saints we pretend to be."[29] This has tremendous implications for renewal of clergy marriage and family life as well, both of which depend on the capacity for being emotionally vulnerable, transparent and authentic in relationship. Self-denial does not entail self-unawareness any more than dispassion involves lacking passion. Often it is precisely in the forgotten and overlooked places that hope and trust in Christ has suffered wounding — either from within the clergy's own heart from sin and spiritual deception or through being worn down by encountering the rough places of parish ministry and the offenses and temptations of a materialistic, sensationalist and consumer driven worldly culture that seems often in competition with the ancient and authentic Christian path that leads to life.

Hope in Christ regained makes the difference between renewal and defeat. Ironically, but not surprisingly, this often comes by discovering Christ anew in the places within ourselves, in the marriage partner and in the parish which, for one reason or another, we have

---

[27] W. E. Conn, "Pastoral Counseling for Self-Transcendence: The Integration of Psychology and Theology." *Pastoral Psychology* Vol. 36, No. 1 (1987): 45

[28] John 15:5.

[29] A. Bloom, *Beginning to Pray* (New York: Paulist Press, 1970).

been most reluctant to embrace, in the questions we have been afraid to voice and in the God whom we have not seen, but have come to know through love and acceptance of the world and the people around us which we have.

CHAPTER SEVEN

He Ain't Heavy, He's My Brother:
On the Unbearable Lightness of Being ... Caregivers[1]

*Come to Me all you who are heavy laden, and I will give
you rest, for My yoke is easy and My burden is light.*
Jesus Christ

*Someone who faces every problem spiritually is not ex-
hausted. The more I am pained by people's sufferings,
the more I pray and rejoice spiritually at telling Christ
everything and having Him take care of it. I notice as
time passes and physical courage diminishes, spiritual
courage increases because love, sacrifice, and compassion for others provide great spiritual strength.*
Elder Paisios of Souroti[2]

Care for the caregiver is a topic which has recently come of age
in the professional world, with a number of helpful books approaching the subject in varying ways, from a focus on resilience[3]

---

[1] Expanded from a presentation given for the 2010 OCAMPR Annual Conference at Holy Trinity Greek Orthodox Cathedral, New York, NY, November 5–6,
2010.

[2] On November 9 and 10, 1993, while suffering greatly from the pain of cancer,
Elder Paisios "stood holding on to a chair and gave his blessing to approximate-
ly thirty thousand people who passed by that day." Geronda Paisios, *Spiritual
Awakening, Vol II of Elder Paisios of Mount Athos Spiritual Counsels* (Souroti,
Thessaloniki, Greece: Holy Monastery of the Evangelist John the Theologian,
2008), 347.

[3] R. Wicks, *Bounce: Living the Resilient Life* (New York: Oxford University Press,

and the neurobiology of exhaustion[4] to contemplative self-analysis[5]
and the latest theory, research and treatment for compassion fatigue
and burnout for those who empathically engage traumatized persons
on a regular basis.[6] These are all very helpful approaches, but they do
not address the theological mystery of the relationship between care
for others and care for self, which is rooted in Christ.

Among professionals, care for the caregiver is often the 'tail of the
dog,' so to speak. While the tail may not seem very significant, it can
be a pretty good indicator of what is going on. It is that part that wags
furiously without the dog even realizing it, excited and totally focused
on whom he loves, pleading and hoping for some kind of personal
attention. If that does not work, he barks, jumps up and down, brings
you a ball to throw or rolls over on his back hoping to attract at least a
perfunctory scratch. Sometimes when the dog is alone with no one to
play with, the tail wags so hard the dog begins to notice it and chases
his own tail in a circle to make up for the absence of nurture from a
real human being. If you leave him alone in the house too long, he
is capable of pulling all the stuffing out of the chair and clawing and
chewing his way through a solid wood door when confined for too
long without company and anxiety gets the best of him.

Professional caregivers are not so different. The caregiver's own
self is often the last to be noticed by others and allowed to receive
personal attention. On the surface, this may resemble the spiritual
action of self-denial along the lines of Jesus' counsel that "whosoever

---

2010). The author has a wide ranging and very comprehensive bibliography for
further reading in the Appendix of his engaging and helpful book.

[4] B. Rothschild, *Help for the Helper: The Psychophysiology of Compassion Fatigue
and Vicarious Trauma* (New York: W. W. Norton & Co., 2006).

[5] R. Wicks, *The Resilient Clinician.* (New York: Oxford University Press, 2008).

[6] C. Figley (ed.), *Compassion Fatigue: Coping with Secondary Traumatic Stress
Disorder in Those Who Treat the Traumatized* (New York: Routledge, Taylor &
Francis, 1995); C. Figley, *Treating Compassion Fatigue* (New York: Routledge,
Taylor & Francis, 2002); R. Wicks, *Overcoming Secondary Stress in Medical and
Nursing Practice: A Guide to Professional Resilience and Personal Well-being*
(New York: Oxford University Press, 2006).

seeks his own life will lose it, but whosoever loses his life for My sake
and the Gospel will keep it for eternity" (Mt. 10:39). But, depending
on how this is understood and put into practice, all work, no pray and
no play can be a recipe for burnout. Elder Paisios explains how the
paradoxical spiritual situation of "one who helps himself rest through
tiring himself" is possible only when there is freedom and purity of
inner intention.

> One who has the spirit of sacrifice, will, for example, if he sees
> someone physically weak working and tiring himself, tell him,
> "sit down and rest," and do the work. The weak person will get
> physical rest, but the other will experience spiritual rest. What-
> ever one does he must do it with his heart, otherwise he is not
> transformed spiritually.[7]

Freely offered[8] and from the heart are the keys to the paradox of
how it is that the one who bears the greatest burden in creation
invites the rest of us, "Come to Me you who are heavy laden and I
will give you rest, for My yoke is easy and My burden is light" (Mt.
11:28–30). One who is obedient to the Holy Spirit, completely sur-
rendered in love, is truly free and is helped by God in ways that
surpass human understanding.

To the degree that there are other competing motives cluttering
the heart, disturbing its unity, the caregiver can be gradually depleted
in ways that go unrecognized until too late. Freedom arises to the degree that we are obedient to the Holy Spirit. Perfect obedience equals
perfect freedom. Though we are students of this Way, there is much

---

[7] Geronda Paisios, *Spiritual Awakening, Vol II of Elder Paisios of Mount Athos
Spiritual Counsels* (Souroti, Thessaloniki, Greece: Holy Monastery of the Evangelist John the Theologian, 2008), 221.

[8] Even at the purely physiological level, freedom is essential to growth. Studies
with mice reveal that significant growth in brain cells is stimulated by exercise
but *only* when mice *voluntarily* choose to exercise, and not when they are forced
to. S. Begley, *Train Your Mind Change Your Brain* (New York: Ballantine Books,
2007), 68.

to learn about our motives and our resistance to receiving the love and care from God that in our willful striving, we seek to offer others. Like the Apostle Peter, there are many ways we refuse to have our own feet washed while yet expecting to be able to do this for others.

PATHS TO BURNOUT. The kind of false 'self-denial' that results in burnout, in contrast to spiritual transformation in Christ and the discovery of a deeper spiritual dialogue with the Holy Spirit birthing humility, loving kindness, mercy and joy in a person, has a variety of roots. Burnout is a general term for the end result of a variety of contributing streams that can deliver the caregiver into its unloving arms. Unconscious childhood pain that results in compulsive caregiving and workaholic tendencies is one of those ways. Another road to burnout is the result of the gradual build-up of compassion fatigue,[9] secondary and vicarious trauma affecting the caregiver who has begun to work out of a stance of functional atheism — as if all depended on him/her rather than in partnership with God. Jesus warned His disciples that while they would face persecution in the world if they were truly following Him, He did not predict that they would burn out. At root, burnout is a consequence of not allowing oneself the same care that one seeks to offer others — from both God and from family and friends.

This actually amounts to a denial of the Lord's own words to "Love your neighbor *as being* yourself." The truth is that I love only because I am first loved.[10] Caregiving is a reciprocal relationship that grows out of what we ourselves are receiving. Apart from this, we are much more vulnerable to falling into self-deception and gravitating toward various forms of self-medication that numb the organism

---

[9] C. Figley (ed.), *Compassion Fatigue: Coping with Secondary Traumatic Stress Disorder in Those Who Treat the Traumatized* (New York: Routledge, Taylor & Francis, 1995).

[10] E. Gassin & J. S. Muse, "Beloved To God: An Eastern Orthodox Anthropology," in E. T. Dowd & S. L. Nielsen (eds.), *The Psychologies in Religion: Working with the Religious Client* (New York: Springer Publishing Company, 2006).

rather than open it up to greater vulnerability to God and to the authentic joy of relationships with others and the natural world. If monitored and recognized early on, it is possible to make changes consciously that help restore balance by making sacrifices needed to honor one's priorities.

An internist traveled 100 miles for a consultation about his vocational dissatisfaction. He said he was experiencing a sense of growing unfulfilment in his work. His group practice was successful, but he felt increasingly pinched by managed care and found himself spending less time with his patients in order to make up for his falling salary. In our discussion, I discovered he was an adult child of an alcoholic and had never really taken a good look at his own emotional needs. Sadness started welling up in him as we talked, and it surprised him. His body confirmed the truth of the words he spoke. He was unaware of the changes in his face as he spoke until I called his attention to them, and then he began to notice it for himself *from within*. This intensified the importance of what he was discovering — that he had lost contact with his own body and presence — so much so that he decided to make time in his schedule to travel two hours on a monthly basis in order to meet for an hour and a half to reflect on his life, his marriage and his relationship with his children along with how he was finding it difficult to carry out his vocation as a physician in his current practice.

Once he was clear about what he really cared about and what it would take to find balance, he decided to have a personal, sit down, face to face meeting with each physician in his group practice to see what their values were and where they stood on the things he cared about. He was inviting them to place quality of care, care for the caregiver and vocational satisfaction on par with making money. A couple were interested, but the others, he discovered somewhat to his surprise and disappointment, were not. He was now clear that he could not be happy in the long run in that practice and he did diligent preparation for a move, paying a huge price financially because of the loss of his initial investment and a non-compete clause he had signed when initially putting the partnership together. Still, he was a man at peace with himself, able to care for his patients as he wanted, and his joy and vitality were evident when he had made the move and we concluded our work together.

THE CHILDHOOD ROOTS OF WORKAHOLISM AND BURNOUT. Another path to professional burnout is related to a propensity toward overwork as a cure for overworking. The compulsive workaholic caregiver's own care always comes as an afterthought if it even becomes a thought.

A general practice physician was working harder than ever to overcome the financial challenges created by restrictive HMO's[11] while still trying to serve his patients at the level of care which had been his vocational desire when he took the Hippocratic Oath. Very bright, he had always been a high-achiever but received little emotional tending from family members beginning in childhood and had in that way learned to ignore his own emotional needs as being normal. Now some twenty five years later, he lamented with great anguish during a marital session that he was "jealous of the care my wife gives the family dog!" He complained of missing her attention in the form of the abandon they once knew in their younger days when sex had been carefree and they had both enjoyed liberal libations together. Now she no longer drank and was not much interested in sex, because he was never around and she felt out of connection emotionally with him when he was because he did not share himself emotionally with her. He was unable to make his deeper emotional longing known and love evident to her because he was focused increasingly on eliciting her sexual interest. Feeling empty and depressed, he had fallen little by little into the habit of increased self-medicating with his two drugs of choice, alcohol and more work. His vocational satisfaction was on the wane, and his mental

---

[11] S. Muse, J. Brende, "Physicians Heal Thyself!" *HumaneHealthCare.com* (formerly *Journal of Humane Health Care*). Vol. 3(2) (2003): 1–20.

and physical health were suffering. If he did not take steps to correct the imbalances in his life, it was only a matter of time before this would precipitate medical error, health problems, divorce or an affair resulting from unacknowledged and unmet emotional needs for mutual intimacy with another human being. This kind of long-term self-neglect is often the case in professional boundary violations among the clergy involving their parishioners.

Clergy, physicians and counselors who burn out in this way are frequently conscientious, intelligent and talented people who come from families where they learned to care for parents who suffered from alcoholism, mental illness, chronic pain, intense marital arguments or other problems that compromised their ability to attend consistently to their children's need for protection, safety, nurture and personal attention. Children in families like this often seek to find compensatory meaning and personal worth as adults through achievement in the field of professional caregiving in one form or another.

A legitimate sense of vocational call to caregiving that matches one's aptitude and inclinations often carries with it the unconscious needs of the parentified child whose antennae have grown three feet long designed to notice any impending danger or distress in persons around them as they learned to do in childhood. They come to feel it as 'natural' to ensure everyone else's well-being before their own, even as the sea of human need around them continues wave after wave like the ocean, without end. Compulsive caregivers have learned to live their whole lives unconsciously in caregiving mode, not altruistically, but *in order to survive*, unconsciously carrying out their childhood scripts still trying to prevent a new disaster — dad hitting mom, or mom embarrassing everyone by being tipsy or by just learning to lay low to avoid upsetting the uneasy peace in the household.

A man told me how he looked out at the moon one day while his parents hashed it out in one of their intense screaming matches, and he bargained with God: "If You will make them stop, I'll give my life to You." He eventually became a pastor and burned out after trying to do the same things for his parish that he had unsuccessfully tried to do for his parents, feeling demoralized and unfit for ministry as a result, a familiar scenario for clergy.[12] Here is the treatment plan (see opposite page) of one clergy who waited until he was burned out before seeking help through an intensive clergy in crisis week

Part of the restoration project for burned out professionals is to invite compassion in them for the child they once were. It is as though their early capacity for attachment — the so-called 'child within' has been cast out into the wilderness, a kind of scapegoat doomed to ignore its real needs all its life. Children who do not receive sufficient nurture, who are abused, or who are pressured to perform rather than appreciated and supported in 'being' who they are also learn to ignore their our own legitimate needs by being totally other focused and continue doing so as adults, having internalized this way of being as 'normal' as a means of self-protection. They have difficulty being open to dialogue with their own somatic and visceral self that is part of their inner life, their awareness that 'I AM' at any given moment, because they did not experience themselves doing this in relation to their parents' genuine interest and attention. Such children often compensate by becoming overachievers whose compulsive care and over work are rewarded vocationally and by public esteem bolstering their false selves, while their family life suffers and they are inwardly plagued with unacknowledged grief, self-doubts and an inability to stop 'doing' in order to wonder, appreciate, worship and give thanks for the *thatness* of life as in the case of this pastor.

As witnessed in the lives of some exceptional ascetics and saints, apart from continual prayerfulness, worship, regular confession, trust in a spiritual father, and faithfulness within marriage and community that characterizes authentic spiritual life, it is only possible for people in the world to ignore legitimate human needs[13] and intimate per-

---

[12] Cf. S. Muse, "Keeping the Wellsprings of Ministry Clear," in S. Muse (ed.), *Beside Still Waters: Resources for Shepherds in the Marketplace.* (Georgia: Smyth & Helwys, 2000).

[13] Cf. Four Realms of Human Needs — Appendix II.

Pastoral Institute Clergy in Crisis Care Plan

Professional Exhaustion as Evidenced by:	Goals:	Interventions:
		Psychosocial:
<u>anxiety</u> difficulty concentrating, paresthesias, chest pain, panic attacks, diarrhea (worse on Sundays) x 1 year	1. Regular aerobic exercise 3–4x week for minimum 30 minutes.	Intensive individual pastoral psychotherapy to include:
	2. Evidence increased tolerance of emotional discomfort for sake per personal and/or partner's growth.	assessment & feedback
<u>unresolved grief & secondary trauma</u> related to multiple deaths of friends in parish over past year & PTSD Sx from childhood abuse		identify support systems
	3. Ability to maintain interpersonal boundaries congruent with personal integrity, faith, values, pastoral vocation and marital covenant.	identify self/other representations & family of origin scripts distorting perceptions of pastoral vocation & capacity for self-disclosure and intimacy
<u>professional burnout:</u> compulsive overwork, inability to set limits and priorities; lapse of judgment compromising professional and personal boundaries out of unrecognized unmet personal needs.		
	4. Evidence freedom to identify and express full range of feelings appropriate to content and circumstance.	**Metabolic:** Rx evaluation & nutritional assessment
		Behavioral:
<u>loss of marital trust:</u> related to emotional over-involvement with married woman & former parishioner	5. Establish friendship with 1–2 males outside parish.	self-care issues introduction to relaxation training and sensory awareness
	6. Marital therapy to address trust issues, intimacy and communication.	
<u>emotional abuse of partner</u> in form of negative feedback loop of periodic rages leaving spouse feeling unsafe and diminished, which in turn "confirms" that client is "like my father" and will "never be the man I desire to be" in a recurring negative feedback loop.	7. Begin spiritual direction and regular confession.	**Spiritual:** prayer & spiritual discernment issues
	8. Take 1 day per week for relaxation and restoration.	**Professional:** leadership assessment and interest inventory suggested readings as appropriate

sonal relationships for so long before some kind of spiritual deception arises, some kind of imbalance develops and compensatory self
medication is sought out in one form or another.

An important longitudinal APA research project studied parental
interaction with children at intervals from preschool to age 18. Researchers discovered three distinct groups with respect to drug use:
frequent drug users, experimenters and abstainers, which

> could be traced to the earliest years of childhood and related
> to the quality of parenting received. The findings indicate that
> (a) problem drug use is a symptom, not a cause, of personal
> and social maladjustment, and (b) the meaning of drug use can
> be understood only in the context of an individual's personality
> structure and developmental history.[14]

The implications of this excellent and methodologically well-con-
ceived study went directly in contrast to the efforts of the Reagan
administration at the time, and that have largely continued subsequently, which focus on preventing drug abuse at the symptom level
rather than addressing the characterological structures derived from
poor quality parental care and support that begins at an early age to
render people vulnerable to drug abuse because they lack the internal structure derived from secure attachments with the parents. For
example, the mothers of frequent drug users were

> hostile, not spontaneous with their children, not responsive or
> sensitive to their children's needs, critical and rejecting of their
> ideas and suggestions, not supportive and encouraging, making
> the test situation grim and distasteful rather than fun, pressur-
> ing their children to work at the tasks, under protective of their
> children, overly interested in and concerned with their chil-

---

[14] J. Shedler and J. Block, "Adolescent Drug Use and Psychological Health: A
Longitudinal Inquiry," *American Psychologist* Vol. 45(5) (1990): 612–630.

dren's performance, conducting the session in such a way that their children did not enjoy it.[15]

The mothers of the drug abstainers were described in almost exactly the same way as being

> hostile, not responsive or sensitive to their children's needs, critical of their children and rejecting of their ideas and suggestions, frustrated by an inability to find adequate strategies for teaching their children, not valuing their children's originality, not supportive and encouraging, overly interested in and concerned with their children's performance, impatient with their children and appearing to lack pride in and be ashamed of their children … pressuring their children to work at the tasks and conducting the session in such a way that their children do not enjoy it.[16]

Most significantly, the overachievers were revealed to *have similar personality structures* as the drug addicts, *only their drug of choice was achievement.* The so-called "experimenters," who had the most responsive parents able to love and appreciate them, also had the healthiest, most resilient character structures which seemed to act as a prophylactic against losing themselves in self-medication. They could and did 'say no' to drugs, because they were able to say 'Yes' to life as being qualitatively better than the drugs.

This is also true for the Orthodox Christian ascetical struggle, which has nothing whatsoever to do with pressure to be good or 'getting better,' but rather with the willingness and desire to say 'no' to whatever impedes a person from saying 'Yes!' to life and to belovedness to God with one's whole being, body, mind and heart. As St. Paul observed, for the Christian, "everything is permissible but

---

[15] Ibid., 621.
[16] Ibid., 621.

not everything is profitable" (I Cor. 10:23). Depending on societal norms, drinking alcohol is permissible and socially accepted along with plopping in the Lazy Boy with the remote at the end of the day and flipping TV channels every evening for hours while eating pop-corn and ice cream. So is neglecting one's health and family in order to work more. But St. Paul also added, "I will not let anything control me" (I Cor. 6:12 ISV).

Christ aims to set us free from compulsivity at the deepest level of the core of our being in order to free us to be loved and to love. The reason that life in Christ is the cure for illness and offers freedom from oppression is because He is the source of all love, life, goodness, beauty and joy. "Apart from Christ, we can do nothing" (John 15:4). The spiritual discipline and effort of asceticism is rightly entered into when we understand that it is for the purpose of supporting life, not destroying it. It is not possible to cure a lesser love except with a greater one, and no one can be faithful to Christ while still partaking of those things that blind and harden us to what is good so that we cannot appreciate it.

The experiences of the quality and tone of maternal and paternal relationships are internalized at a young age and operate outside of consciousness, continuing coping patterns into adulthood, regardless of the intellectual prowess and professional competence of the adult. The pastoral counselor's task is often one of helping professionals recognize what is going on in this domain and to facilitate through mindfulness and critical reflection, giving themselves permission to put down the compulsive cross acquired in childhood to survive their situation so that the adult that they are can *freely* pick it up.

This is what lightens the burden and makes it an act of freely-giv-en love rather than one of compulsive self-preservation. This requires compassion and empathy for the child they once were. Another way of putting it might be "to experience one's own self being loved as we wish to love our neighbors." As God becomes central in our lives, not ideologically, but personally, the world becomes increasingly sacra-mental and the work of caregiving a continuing spiritual formation process in which we are forever in call and response with God around the encounters we have with others, which stirs questions, elicits pain of heart through compassion and reveals marvels along the way that evoke wonder and gratitude to God for being able to be a part of seeing people come alive. This is the true reward of every caregiver.

IATROGENIC ARMORING: WHAT PROTECTS CAN ALSO INJURE. There is a children's story, called the Rusty Knight, about the problems encountered when a noble knight is unable to remove his armor after battle. It is a parable of sorts, serving to illumine the dangers of becoming trapped in the 'skins' necessary to provide objectivity at times in order to fulfill one's professional role. I call this phenomenon resulting from the build-up of secondary trauma encountered by physicians, EMTs, police and firefighters who face life and death scenarios frequently, 'iatrogenic armoring,' a form of psychic numbing that gradually intensifies until it separates the caregiver from his/her felt human presence. While initially offering protection from being overwhelmed by the intensity and demands of dealing with life emergencies, the grief connected with human suffering and the inevitable multiple losses that accumulate over time in both medicine, public health and the priesthood, we can get stuck in our armor like the rusty knight, making it difficult or impossible to be tender and vulnerable in our closest potentially intimate relationships. Irritability and aloofness surface that ruins marriages and friendship alike, even if by just keeping them superficial. Like the knight, the professional caregiver finds it difficult to move between the demands of the battlefield of healthcare delivery or the rough and tumble 24/7 demands of the parish priesthood and the very different, but equally vital demands for transparency and emotional availability that are at the heart of marriage and family life. The caregiver begins to withdraw and self-medicate rather than open up in dialogue regarding the pain and loneliness building up underneath, and colleagues around him turn a blind eye if they notice it.

A certain degree of dispassion rooted in genuine human presence that is necessary for the professional role becomes counter-

productive and even dangerous when it extends beyond this into
one's personal life as a result of unaddressed growing compassion
fatigue. As many as 14% of mental health practitioners who work
with trauma victims report traumatic stress levels similar to those
experienced by persons suffering from PTSD.[17] It is vitally necessary
for the caregiver to be deft in the skills of noticing one's inner proprioceptive state on a regular basis in order to support the ability to
transition intentionally from the other-centered world of technical
precision, medical procedures, counseling and hearing confessions
to the interpersonal world of mutual intimacy where self-transpar-
ency, playfulness, friendship, wonder, joy, awareness and vulnerability are the stuff of personal encounter. For professional caregiving
to be genuine, the role must not be unconsciously cut off from the
genuine human person underneath. It is only people, not professional roles, who are bearers from the heart of what Elder Paisios
refers to as *philotimo*.[18]

Just as confession shames the ego while refreshing the soul, daily life
experiences that touch us beneath the professional roles we can come
to identify with, are essential to the caregiver's well-being. One's spouse
and friends, the disrespect, criticism and challenge of adolescents and
the innocence, spontaneity, intensity and directness of little children as
well as physical labor, contact with animals and the natural world, all
offer correctives to the lofty illusions accruing to persons whose positions of power and competency in the face of human need creates an
idealization in which we can foolishly begin to believe. Adversity and
conflict in this regard help restore sobriety, perspective and renew a
spirit of repentance which opens up access to gratefulness and joy in the
world over everyday life which reveals the glory of God in small ways.

Too much armoring, supported by brilliance, personal charisma, a
strong will and a sense of entitlement, which are often the characteris-

---

[17] B. Rothschild, *Help for the Helper: The Psychophysiology of Compassion Fatigue and Vicarious Trauma* (New York: W. W. Norton & Co., 2006), 98.
[18] A tender, humble self-offering of love for others and for the created world that
is full of gratefulness.

tics of successful physicians, priests and psychotherapists, lacking ways of recovering humility can create vainglorious illusions which become a barrier to empathy. The word humility is related to the word *humus*, for earthy, fertile soil. Humility involves the ego coming back down to earth from its lofty perch above, as in the bow of a *metanoia* and the entreaty of the Jesus Prayer which remind us that the way of spiritual ascent is always equally linked with the way of loving descent. Those who would be great must be servant of all — not compulsively, but freely, recognizing that it is God who is the healer and we are the midwives. This lesson is taught to all who remain attentive to the fact that the true healer also remains the patient and the perpetual student of life.

L EARNING COMPASSION AND HUMILITY THROUGH WEAKNESS. I will forever be grateful to my friend and colleague George Zubowicz, MD, who gave me the gift of seeing this made visible in a marvelous way during the last days of his life through his vulnerability and willingness to be transparent. Respected and beloved, George served many years as medical director of the psychiatric hospital and then on our out-patient staff at the Pastoral Institute, Inc., where we became good friends. At his request, I helped conduct his beloved wife Charlotte's funeral as well as his own a few years later. George had a distinguished career. He was a Menninger-trained psychiatrist who valued the integration of spiritual, medical and psychological care and was one of the founders of the Pastoral Institute, Inc., in Columbus, Georgia, where I work. This outwardly stern Russian bear-of-a-man was the one person the staff would go to when an unstable patient went AWOL against medical advice, leaving the building in reactivity. George would lumber out the door quietly and slowly, and in a few minutes, as our receptionist at the time loved to say when she told the story, "Here would come the person following behind Dr. Z. as docile and obedient as a lamb." This brilliant physician was still discovering things about the limits of human power and the importance of vulnerability and compassion in his life and work by undergoing self study and repentance up to his last breath. He, like

St. Augustine, had become a question for himself as he reflected on his life made visible in a new way by the cancer which was wrecking his body and sapping his strength daily.

On my visits with him, we would talk together about what he was discovering. This man, who had been an Olympic athlete and was still winning Senior Olympic swim meets in Europe in his eighties, who as they say "had never been sick a day in his life," described what he was experiencing as he was growing weaker and weaker. At one point, I said to him, "It seems to me that your biggest surprise in all this is that your 'I,' which does not feel weak at all, can exist in this body which cannot even find the strength to make it to the bathroom." He responded with excitement and vigor from his frail body in his thick Russian accent and rational manner, "That is correct. You understand me exactly!" Then he told me,

> "You know I had a contract for many years with the nursing home. I would visit and ask each person, 'How are you doing?' and they would say, 'Fine.' And I would write this in my book and go on to the next one. You hardly have time to do more than that, but now that I have had this weakness, *I realize that I did not really ask them how they were.* This is because they were sick and helpless and I had never felt this in my life. Now I understand what this means. Can you imagine that!?"

He said gently, with sober and tender compassion, wonder and a hint of regret that moves my heart even now as I recall it eight years later: "*For fifty years, I have been a psychiatrist, and I did not really know how to ask people how they are in a way that really means it?*"

There is in this statement, and how he came to understand it, a whole course in what it takes to become a good physician and psychotherapist. Our Lord Jesus Christ showed us the path to this in His own life. The willingness to value, study and learn from the experience of one's own vulnerability is not only the best possible foundation for training good physicians and pastoral caregivers, but it is also the best possible foundation for the caregiver receiving the care that only humility can make it possible for us to receive, like the earth soaking in the rain. Vulnerability is like the intelligent membrane of the cell wall which permits inside what it needs to function and keeps out what is injurious, constantly regulating the flow in an intelligent way that can only occur if the membrane remains alive and in communication with both inside and outside and is able to discern what is needed for the well-being of the larger body. Compassion and empathy cannot penetrate a dissociated armor. Too far removed from our humanity, illness and error arise.

BURNOUT AND RELATIONSHIPS. So what exactly is happening in conditions of compassion-fatigue and burnout? A good self-check instrument identifies the symptoms of compassion fatigue and can give a quick reading of one's current state.[19] Compassion fatigue is a collection of symptoms indicative of the chronic stress of over-functioning without refreshment, beginning to affect the vitality of the physical organism. Symptoms include being keyed up, over utilizing 'emergency emotions' that overwork the adrenal glands leading to physical fatigue, loss of energy, exaggerated startle response and increased anxiety as we find ourselves 'going in 60 million directions,' responsible for too many things. With some time off and interpersonal replenishment, good food, relaxation and inner stillness, it is possible to rebound with renewed energy ready for the next round. If ignored, compassion fatigue can degenerate into the more serious territory of burnout with its toll on both physical and mental health.

The signs of burnout are very similar to those of post traumatic stress — increased irritability, psychic numbing, sleep disruption, decreased physical energy and diminishment of joy in one's work, depression, loss of idealism and a growing demoralization that at-

---

[19] Cf. B. Hudnall Stamm, 2009. *Professional Quality of Life: Compassion Satisfaction and Fatigue Version 5 (ProQOL)*. It is a useful self-scoring inventory for checking compassion fatigue and burnout levels. http://www.isu.edu/~bhstamm or http://www.proqol.org.

tacks the root of vocational satisfaction to the point of causing the caregiver to question his or her personal self-worth and vocation as a physician, minister or counselor. The loss of capacity and interest in really encountering people seems only to confirm this. Burnout also brings with it an increased potential for medical error, ethics violations,[20] lowered immune system functioning with increased susceptibility to disease.

The average life expectancy for people living in the United States is approximately 78 years, compared with 75.4 ten years ago. Yet, the average life expectancy for American physicians is 69.7 years, approximately eight years less than the national average for men.[21] There is a growing body of research indicating that much more is needed to preserve the health and well-being of caregivers than exercise, good genes and a healthy diet. At age 45, even when in perfect physical health, depression alone increases the possibility of heart attack by 50–100%.[22] Among the most significant overlooked variables relevant to caregivers is the quality of the interpersonal relationships we have, the degree of playfulness and emotional intimacy in our lives and rootedness in our religious faith and practices.

At Southern Methodist University, researchers under the direction of Dr. James Pennebaker asked a group of students to spend a mere 20 minutes each day for only four days writing in a journal about a traumatic event in their lives. A control group was asked to write

---

[20] Dual relationships, including sexual misconduct (60% between male therapist and female client, 20% female therapists and male clients and 20% among same sex pairings), were the cause of most disciplinary actions among therapists from 1983 to 2005, and alleged boundary violations were the leading cause of malpractice suits against all mental health practitioners during that time period (Boland-Prom, 2009; Daley & Doughty, 2007; Pope & Vasquez, 2007; Strom-Gottfried, 2000) cited in M. D. Corley, "Staying out of Trouble: The Importance of Boundaries for MFTS," *Family Therapy Networker*, July-August (2010): 40.

[21] National Center for Health Statistics.

[22] H. E. Marano, "Depression: Beyond Serotonin," *Psychology Today* Mar/April (1999): 72.

the same amount of time but about trivial events. Blood samples were then taken from both groups before and after this four-day period. Results showed an increase in immune activity in the self-disclosing group and no change in the control group. Pennebaker's conclusion was that "failure to confide traumatic events is stressful and associated with long-term health problems. Inhibition of thoughts, feelings, or behaviors was associated with physiological work, resulting in increased autonomic nervous system activity."[23]

The John Wayne school of medicine that teaches doctors to hold their feelings in puts chronic stress on the heart and on the immune system. One newly minted doctor in the local family practice residency used to come to therapy for periodic visits "so I can cry. You can't do that at the hospital." He felt estranged from his colleagues who did not show their feelings, and he felt trapped. Not being allowed to have feelings was incongruent with his desire to care for people and the reason he entered the medical field in the first place. More than that, twenty years of research is pretty definitive that holding in feelings does not make good sense medically. Emotional isolation is unhealthy.

An Ohio State University College of Medicine study revealed that patients who scored above average in loneliness also had significantly poorer immune functioning. At Stanford University School of Medicine, Dr. David Spiegel researched women with metastatic breast cancer who were randomly assigned to one of two groups. Both groups received the usual medical care. The experimental group, however, also received weekly 90 minute group support meetings for a year. Five years later, the support group survivors had *twice the survival rate* of the control group.[24]

At the University of Houston, rabbits were fed high cholesterol diets designed to cause atherosclerosis. Unexpectedly, researchers found that the rabbits (who were stacked in cages up to the ceiling) in the higher cages developed more atherosclerosis than the ones in

---

[23] D. Ornish, *Dr. Dean Ornish's Program for Reversing Heart Disease.* (New York: Ballantine Books, 1990).
[24] Ibid., 91.

lower cages. Further investigation uncovered the unexpected variable of a lab technician who was responsible for feeding them played with the rabbits on the lower levels she could reach and they did not develop the same degree of cardiovascular problems. What was going on? A controlled experiment was then carried out which confirmed that the rabbits who were played with showed *more than a 60% reduction in the percentage of atherosclerosis* when compared to a control group of genetically identical rabbits fed the exact same diets but given only routine laboratory care. Most significant of all was that this was true *even though blood cholesterol levels, heart rate, and blood pressure were comparable in both groups of rabbits.*

Love and intimate relationships make a huge difference in our health and longevity. Several studies involving more than 10,000 subjects tracked over a period of 5–9 years revealed the critical importance of intimacy, underscoring Orthodox anthropology which views soul and body as seamlessly joined. This study revealed that those who were socially isolated had a two- to three-fold increased risk of death from both heart disease and from all other causes when compared to those who felt most connected to others. *These results were independent of other cardiac risk factors*, such as cholesterol level, blood pressure and genetics. Similar results were found in 2,059 subjects from Evans County, Georgia, where the greatest mortality was found in older people with few social ties.[25]

At Yale University School of Medicine, researchers studied 119 men and 40 women undergoing coronary angiography and found that *the more people felt loved and supported, the less coronary atherosclerosis they had at angiography*. As in the other studies, these results were independent of other expected medical risk factors such as age, sex, income, hypertension, serum cholesterol, smoking, diabetes, genetics and hostility.[26] A similar study at Duke University of 1,400 men and woman who had undergone coronary angiography

---

[25] Ibid., 89.
[26] Ibid., 90.

found that five years after the procedures, those patients who were not married and who did not have one or more close friends suffered mortality rates three times that of those who had emotionally intimate relationships.[27]

Hospital cost effectiveness studies related to incorporating spiritual aspects of human health, which include a strong interpersonal dimension of care, begun in the 1980's generated initiatives in "Whole Person Health Care" by integrating physical, mental and spiritual components under the larger heading of pastoral health care.[28] Psychiatrist Harold Koenig, MD, of Duke University is one of the leading researchers in the area of the relationship between religious faith and practice, physical health and medical costs,[29] which suggest similar conclusions.

- Recent and lifetime alcohol problems were lower among those who attended religious services regularly. Those attending weekly had less than one-third the rate of alcohol abuse of those who attended less frequently.[30]
- People who regularly attend church, pray individually and read the Bible were 40% less likely to have diastolic hypertension than the less religious (1 in 10,000 probability of being explained by chance alone) *This was true even after controlling for differences in body-mass, socioeconomic status and smoking.*
- People who attend church regularly are hospitalized much less than people who never or rarely participate in religious

---

[27] Cited in R. Wicks, *Bounce: Living the Resilient Life* (New York: Oxford University Press, 2010), 75.

[28] E. McSherry, *Journal of the American Scientific Affiliation* Vol. **35** December (1983): 217–224.

[29] H. Koenig, (2001) *The Healing Power of Faith: How Belief and Prayer Can Help You Triumph Over Disease* (New York: Simon & Schuster, 2001); *Medicine, Religion, and Health: Where Science and Spirituality Meet (Templeton Science and Religion Series)* (Pennsylvania: Templeton Press, 2008).

[30] Koenig, (2001), 88.

services (e.g. an average of 14 more days at $4,000 per day at Duke Hospital = $54,000 per person savings) than persons with no religious affiliation.

- People with strong religious faith are less likely to suffer depression from stressful life events, and if they do, they are more likely to recover from depression than those who are less religious (n = 87; This takes into account 28 different variables, including quality of life, family history of psychiatric illness, severity of physical illness, social support, antidepressant Rx, etc.).
- For every 10 point increase on intrinsic religiosity score, there was a 70% increase in speed of recovery from illness.
- People of strong faith suffering from physical illness have significantly better health outcomes than less religious people.
- People who attend religious services regularly have stronger immune systems than their less religious counterparts (e.g. churchgoers had significantly lower blood levels of interleukin-6, which tends to rise with unrelieved chronic stress).
- Religious people live longer, are healthier in later life and have less cardiovascular disease and cancers (n = 5,286, 1965–1994). Frequent church attendees had more health problems than average, but a 23% reduced risk of dying during the same period than those not attending church.
- Children in disrupted families were nearly twice as likely as those in mother-father families to have developmental, learning or behavioral problems
- 83% of regular church attendees were still married to their first spouse.

Dr. Elizabeth McSherry, a Veterans Administration cost effectiveness consultant, was able to show that utilization and length of hospital stay was significantly lower "if spiritual issues are adequately dealt with." For example, at the University of Virginia Medical Center, orthopedic injury patients receiving chaplain visits required 66%

less pain medication, made two-thirds fewer calls on nursing staff and were discharged two days earlier than patients with similar diagnoses and no chaplain visits. McSherry conducted a study in the Veterans Affairs health system using the Spiritual Profile Assessment — a questionnaire that helps pastoral counselors understand a person's religious strengths and vulnerabilities. McSherry wanted to find out if more intense and focused chaplain visits would further affect total length of stay. Her results were that open heart surgery patients receiving daily chaplain visits averaged two days less length of hospital stays compared to those who received no chaplain visits. Patients receiving pastoral care suffered less post-surgery depression. McSherry argued that better use of pastoral care programs could save the hospital more than the cost per patient incurred by hiring salaried VA hospital chaplains. In a 1993 Veterans Affairs Hospital study conducted over a 30 month period with 700 cardiac patients, McSherry "discovered that those in the group who received daily chaplain visits on average left the hospital three days earlier than those who only saw the Chaplain for a few minutes during their stay in hospital, (at an) estimated savings of up to $4,000 per patient."[31]

SPIRITUAL ROOTS OF SUSTAINMENT. Care for the caregiver means caring for body and soul by protecting the capacity for inner stillness and peace of heart that support compassion and professional competence as well as capacity for emotional intimacy and vulnerability with others in one's personal life that includes a sense of wonder and gratitude for life that replenish and nourish the inner being. This way of being is rooted in humility and obedience which stem from repentance in the face of divine love that gradually converts and purifies the heart over a lifetime.[32] The ancient patristic sci-

---

[31] E. McSherry, "Study Undertaken into Cardiac Patients at the Veterans Affairs Hospital, Brockton Mass.," cited in T. Hudson, "Measuring the Results of Faith," *Hospitals and Health Networks* September 20 (1996): 23–28 (normal fiscal extrapolation would apply).
[32] Cf. Archbishop Chrysostomos, *Themes in Orthodox Patristic Psychology: Hu-*

ence of the hesychastic Fathers contained in the *Philokalia* describes
the conditions necessary to protect and grow human persons toward
theosis, which requires a special kind of attention devoted to awakening consciousness of God that is renewed on a daily basis so that it
preserves the inner being from dissolution by worldly fragmentation
and dissociation in the face of human suffering. Fr. Nikon, a monk
on Mount Athos, writes in the foreword introducing the first English translation of a portion of the *Philokalia* regarding the conditions
needed for the traditional Orthodox Christian Way of prayer and love
that include self-knowledge acquired through the lifetime psychotherapy of continual repentance and spiritual struggle in response to
God's love. This is the heart of an Eastern Orthodox foundation for
caregiving, which is rooted in an intentional trialogue between God,
self and others in the world that reveals the limits of human strength
and the boundless power of God's Grace.

> The primordial condition and absolute necessity is to know
> oneself... to be alive to the many-sided possibilities of the
> ego... Silence and quiet are indispensable for concentration.
> Practice of the Jesus Prayer is the traditional fulfillment of the
> injunction of Apostle Paul to "pray always"; it has nothing to do
> with mysticism which is the heritage of pagan ancestry... the
> essential conditions which allow hope for success are genuine
> humility, sincerity, endurance, purity...
>
> Whenever human consciousness begins to be alive to the
> questions, Who am I? Whence do I come? Whither do I go?
> Then there arises the possibility of taking and following the nar-
> row, long, blessed path to wisdom.
>
> By and by circumstances show that our individual capaci-
> ties are quite insufficient, and Supreme Help is vitally needed.
> The obstacles that arise are numberless and multiform, such as

---

mility, Obedience, Repentance, and Love (Etna, California: Center for Traditionalist Orthodox Studies, 2010).

will lead us, if possible, in a false direction and make us lose sight even of the ultimate goal.

The two principal Commandments include the absolute necessity, the duty, of Love, which for those practicing the Prayer is more than essential. If the Path is taken and followed in the spirit of genuine Love, irrevocable self-denial and humility, there is a great chance of successful attainments in this life leading imperceptibly to the farthest future.

These holy Fathers were of the Christian Church of the first millennium and their teachings, instructions and help are accessible only in the light of genuine, primordial Christianity, devoid of any human considerations, additions and alterations, in its integrity and purity of the time of the holy Apostles.[33]

Is such a Christianity possible apart from monastic seclusion in the routine demands of daily life? Can one find the door to the closet of one's heart to abide there in the midst of daily life so that we are not dissipated by poor attention and the "cares and worries of the world" that choke the spirit, leaving us on our own again? I remember psychiatrist Gerald May,[34] who sought to integrate a contemplative dimension of prayer into his daily routine, many years ago during a talk he gave in Valdosta, Georgia, revealing that, try as he might, he was not able to pray the Jesus Prayer during his hospital work. Over and over again, he found himself beginning it when he walked in the door only to realize he was remembering it again as he was walking out. Romanian theologian Dumitru Staniloae said somewhere that he had been able to find continuous prayer impelled by Grace in his heart while imprisoned in the gulag, but had lost it after his release back in the daily world of priesthood and the de-

---

[33] Kadloubovsky & Palmer, *Writings From the Philokalia on Prayer of the Heart* (London: Faber & Faber, 1975), 5–7.
[34] G. May, *Will and Spirit: A Contemplative Psychology* (New York: HarperOne, 1987); *Addiction and Grace: Love and Spirituality in the Healing of Addictions* (New York: HarperOne, 2007).

mands of his scholarly writings and was never able to find it at that depth again. The beloved parish priest St. John of Kronstadt,[35] on the other hand, St. Luke the Surgeon[36] and others like Fr. Arseny,[37] were granted miraculous Grace in their daily lives in the world. What accounts for the difference?

Clearly, there is abundant evidence that there is life in Christ of a depth and power as remarkable and vital as what is depicted in the Gospels and has been confirmed again and again throughout the centuries. This certainly gives us hope and definite direction, but we must also realize that work itself can and should be approached as a way of prayer of dialogue with God and not as a distraction from prayer. The caregiver's vocation of healing, whether as physician, priest or psychotherapist, is rooted in the trialogue with God, self and the world that is the precondition for sustaining the work of caregiving as part of the same spiritual formation process as the ancient Orthodox Christian path in Christ. This trialogue involves a subtle but definite inner taste of 'being present' that is a function of turning toward the 'spiritual closet' of one's own presence before Christ, here and now, whatever one is doing, wherever one is, whenever one can. Since we cannot all live our lives in monasteries, our task is to discover in our respective settings what supports this kind of intentional neptic presence in our ordinary daily lives and relationships in the world.

Brother Lawrence in his classic autobiographical reflections, *The Practice of the Presence of God*, points us in this direction where a degree of love and humility can overtake a person who approaches every action in this way from moment to moment, even the flipping of a pancake on the griddle.

---

[35] J. Kronstadt, *My Life in Christ* (Russia: Holy Trinity Monastery, 1911).
[36] V. Marushchak, *The Blessed Surgeon: The Life of Saint Luke of Simferopol.* (California: Divine Ascent Press, 2002).
[37] *Father Arseny, 1893–1973: Priest, Prisoner, Spiritual Father: Being the Narratives Compiled by the Servant of God Alexander Concerning His Spiritual Father* (Crestwood, NY: St. Vladimir's Orthodox Press, 1998).

I cannot express to you what goes on in me now. I sense no distress
nor any doubt about my state. I have no other will but God's will,
which I seek to fulfill in all things, and to which I am so committed that I would not wish to pick up a piece of straw without His
command, and from any other motives than pure love of Him.[38]

Recent developments in neuro-imaging of the brain confirm the
value of integrating mindfulness and attentive presence, which have
traditionally been associated with the monastic path of religion, into
one's life as a daily practice and demonstrate that this actually changes the brain,[39] enabling people who persist in this to grow a brain that
makes it more possible to maintain equanimity under greater degrees
of stress than otherwise possible.

Meditators showed significantly larger volumes of the hippocampus and areas within the orbito-frontal cortex, the thalamus
and the inferior temporal gyrus — all regions known for regulating emotions. "We know that people who consistently medi-
tate have a singular ability to cultivate positive emotions, retain
emotional stability and engage in mindful behavior.[40]

While meditation and the cultivating of a high quality of attention
and freedom from identification with the *logismoi* that lead to passions is part of the ascetical conditions for responding to God's Grace,
the crux of the matter is how to do this while staying in relationship
with both our work and interactions with people in the world and
with God at the same time.

[38] Brother Lawrence, E. M. Blaiklock (trans.), *The Practice of the Presence of God*
(Nashville: Thomas Nelson Publishers, 1981), 44.
[39] Cf. S. Begley, *Train Your Mind Change Your Brain* (New York: Ballantine
Books, 2007).
[40] Cf E. Luders, A. Toga, N. Lepore, C. Gaser, "The Underlying Anatomical
Correlates of Long-term Meditation: Larger Hippocampal and Frontal Volumes of Gray Matter," *NeuroImage* Volume 45, Issue 3 (15 April 2009): 672–678
doi:10.1016/j.neuroimage.2008.12.061.

The usual slow and gradual movement in the direction of loss of inner attention to personal relationship with God and other people inevitably involves increasing addictive compensations sought out to stimulate an overly tired body and an undernourished and overburdened heart, providing momentary mood enhancements that mask the underlying psychic numbing and mild depression that are signals of imbalance. This often happens in small innocuous ways at first without even realizing it. Prayer and mindfulness give way to a bowl of ice cream, a glass of brandy, television, internet or other forms of stimulation which involve a loss of the sense of presence and fineness of heart, that arise in the stillness that is cultivated within as part of daily prayer, participation in Divine Liturgy and the intentional feasts and fasts of the Church calendar. This poor quality of attention, dissociation and captivity to the passions interferes with the caregiver's ability to be present, and the mind becomes more vulnerable to suggestions of alternative 'quick fixes' to brighten the mood. This gradually gives way to secular pursuits as a change slowly comes over us, often without noticing because it is so gradual. In and of themselves, these things are not much of a problem, but repeated enough with the gradual loss of inner dialogue with God, spouse, friends and the natural world, they become poor substitutes for the very high quality mental, emotional and physical nutrition which can only come from attention to God's presence. This in turn trains the brain to look for satisfaction through dopamine and adrenaline surges related to instinctive cravings rather than the finer qualities of spiritual refreshment that are afforded by the struggle to have the mind in the heart.

THE NEUROPHYSIOLOGY OF BURNOUT. Burnout is a phenomenon caused by chronic over stimulation of the body's fight-flight protective mechanisms of the autonomic nervous system (ANS), which consists of the sympathetic (SNS) and parasympathetic (PNS) branches. Learning to be aware of the physical symptoms of ANS activity and intentionally creating relaxation and stillness physically, as well as in the *nous*, wherever possible, is part of neptic awareness that helps prevent compassion fatigue and burnout. This is a must for professional caregivers, particularly those who work with people in significant pain, severe illness and trauma, as these are the ones most vulnerable to accumulating vicarious trauma. "We can become so focused on the distress of those in our care that we neglect our own growing discomfort"[41] in the process.

Signs of SNS activity are indicative of the body's mobilization for fight or flight and include movement of circulation away from digestion toward the large muscles of the body. Blood platelets thicken in preparation for quick clotting in case of injury; respiration and heart rate increase oxygenation of the muscles; pupils dilate for better vision; and peristalsis slows as the body shifts energy toward improving reflexes for fight or flight. By contrast, the PNS prepares the body for relaxation, conversation, sexual enjoyment, rest, digestion of food and the activities of intimacy and relationships that occur in safety.

Signs of PNS activity include slow, deep respiration and heart rate as in prayer and meditation, dry warm skin indicating circulation being shunted away from major muscle groups and a general sense of well-being. When both branches of the ANS become activated simultaneously in the face of perceived helplessness and danger, instead of fight or flight, the 'freeze' response occurs, which is associated with dissociation that is characteristic of post-traumatic stress.

> During freezing there is an altered sense of time and space, reduced registration of pain, and dampened emotion. Those who have frozen under threat report a kind of dissociative experience. Time slows down and they are no longer afraid. As such, freezing is also an extremely valuable survival defense. However, it has greater consequences in the aftermath of trauma than does fight or flight. Studies demonstrate that those who dissoci-

---

[41] B. Rothschild, *Help for the Helper: The Psychophysiology of Compassion Fatigue and Vicarious Trauma.* (New York: W. W. Norton & Co., 2006), 103.

ate during trauma have a greater chance of developing PTSD
than those who do not.[42]

These responses, whether fight, flight or freeze, are generated by sub-
cortical processes designed to keep the organism alive by initially
bypassing the slower rational thought. However, with training and
practice in tuning into the sensation of the body, noticing the feelings and cultivating a quiet, silent inner prayerful mind, it is possible to increase facility in more rapidly deactivating limbic responses
that are not actually necessary. This is part of the 'twin missions' of
soldiers as well as healthcare professionals: to be able to function in
battle and then to be able to function at home without the need for
battle-ready emotions.[43] It means gaining more recognition of and
control over the ANS and the PNS through uniting mind and body in
greater mindfulness and increased capacity for vulnerability.

It is what we *believe* to be true to which our bodies respond, rather
than what actually is. Increased vulnerability to heightened activation
of ANS stems from perceived threat as well as through empathic connection with others involving secondary and vicarious trauma. This
can take many forms, including the claim on the nervous system that
is created by feelings of personal responsibility for the health and welfare of one's patients and clients that goes beyond professional care
into one of 'functional atheism' in which the caregiver professes faith
in God, but acts and feels as though everything depends on one's own
self. The ANS nervous system does not distinguish between an attack
by a saber-toothed tiger and the same kind of life and death situation
that is elicited by the intense sense of responsibility the caregiver begins to feel for those she or he serves. In such moments,

> an alarm from the amygdala activates the hypothalamus, setting
> in motion two parallel actions. One activates the SNS while the

---

[42] Ibid., 102.
[43] S. Muse, "Fit For Life, Fit For War: Reflections on the Warrior Ethos," *Infantry*
March -April (2005): 11–15.

other provokes the pituitary gland. The SNS triggers the adrenals to release epinephrine and norepinephrine, which mobilize the body for fight or flight. The pituitary action also stimulates the adrenals to release something different: cortisol. Following a successful fight or flight, cortisol will quiet the amygdala's alarm and return the nervous system to a state of homeostasis.[44]

A problem arises when this psychobiological system is chronically activated and goes unnoticed. Instead of cortisol in combination with regular worship, prayer, aerobic exercise and nutritious diet, along with relaxed conversation with friends that lowers stress levels and replenishes the person, the overworked caregiver begins to neglect these and starts to self-medicate in a variety of ways.

THE NEUROBIOLOGY OF ADDICTION AND PATRISTIC PARALLELS. Modern understanding of the neurobiology of addiction and the struggle to maintain abstinence and achieve sobriety almost exactly parallels the traditional patristic teaching on spiritual warfare and guarding the heart leading to what is called 'mental sobriety.' Though detailed in different stages by various Church Fathers who have made careful self-observation of this process aided by the Holy Spirit, the basic schema is one of recognizing how the attention is subtly captured by *logismoi* (thoughts) that come through the mental space activating the imagination through the energy of the attention and then drawing off enough psychic energy to involve the will in carrying out 'purchase' of what is offered, by paying for it with the energy of the human organism that would otherwise have been available for real life. "The main concern of patristic asceticism is not with external manifestations of sin, nor individual instances of sin, but rather with their cause, i.e. the vices and passions rooted in the soul, or diseases of the soul and hidden states of sin."[45]

---

[44] Op. cit., 101.
[45] I. M. Kontzevitch, *The Acquisition of the Holy Spirit in Ancient Russia* (Platina, CA: St. Herman of Alaska Brotherhood, 1988), 39.

Using modern cybernetic metaphors we can look at these stages[46] leading to addiction as first receiving an email from the devil who is a spammer. It comes unbidden into the psychic space of our outer consciousness. We must decide whether to allow it to pass on through to the spam folder or attempt to open it. The first stage of suffering comes in the form of hesitating before this question, wondering whether or not to open it. As discernment grows with experience, one senses whether it is dangerous and moves it to the spam folder without having to deliberate over it. If, on the other hand, the operator is tired and seeking some kind of diversion, there is a greater vulnerability to 'gambling' and 'curiosity.' These states of mind are linked with biofeedback mechanisms that trigger dopamine release in the brain, which act like magnets. With this, the second stage of spiritual beguilement has been entered, in which the attention has connected the advertisement of the email (*logismoi*) to consciousness of desire. If, after opening up the email, the inner content is attractive or 'salient' to the reward center of the brain, then it captures more energy. The struggle intensifies and, if not interrupted voluntarily by pre-frontal cortical control which is starting to give way, it can lead to clicking on the attachment contained in the email which redirects the browser to another site. This exposes an even deeper level of the psyche to a more intense involvement with the intent of the seemingly innocuous email or advertisement. In this way, the initial email becomes the connecting agent between the psyche and the sender of the email through the attention which, due to tiredness, negative thoughts and the need for distraction, is now beginning to serve immediate short-term pleasure for its own sake, apart from discernment of what is good for the whole over the long term.

Psychic energy of desire is siphoned off through the 'straw' of the attention infusing the power of the imagination with life in this particular form, which temporarily fills up the psychic space, further

---

[46] Various patristic writers break down the stages of spiritual beguilement differently, but along the same lines. Cf. I. M. Kontzevich, (1988), 39–43, for a fuller detailed description of the inner process leading to captivity of the will.

exciting and training the craving centers of the brain, the nucleus accumbens and ventral tegumental areas, which are devoted to the dopamine reward system. This is what happens for crack addicts who, just by thinking about smoking crack, or entering into an area where they once used, begin to have an anticipatory dopamine surge that creates a sense of craving. The brain never forgets what gives the body its most intense pleasure. This is the third level of spiritual beguilement.

As the imagination further excites the pleasure-craving centers of the brain that remember having been previously stimulated in the same way, added emphasis is given to the content and direction of the advertisement which now begins to involve the will in carrying out the impulse to click on the link to purchase whatever it is that is desired. At this point, imagination and desire have fully 'captured' the attention of the person, which carries out the action to achieve the anticipated reward. If repeated, this acting out becomes 'captivity' or addiction — the final stage of spiritual beguilement where instead of obedience to God and the freedom entailed in this, the heart of the person is subjected to the suffering of captivity to an addictive pattern or 'passion' in which sensitivity to what is good is deadened and freedom to choose is subverted. The soul is now held captive to the craving of bodily instinct, blind to the Spirit, instead of the body being illuminated and made sensitive by the Spirit which fills the soul who abstains from all that impedes it. Captivity to vainglory, pride and other forms of self-will and self-adoration are more subtle than the instinctive bodily appetites and harder to notice, but equally destructive. They can occur in outwardly pious and religious persons who are relatively free of distortion by bodily passions, yet secretly feed on these 'delights' which block the action of repentance and reception of Grace in the heart so that there is a lack of compassion and mercy for others.

What modern studies of the plasticity of the brain and its neurochemistry reveal is that each of these steps, when repeated, stimulate the brain to grow and develop in the direction of supporting the addictive compensations (or learning to avoid them). Like adding 'cookies' to the human bio-computer so it can connect faster and more completely to a given internet site the next time. In this way, the brain gradually adapts to the addictive compensations so that the person begins to be submitted to control of the addiction, rather than have freedom of choice to pursuing life in Christ.[47]

T HE POWER OF ADDICTIVE COMPENSATION. In 2005, (SAM-HSA) estimates are that $276 billion was spent or lost as a result of drug and alcohol related abuse in the United States.[48] Along with growing illicit drug use, Americans are fast becoming a legally drug-dependent country, medically and economically. In 2003 alone, pharmaceutical companies spent more than twenty five billion dollars marketing and promoting prescription drugs,[49] helping to beguile the public into greater expenditures in this area. Television commercials inundate the consumer with suggestions to "ask your doctor" about one or another prescription drugs, a rather strange request when you stop to think about it, except that it is propelled by an enormous corporate economic engine whose ethics are determined purely by whether any damage done by a given drug will be sufficiently outweighed by revenues received. What kind of message is this which corporate sponsors want us to become used to?

Between 1992–2003, the number of Americans who admitted abusing prescription drugs in the U.S. doubled from 7.8 million to 15.1 million. This represents a twofold increase more than marijuana use, five times greater than cocaine, and sixty times greater than

---

[47] Cf. A. Lazar, "The Neurobiology of Sin," talk given at the International Orthodox Psychotherapy Conference in Chicago, June 2010.
[48] "The Five Most Expensive Addictions," Forbes.com, 10-31-2006 12:00 AM ET. http://articles.moneycentral.msn.com/Investing/Forbes/The5MostExpensiveAddictions.aspx.
[49] 'Pharmaceutical Marketing and Promotion: Tough Questions, Straight Answers," Pharmaceutical Research and Manufacturers of America, July 2008, http://www.phrma.org/files/attachments/Marketing%20and%20Promotion%20Facts_071108_FINAL.pdf.

heroin.[50] Of the twenty one million adults in the U.S. diagnosed with mental heath problems between 2000 and 2001, 79% received prescriptions for psychoactive drugs while 40% of these received no psychotherapy at all. A pill was expected to be quicker acting and to replace dialogue with a human being even though 40 years of research strongly shows exactly the opposite to be the case.[51] The number of prescriptions written in the U.S. doubled from two billion in 1994 to four billion in 2004. This represents approximately 13.6 prescriptions per person in America.[52]

There is overwhelming evidence that many of the maladies whose symptoms are treated by prescription are actually the result of poor nutrition, bad spiritual and mental hygiene, lack of exercise, overwork and poor quality human relationships. Addictive compensations (and in some cases prescription medicines) used as substitutes for the loss of inner clarity and sensitivity that result from these imbalances creates a vicious, snowballing addictive cycle. The problem is that addictive compensations gradually train and grow the brain to crave more of the artificial substances that initially offer immediate gratification, at the expense of creating further imbalance in the other biological systems. This, in turn, stimulates greater cravings for the addictive compensation which is no longer effectively eliminating the pain or shifting the mood that it was initially used for. This is the basis of all captivity to addictive cycles, regardless of the substances,[53] so it is not surprising that a return to religious foundations is implicit in achieving and maintaining sobriety.[54] For example, after a year into recovery from heroin abuse, those in the religious-based recovery programs were almost eight times more likely to report ab-

---

[50] C. Prentis, *The Alcoholism and Addiction Cure* (California: Power Press: California, 2007), 30.

[51] B. Wampold, *The Great Psychotherapy Debate: Models, Methods and Findings* (London: Lawrence Erlbaum Associates, Publishers, 2001).

[52] Op. cit..

[53] Cf. R. Ruden, *The Craving Brain* (New York: HarperCollins, 1997).

[54] M. Weber, *Steps of Transformation: An Orthodox Priest Explores the Twelve Steps* (California: Conciliar Press, 2003).

stinence from opiates than those who received purely secular treatment.[55] Orthodox teaching as a whole is in direct opposition to captivity of any kind, whatever the medication, seeking instead to restore
organic harmony and balance that support greater receptivity to the
Divine Energies of Grace and vulnerability to the joys and sorrows of
life that are part of loving and being loved.

As Jesus told the devil on the mount of temptation, who was suggesting this alternative, depersonalized, Godless path to Him, "Man
does not live by bread alone, but by every word that proceeds from
the mouth of God" (Mt. 4:4). What is necessary to feed on the word
of God? Apart from the personal energies of Divine Grace, flesh and
blood cannot recognize the Kingdom of God. The patristic witness is
clearly one in which the path of the Orthodox Way is one of preparing
and sustaining human beings in feeding on the 'bread from heaven'
on a daily basis in a variety of forms over an entire lifetime. Captivity
by addiction in any form competes with and impedes digestion of the
energies of Grace and ultimately impedes human growth and well-
being into the full image and likeness of the Holy Trinity.

Neurobiologically, according to current understanding, addiction places the craving brain located in the nucleus accumbens and
the ventral tegmental area responsible for regulating dopamine release, in power over the pre-frontal cortex, which is able to weigh
options, determine meaning and recognize what kind of executive
control needs to be put in place to keep the entire organism functioning optimally. By adding the intention of continual prayer and repentance to the program, along with fasting from poor quality nutrition
at the bodily, emotional and mental levels, the way is made clear for
'the coming of the Lord,' whose presence in a properly functioning
organism can open the heart to *theoria* (the vision of God). That is
not to say that God cannot transform people instantaneously whose
bodies and minds have been broken by a lifetime of addiction. Evi-

[55] Matthews, Larson & Barry, (1993) "The Faith Factor: An Annotated Bibliography of Clinical Research on Spiritual Subjects, Vol. 1," *National Institute for
Health Research* (1993): 72–73.

dence is clear that this too occurs as in the case of the suicidal man with chronic alcoholism who sought Elder Ambrose's help. However, evidence is also abundant that those whose lives have been devoted to the kind of high quality neptic attention and vulnerable relationship to which Fr. Nikon alludes, *have grown different kinds of brains*, indicating that a healthy body, mind and heart are more conducive for the Holy Spirit to remain and enliven the organism, than one which is constantly choosing to activate biological systems that work against these and shut down those that do.

Advances in brain-imaging and a growing body of associated research in the neurophysiological mechanisms of addiction are revealing the significant role played by the neurotransmitter dopamine. Dopamine is one of the primary neurotransmitters that lets a person know whether something is worth paying attention to or not. Dr. Nora Volkow, MD, Director of the National Institute on Drug Abuse (NIDA), explains:

> The dopamine system ... responds to salient stimuli — to something that is either pleasurable, important, or worth paying attention to. Other things can be salient as well, such as a novel or unexpected stimuli or aversive stimuli when they are threatening in nature. So dopamine is really saying, "Look, pay attention to this — it is important." Dopamine signals salience. But dopamine generally stays within the synapse for only a short time — less than 50 microseconds — before it is recycled by the dopamine transporter. So under normal circumstances, dopamine receptors should be plentiful and sensitive if they are going to pay attention to a short burst of dopamine that is intended to carry the message, "Pay attention!"[56]

When people begin self-medicating with drugs that flood the brain with dopamine when it is not in harmony with the rest of life, the

---

[56] J. Rosack, "Volkow May Have Uncovered Answer to Addiction Riddle," *Psychiatric News* (American Psychiatric Association) Volume 39, Number 11 (June 4, 2004), 32.

brain gradually loses sensitivity to ordinary life, which no longer reaches the threshold of awareness as being 'important' or 'salient enough' to pay attention to. This accounts for the dullness and lack of interest in the ordinary that begins to shadow addicts. When the priest invites throughout the Divine Liturgy, "Let us be attentive," he is inviting us to recognize as vivid and present the images represented by the icons, the smell of the incense, and the words of the Liturgy, all signaling the invisible presence of God, which reveals the quality of all life as being 'salient' and declaring the glory of God. For this to occur, we must begin to become responsible for our attention. Instead of looking for stimulation passively from the outside, Orthodoxy teaches us to train the mind to find salience in ordinary life illumined by God's Grace by attending to the present moment and awakening the mind (nous) receptively within in the heart.

Worldliness, by contrast, is just the reverse. Instead of being able to be refreshed and strengthened by attendance in the Divine Liturgy and on one's knees in prayer or in conversation with one's spouse and friends because of a high quality of attention and a heart purified and on guard against identifying with *logismoi* that lead to suffering, the addict seeks stimulation to fill the emptiness or mask the pain of a poorly directed attention. In this sense, we are all addicts, struggling to free our attention (and thereby our hearts) from superficial distractions that gradually accumulate as replacements for fully encountering life. Chronic use of self-medication by seeking stimulation of daily television viewing, internet, junk food, shopping, sexual titillation (in contrast to eros as part of a committed, spiritually rooted, dialogical love relationship), and preoccupation with afflictive emotions or 'passions,' of envy, gossip, negativity, greed, vainglory, etc., begin to dull the capacity for finding salience in ordinary life. This may in turn lead to compounding the problem by taking it to another level as in the use of manufactured chemical cocktails of the illicit drugs (and in some cases prescription drugs), all of which train the brain to depend on these for relief and stimulation, instead of the organically natural and harmonious processes that are vital to health and well-being. They block the heart's receptivity to Grace and make it difficult to 'attend' to God's presence. One loses the 'taste' and 'feel' for God who becomes at best a mere 'idea'. Volkow explains the neurophysiological basis for this:

> Most drugs of abuse block the dopamine transporter in the brain's reward circuits, allowing the neurotransmitter to remain in the synapse for a comparative eternity. This results in a large and lasting reward, even though the individual has reduced numbers of receptors. Over time, addicts learn that natural stimuli are no longer salient, but the drug of abuse is. Other research is showing that inhibitory control; reward, motivation, and drive; and learning and memory circuits are all abnormal in individuals with an addictive disorder.[57]

In effect, what happens is that by failing to 'work the steps' of Orthodox life on a daily basis, and falling prey to self-medicating with sin as a way of addressing unacknowledged compassion fatigue and vicarious trauma, health professionals become vulnerable to a kind of spiritual beguilement in which we tell ourselves cognitively, "I'm in control," when in actuality, the pre-frontal cortex has given way to control of the instinctive craving brain that is increasingly calling the shots. If burnout reaches the point of a full-fledged addiction, an integrated intervention is called for, which addresses body, mind and heart within a communal context of interpersonal support in order to expose and begin to correct the imbalances. One cannot do it alone or simply by taking a magic pill, which is already the bane of every addict's thinking. *What must be clearly understood to be at the heart of the problem is the monologue that enshrouds every impaired professional who increasingly isolates and feels shame and guilt over being out of control. While working harder and blaming oneself for no longer caring like you once did, the impaired professional falls into the same trap*

---

[57] Ibid.

as the addict: "I ought to be able to stop this on my own." The fact of the matter, as Volkow stresses, is that "no one chooses to become addicted, they simply are cognitively unable to choose not to be addicted."[58]

Theologically, it is the same with regard to passions. Repeated sins and compensations sought out in order to avoid being present, when repeated enough, become deeply rooted to the point that they take the heart captive so you cannot *not* do them. As we become aware of this condition and begin to struggle, it causes a lament to build in the heart like St. Paul: "The good I would do I do not and the evil I would not do that I do! Who will free me from this body of death?" (Rom. 7:19). Fortunately, God's love is just the reverse of addiction. God refuses to take captive our freedom to resist Him. God is without compulsion. At its most extreme, captivity to a passion seems all powerful and God utterly helpless, abandoning. Unavailable. We are alone with our suffering and the sea of human misery. Freedom, on the other hand, is found in the mystery of Christ freely assuming human nature and the cross and when He seemed most vulnerable, most overpowered, He was actually opening up the possibility of humanity freely responding to God's love. Choosing to turn and let ourselves be loved by God in the abandoned places and at the moments we feel most compulsively unable too and most unworthy of love is paradoxically the first step toward freedom to love. According to St. Isaac the Syrian, "nothing is stronger than despair, for it is then that we discover God's strength and grace, not in comfort."[59]

A N ORTHODOX APPROACH TO HEALTH AND WELL-BEING. With respect to Jesus' admonition that the heart of the law is to "love God with *all the body, all the mind* and *all the heart* and your neighbor as being of one life with yourself," the curative prevention and remedy for compassion fatigue, secondary and vicarious trauma, burnout and the myriad health consequences that are their sequellae,

---

[58] Ibid.
[59] Cited by Rev. Vasileios Thermos — personal correspondence with the author.

is *metanoia* — a revolutionary Copernican shift of mind that results in a renewal of harmonious relationships in life. Love of God (*philotheia*) is at the center of the heart instead of self-love (*philautia*). Becoming attentive to the glory of God (*orthodoxia*) instead of seeking entertainment and stimulations of vainglory (*kenodoxia*) become the aim of everyday life. Body, mind and heart all require a special kind of nourishment that comes from the dialogue that results from this. Vigilance and ascetical restraint, which are part of the Orthodox Christian path, are needed to ensure that instinctive cravings do not overpower the finer intelligence that can govern the whole in accordance with the 'still small voice' of the Holy Spirit.

The physical body must have high quality nourishment in proper balance.[60] The natural order has an immense interdependent system of checks and balances that promotes and sustains biological life at optimal levels. In the same way, the hesychastic witness of the Church over millennia attests to the fact that the heart requires a very pure diet of high quality impressions in order to become receptive to the energies of Divine Grace. Neptic vigilance utilizes the attention in order to avoid 'eating' poor quality *logismoi*, which deplete energy by wasting through infusing *phantasia*, which do not nourish the soul and which harm the brain. Drawing into the heart the untransfigured afflictive emotions of the passions blinds the heart to God's presence which in turn stimulates further cravings for 'junk food' impressions. Like powerful drugs, these burn up the 'oil' of neurotransmitters in the brain at a rate that leaves the *nous* as a 'lamp without oil' unavailable for attentive receptivity when the bridegroom of Grace arrives unexpectedly.

---

[60] Cf. J. Fuhrman, MD, *Nutritarian Handbook* (USA: Nutritional Excellence, LLC, 2010). Dr. Fuhrman's approach, in this author's experience, makes the most sense medically as well as in terms of its feasibility for everyday life. It fits beautifully with an Orthodox approach to fasting and feasting and offers the best chance for optimal nutrition that serves both the body's health and the mind's clarity, freeing us from subtle food cravings that create addictive cycles of dopamine stimulation which compensate for loss of inner clarity. His website can be found at EatRightAmerica.com. Highly recommended.

St. Isaac the Syrian notes, "Knowledge of God does not abide in persons who love comfort." What we put into our bodies, and how much, affects the quality of our attention. The quality of our attention is even more important than the quality of the physical nutrients themselves, for it is the quality of attention that allows us to begin to metabolize our true spiritual food which are the finer 'nutrients' of Grace itself, our 'daily being bread'[61] on a moment to moment basis.

Looking at the traditional ascetical disciplines of the Orthodox Christian faith, one notices that all have an element of fasting in them. Fasting requires intentionality and discernment. It is not a mechanical act. Fasting from food cravings frees the organism from domination of pleasure as our master. Fasting from self-centered preoccupation, through acts of charity, opens up room for the joy that comes from loving and giving of oneself for others. We are freed from captivity to greed through almsgiving and from slavery to sin through making confession to God in the presence of the priest, thereby dissolving the monologue that is most dangerous of all. All these no's to captivity by lesser idols open the door to freedom to say Yes! to offering ourselves in love to the One who is always doing this for us. We begin to see God represented in all people as living icons and now life takes on more and more the character of being in God's presence in all places of our ordinary lives.

There is, indeed, 'struggle' in the Orthodox Christian Way of life. It is the struggle of seeking freedom from all oppression in order to respond fully to God's love for us. The fruit of this path is freely forgiving and loving others as God loves us. St. Silouan the Athonite observes that freedom is to be found in obedience to the Holy Spirit. This alone, from the Orthodox Christian standpoint, is the path to health and well-being and the source of God's care for those who co-creatively care for others in God's name with God's power.

---

[61] Origen and others have commented on the Greek word 'epiousion' in the Lord's Prayer, which is translated into English as 'daily' bread, suggesting that it carries a connotation of 'super substantial' or 'heavenly' bread that goes beyond physical substance to an essential nourishment for the soul.

Orthodox Christian patristic tradition, as noted by Fr. Nikon in the introduction to the *Philokalia*, is about training the mind to stand guard in the heart over a lifetime to prevent spiritual beguilement in all its forms in order to achieve what is called 'mental sobriety.' This is the foundation from which Grace is metabolized to develop people toward full potential as human beings in relationship with God and each other. By standing and repeatedly bringing ourselves to pay attention in Liturgy and by entering deep stillness in hesychastic prayer, we grow healthy brains as well as healthy hearts. The same is true for making the efforts involved in the other ascetical disciplines of fasting, confession, almsgiving. Learning to be present and obedient to God in all things in daily life is the clear path toward human wholeness and well-being. And more than that, as Eastern Orthodoxy has shown, it is the path toward communion with the Holy Trinity, with humankind and the natural created world as it was intended to be.

T HE PRIMARY THEOLOGICAL AND ANTHROPOLOGICAL QUESTION OF CARE FOR THE CAREGIVER. Having noted the twin predisposing vulnerabilities to burn out, which are the psychodynamic internalized family of origin patterns in the caregiver and the occupational hazards of intensely demanding schedules and contact with human suffering, the central question arising from the Orthodox Christian perspective that should strike us as very odd and something of an important puzzle to solve is how it is that the being in the universe who bears the greatest burden and the heaviest yoke of caregiving, beyond all comprehension, can say to the rest of us, "Come to Me all you are heavy laden, and I will give you rest for My yoke is easy and My burden is light" (Mt. 11:28–30).

Archimandrite Sophrony describes Jesus as being the keystone at the point of an inverted pyramid holding up all creation. God *is* love, and love's burden is the greatest of all, for it bears all who cannot bear themselves. So how can this burden be 'easy and light'? This question relates to what I view as the 'caregiver's Trinity' — the threefold related areas of vocational satisfaction, quality of care, and the personal well-being of the caregiver, which evidence suggests that all three are interdependent on one another. If one fails, the other two are also in danger.

The Eastern Orthodox path is one that is wholistic in supporting well-being by anchoring vocation in the co-creative partnership with Christ, who offers His life not compulsively, but freely for love, out of recognition that all life is one and that the basis for caring for the other is loving others in the same way that one is loved by God. Jesus' new commandment to "love one another as I have loved you" (John 13:34) does not mean to go it alone, caring for others while neglecting one's own legitimate needs. Even the ox is allowed to eat from the threshing floor. How much more a human being?

We must keep in mind that Jesus did not exhaust Himself going beyond physical human limits during His ministry. He did not let people throw Him over cliff or stone Him to death when the incited mobs wanted to. He ate all organic food, walked everywhere He went, prayed regularly and for extended periods, fasted, climbed mountains, went boating, kept learning and teaching, spent time with friends like Mary, Martha and Lazarus, whose house He frequented. He went away by Himself when He needed to, even when His disciples told him there were still people in need who were clamoring for His help. Prayer helped Him keep His priorities and determine His actions, "I do whatever I see the Father doing. I do nothing on My own." He kept priorities that allowed Him to do what the cell wall in the body does to preserve life; having an intelligent membrane that stays constantly in touch with both the inner and outer world, balancing potassium and sodium and other nutrients, while keeping out what is harmful, in order to enhance life.

The *unbearable lightness of being caregivers* is discovered to be mystery of abiding in Christ. Quality of care for others, fidelity to one's vocation and being wakefully present in the rhythms of daily life are all rooted in fidelity to Christ whose life gradually becomes one's own. The love of God offered us, to the degree that we freely and intentionally receive it, invites us to freely offer ourselves in return for one another in the same way.

When the disciples had been working and came together to 'a deserted place' for a well-deserved and needed retreat, we are told that 5,000 people showed up (Mark 6:37–44). They are nervous about the crowd and suggest to Jesus that He send them to buy something to eat. Jesus says no, "you give them something." This is what every overworking caregiver expects of himself or herself already. What do you have to give, and how do you give when you have come to the end of your human resources? It is the burnout question. And to this, Jesus teaches us a most remarkable thing. He finds the appropriate response through the solution offered by one of his clients! A small boy freely offers "five loaves and two fishes." This simple gift is not recognized as significant by the Apostles, who are operating out of a scarcity model and already overworked themselves. Thinking like the corporate experts, they dismiss the inadequate resources of the patient thinking everything must come from the physician. "What are these among so many?"

But Jesus operates out of a co-creative, trialogical relationship between Himself, God and the world. As with the widow's mite, what seemed (and was) insignificant in and of itself, when offered to God was transformative. Jesus sees with different eyes. When He takes the boy's offering, He offers it back to God. "Master of the Universe who are the Giver of all good and perfect gifts, what You have brought forth from the guileless heart of this little child, I return to Thee for Your blessing." All that is given to God is given to the Son of God and the Son of God has emptied Himself of everything so that he could take up the entirety of humanity's helplessness and suffering. As He does with Himself, Jesus breaks what is offered, and gives it to the disciples who discover the miraculous joy of spiritual renewal that lightens their souls and bodies in the act of being midwives between God and the world, freely offering to others, what they themselves have freely received. In this way, they are able to give what they do not think they have to give. All who were present were filled and still twelve baskets were taken up of leftovers.

This miracle of Eucharist offered in everyday language and everyday circumstances, without Temple, Liturgy or monastery, is the miracle of life that is lived in and through Christ in all places and at all times with all people. All that we have received we are free to return to God for blessing — our life, our learning, our impressions during a day, the moments we sit with patients, clients and parishioners. In this way, like a kind of breathing, a heart taking a brief Sabbath rest between giving and receiving, over and over in a day, we are newly equipped to render care for others — not because we are experts who have enough to give, but because we learn in those moments of nothingness between actions, that all life comes from God.

If we learn to pay attention in this way, we can share in the joy of discovering what God is doing in the hearts and lives of those who come to us in need. They too have "five loaves and two fishes." In this way, all is transformed into the body and blood of Christ, whether it is bread and fish, or a comforting touch, a word or a listening presence. Everything becomes the great and only eucharistic medicine of life which nourishes the weary and revives the sick and still is not itself diminished. In this way, we begin to glimpse that my neighbor is indeed myself and the paradoxical mystery entailed in the unbearable lightness of being caregivers is that we are in fact caring for ourselves by caring for one another.

CHAPTER EIGHT

Post-Traumatic Spiritual Disorder and the False History Syndrome[1]

(on the Use of History to Deny Reality and a Call to Healing and Justice through Awakening Conscience in Church and Community)

You shall know the truth and the truth shall set you free.

Jesus of Nazareth

A truth that's told with bad intent beats all the lies you can invent.

William Blake

Take sides. Neutrality helps the oppressor, never the victim. Silence encourages the tormentor, never the tormented.

Elie Wiesel

The individual who has lost his place in the political community risks to drop out of the boundaries of humanity.

Hannah Arendt

If you have come to help me, you are wasting your time. If you have come because your liberation is bound up with mine, then let us work together.

Australian Aboriginal saying

---

[1] This article is a revised and expanded version of one that first appeared in *The Messenger: Journal of the Episcopal Vicariate of Great Britain and Ireland* 3 (August 2007): 3–14. Exarchate of the Ecumenical Patriarchate: Archdiocese of Orthodox Parishes of Russian Tradition in Western Europe and later on the website of the Orthodox Peace Fellowship.

How is it possible for a man to suffer 38 years of paralysis sitting outside the Temple day after day unnoticed by worshippers, priests and Levites serving and all those rushing to the waters of the pool of Bethesda in hopes of being healed themselves? (John 5:1–15). When the afflicted one is asked by Jesus the critical diagnostic question, "Do you want to be healed?" his plaintive reply says it all: "I have no person." Indeed, by being invisible to humanity — both the educated, wealthy, religious elite as well as the community of other suffering ones seeking healing themselves — whatever else plagued this man, he was further paralyzed and demoralized by the trauma of depersonalization. He had been so severely 'otherized' by his afflictions that his humanity had become invisible to his community. One who is invisible to others in this way soon begins to suffer the psychic numbing of post traumatic stress, gradually becoming invisible even to himself.

This kind of society-inflicted trauma of depersonalization, on top of the physical and psychic suffering that marginalized persons already experience due to personal trauma, economic hardship, and mental and physical illness, is a function of the symptoms of collective dissociation and psychic numbing of what I call post-traumatic spiritual disorder which afflicts society. Self-medicating with food, fashion, drugs, information, television, video gaming and various other forms of spectator entertainment, including using religion as yet another commodity to serve egoistic purposes,[2] can all be symptomatic of spiritual captivity to various passions that dull and weaken our heart's responsiveness to 'the least of these' among us and within us.

This kind of spiritual beguilement manifesting collectively at the systemic level and seen as normal is the most prevalent undiagnosed and untreated pastoral care problem of our age. Unless these systemic injustices within society are recognized as being integral to

---

[2] J. MacDonald, *Thieves in the Temple: The Christian Church and the Selling of the American Soul* (New York: Basic Books, 2010).

the etiology of human suffering, and therefore relevant to the gnosology and treatment of pastoral care and counseling, then both religion and psychotherapy are too easily privatized and end up serving those very forces that dehumanize persons. Injustice normalized, whether as an ordinary characteristic of society or by being seen purely as being a function of individual 'illness' fails to identify the immense role of the 'powers and principalities' that, like inner *logismoi* on the intrapsychic level, shape national character, world view and at times even possess nations in periods of stress and conflict by way of systemic influences.

The people who ignore the suffering man in this New Testament account all suffer invisible spiritual blindness and paralysis themselves which they do not recognize. They cannot see the glory of God shining forth in a human being, because his suffering is a stigma that renders him invisible. He is not *relevant* to their lives, except as someone whose poverty, illness and pain are *acceptable casualties* which permit things to go on as usual. If he were actually seen, conscience would demand at least a personal response and a change in society so that it is no longer acceptable to lose members of the community in this way. Where the effort, creativity and sacrifice to change things is feared, we turn 'a blind eye' to such suffering in our society just as they did in theirs.

HIV infection, people with convictions and jail time, homelessness, psychotic disorders, PTSD (especially in our veterans) and not being a member of the dominant gender, culture, sexual orientation, age, race or simply being without sufficient capital, have the power to render people invisible to society and, therefore, vulnerable to further traumatization.

The child slave trade, which indirectly serves the interests of large corporations seeking cheap labor overseas without being responsible for the true cost, is an unfortunate and alarming example. In 2000, Americans spent 13 billion dollars enjoying the pleasure of 3.3 billion pounds of chocolate without being aware of the fact that the majority of the cocoa beans used to make it were grown in West African countries from beans harvested by child slave labor under inhumane conditions. What makes it possible for this atrocity (which few would tolerate in our own families and which would be against the laws of our own country) to remain hidden behind warm and fuzzy familiar brand names like M&M's and Nestle's cocoa? How can we knowingly continue to receive Hershey's 'kisses' without taking steps to require corporations to assume responsibility for ensuring that fair trade regulations provide for humane working conditions for those who harvest the cocoa beans? By conveniently turning a blind eye to these children's suffering in order to be able to pay less for chocolate, not holding our manufacturers accountable by something as simple as selective purchases,[3] we are in effect aiding and abetting our economic system to succeed based on exploitation. By plucking the fruit of cheap slave labor from the forbidden tree of human misery, corporations act as our proxies to ignore these suffering persons while claiming to be creating economic growth in impoverished African nations. Incredibly,

> *researchers estimate there are more slaves in the world today than there were four hundred years ago* (my italics). Numbers are now reaching over twenty-seven million. Approximately 284,000 of these are children working on cocoa farms with machetes and pesticides. Parents sell their children to traffickers sincerely believing their children will find honest work ... Production companies like Hershey, Nestle, and Mars contract with local governments and militia groups to purchase cocoa beans. Local governments and militia groups turn to local farmers and tax them in order to make a profit with the production companies. Local farmers, being taxed by the government hire cheap labor to make ends meet. This act results in children being trafficked into slavery ... $150 a year and a bicycle was all one fam-

---

[3] There are chocolates, such as 'Divine' and other brands, which evidence 'fair trade,' indicating they have taken steps to ensure humane working conditions.

ily needed to sign on the dotted line. Their child was shipped to Cote d'Ivoire where his only reward was not getting beaten with a bicycle chain. Aly reported having to work whenever the sun was up and being locked into crowded, poorly ventilated rooms at night. He often had nightmares about dying in the cocoa fields. "Though he had worked countless days harvesting cocoa pods — 400 of which are needed to make a pound of chocolate — Aly Diabate has never tasted the finished product. The Global Exchange website cites him as telling the press, "I don't know what chocolate is."[4]

This can be said to reflect the *de facto* state of spiritual beguilement of individual persons in the culture who are not living by conscience on a daily basis.

THE TRUE MEASURE OF A NATION'S SOUL. Research suggests that accruing wealth in and of itself does not stimulate conscience, but just the reverse.[5] If the true measure of a nation's soul is

---

[4] B. Owen, "Jesus vs. Willy Wonka: Supply and Demand," *The Bridge* (July 2010). Cf. Julie Clawson, *Everyday Justice: The Global Impact of Our Daily Choices* (Downers Grove, IL: IVP Books, 2009), 53–56, 58–59, 71, 73. Global Exchange Company, "Fair Trade Chocolate: The Sweet Solution to Abusive Child Labor and Poverty" (online: http://web.archive.org/web/20070208142507rn_1/www.globalexchange.org/campaigns/fairtrade/cocoa/); "Fair Trade: Economic Action to Create a Just Global Economy for Farmers and Artisans" (online: http://www.greenamericatoday.org/programs/fair-trade/whattoknow/index.cfm).

[5] "Psychological tests in nearly 70 countries show that values cluster together in remarkably consistent patterns. Those who strongly value financial success, for example, have less empathy, stronger manipulative tendencies, a stronger attraction to hierarchy and inequality, stronger prejudices towards strangers and less concern about human rights and the environment. Those who have a strong sense of self-acceptance have more empathy and a greater concern about human rights, social justice and the environment. These values suppress each other: the stronger someone's extrinsic aspirations, the weaker his or her intrinsic goals. T. Dyson, "The Values of Everything," http://www.monbiot.com/archives/2010/10/11/the-values-of-everything/; for comprehensive data underlying this, cf. T. Crompton, "Common Cause: The Case for Working With

not to be found in the degree of its military strength or its economic and technological progress, but in its moral fortitude and quality of life shown forth in the capacity and willingness to care for its own and others in the world, so they can lead vital meaningful lives, where do we so-called 'first world' nations stand?

According to God's provisioning for ancient Israel in the law of Jubilee, economic inequities are self-corrected every 50 years[6] so that all God's people would remain equally blessed by God's gifts given to them all. Provision was made for freedom of initiative and creativity among those who were capable and motivated to increase their holdings as well as for the poor and the stranger and those who fell behind in hard times. Could it be that the increasing "degree of class differences today is wrong in the same sense that Lincoln believed slavery was wrong because it deprives billions of people of the ability to participate fully in society and to realize themselves as individuals"?[7]

Stigma and invisibility stemming from societal dissociation renders persons unworthy of the full energy, creativity and attention that would arise if these were seen "as part of our family." Raising questions about the relationship between the *status quo* and a kind of lukewarm Christianity aligned with culture have always proven difficult and dangerous for those that do.[8] From the Eastern Orthodox perspective, we live in a Theocentric world based on conscience awakened in the heart through relationship with God rather than a

---

Our Values," September 2010. http://assets.wwf.org.uk/downloads/common_cause_report.pdf.

[6] Cf. D. Kraybill, *The Upside Down Kingdom* (Pennsylvania: Herald Press, 1978) for explanation of the "Year of Jubilee" and how Jesus affirmed the economic intent of Jubilee which was to ensure the sharing of God's wealth among all the people, balancing freedom to provide for oneself and one's family as well as for the stranger.

[7] R. Bellah, R. Madsen, W. Sullivan, A. Swidler, and S. Tipton, *Habits of the Heart Individualism and Commitment in American Life*. Updated edition (Berkeley: University of California Press, 1996), xxxiv.

[8] Cf. R. Inchausti, *Subversive Orthodoxy: Outlaws, Revolutionaries, and Other Christians in Disguise* (Michigan: Brazos Press, 2005).

post-enlightenment, human-centered world based on reason alone and the meanings created by human beings. A person or a country is not free when it acts individualistically on its own self-will without recognizing an objective duty to life and to God.

Questioning the privileges of any dominant culture and its relationship to marginalized populations within it is analogous to the false self of an individual ego being in dialogue with and questioned by the 'unthought known' of the dissociated, marginalized, mute and paralyzed parts of one's own self as occurs in psychotherapy and in repentance. Both these processes require a willingness to be mindful of and bear the tensions and fear of change that are part of every intentional movement away from the homeostasis of captivity and the mechanisms of self-protective egoism and the characterological defenses. The kind of differentiation of living systems toward second order change of enhanced co-creative mutuality and intimacy welcomed as the holy grail of every marriage and family therapist, always comes at the price of enduring some disorder and confusion in transit between the two.

Guilt-induced first order changes of making efforts to 'help needy persons,' which do not really change the system that produces them, fail to grasp the mystery of the relationship, as with Abraham and Sarah, in which the host becomes the guest. Hospitality offered becomes hospitality received. Apart from this depth, 'philanthropy' is more of an attempt to ensure that the 'helper' is not really affected by the person as one who is equally beloved to God and whose problems are intimately related to one's own and which may be a result of some of the structures which ensure the continuation of one's own privileged status. Elements of co-suffering love[9] and pain of heart[10] are

---

[9] Cf. A. Sopko, *For a Culture of Co-Suffering Love: The Theology of Archbishop Lazar Puhalo* (California: Archive Publications, 2004), 141.

[10] This is a clear theme in Elder Paisios' *With Pain of Heart for Contemporary Man* (2008) and *Spiritual Awakening*, Vols. I–II of Spiritual Counsels (Greece: Holy Monastery of Evangelist John the Theologian) as well as the books of Archimandrite Sophrony: *His Life Is Mine* (Crestwood, NY: St. Vladimir's Semi-

often missing from such one-way human relationships, even those of a 'professional' nature.[11] The 'helper' is depersonalized to the degree to which he or she secretly views the other as an 'untouchable' and not woven of one piece of cloth with all the rest of life. In this way, both are deprived of the essential ingredient of life which Martin Buber calls 'confirmation' of one's humanity, which occurs only to the degree each person is affected by the other through recognition and repeated discoveries of the shared life between them. Pastoral counseling is impossible without this kind of existential stance toward the other that is open to such encounters with the unknown country of Self, Other and God in all places and among all people on a daily basis. This is the nature of love.

The terrible irony, which occurs throughout the Gospels, is that when God's mercy healed people, like this invisible man, so that he could for the first time in 38 years walk and leap for joy among people, lo and behold, there was no celebration. As far as the most precious aspect of him was concerned, his humanity, the man remained just as invisible to the economic and religious elite as he was before. In the second century, St. Ireneos observed: "The glory of God is a human being fully alive." He through whom the love and glory of God now shone forth was not welcomed back into community after he had become alive. He was not noticed for having come alive, but only as one who was doing something unlawful in that society — carrying his squalid mat — the place of his 38-year invisible paralysis, on the Sabbath day which was against the laws of expressing religious piety. This is the kind of upside-down straining-at-a-gnat-and-swallowing-a-camel-situation in which the laws God

---

nary Press, 1977); *And We Shall See Him as He Is* (Essex: Stavropegic Monastery of St. John the Baptist, 1988); *St. Silouan the Athonite* (Essex: Stavropegic Monastery of St. John the Baptist, 1991); C. Yiannitsiotis, *With Elder Porphyrios: A Spiritual Child Remembers* (Athens: Holy Convent of the Transfiguration of the Savior, 2001) and others. The Orthodox approach is one of entering into prayer and love for the world as the fruit of relationship with Christ.

[11] Cf. A. Sopko, *For a Culture of Co-Suffering Love: The Theology of Archbishop Lazar Puhalo* (California: Archive Publications, 2004), 141.

gives humankind to ensure human life and well-being end up serving the forces that deny that life. The spirit that is behind this misuse of religion is that same one that eventually leads to the Lord's own suffering and murder "in the least of these" over and over again, and always 'according to law,' wielded by forces of religious correctness and societal uprightness.

When we, as the privileged, power-possessing, religious and educational elite of 21ˢᵗ century, fail to see the glory of God shining through the humanity of those beloved to God who are hidden behind the faces of poverty and disease, whether they are Orthodox, Muslim, Jewish, Hindu, Buddhist, Bushman, Lakota or other form, we fail to see Christ.

Because this man came from the 'wrong side of the tracks,' was born of seemingly low birth, and was without 'a proper education,' like Jesus Himself, he was accursed. The life and joy of God's glory shining through him was invisible to those for whom life is not life, but a trust in the manmade appearance of propriety legitimized by worldly power, success and righteousness. Jesus, like the blind, deaf and lame whom He loved and healed in His ministry, was 'otherized' by the same societal forces whose power and security were threatened by His aliveness and His vision of God's love reaching beyond the boundaries of society into the marginalized and outcast. It is the same in our time and in every age — a conflict between worldly power and the call of the Holy Spirit. We have within us these same forces at work rendering us blind, deaf and paralyzed with respect to the Lord in our midst.

How we begin to look and listen with the eyes and ears of the heart open to the leading of the Holy Spirit remains the core issue and primary training ground for people seeking to offer pastoral care and counseling. It is about learning to love as God loves and about seeing that justice is ultimately a result of entering into this love beyond the mechanical paralyzing polarities which always lead to stalemate in the public sphere just as they do in chronic marital impasses. Pastoral care and counseling cannot be simply an activity of professional psychotherapists in a consulting room or priests hearing confessions and serving liturgies in the church, though both are essential, vital and necessary. Nor can spiritual warfare be seen simply as an exercise of personal vigilance in one's inner world, though this is also essential. There are also systemic factors that endanger persons and these must be challenged and resisted by the awakening of the conscience that reaches to action in the public sphere.

A good bit of our reluctance to interfere with the *status quo* has to do with the expectation of personal loss in the realms of power and economics, just as it did in Jesus' time when 10% of the people had 90% of the wealth. Social theorist Oliver C. Cox, early in the 20th century, pointed to the U.S. history of slavery, arguing persuasively that Christianity was hijacked early on in America in the service of capitalism and this has not yet been corrected in spite of electing the first biracial president. The American way of doing business required keeping the full humanity of African Americans invisible so that they could be exploited as a labor commodity for the purpose of increasing profits.[12] A bloody civil war was fought over this, which to this day still is not recognized as being primarily about this economic and humanitarian conflict.[13]

Exploitation of people of color has continued less visibly in the subsequent century, both domestically and in so-called 'developing' nations all over the world. Multinational corporate interests supported by lifestyle choices and spending habits are in many cases directly

---

[12] Katie Cannon, "Racism and Economics: The Perspective of Oliver C. Cox," in *The Public Vocation of Christian Ethics* (New York: Pilgrim Press, 1986).

[13] B. Smith, "Civil War's 150th anniversary stirs debate on race," *Columbus Ledger/Enquirer*, Section D Sunday, Dec. 12, 2010. "A few weeks before the first shots of the war were fired at Fort Sumter in Charleston Harbor, Confederate Vice President Alexander Stephens called slavery "the immediate cause of the later rupture and present revolution." But as the war progressed the Confederate government shifted its rationale to states' rights because (Jefferson) Davis knew neither England nor other third powers would support the South in a war to preserve slavery." Intellectual struggles to define history along these lines has continued since then.

contrary to the values Jesus lived and advocated, placing profits and comfort ahead of the welfare of the community, but it takes continuing ascetical efforts to uncover this and an inner vigil supported by prayer to stay in front of it in such a way that it begins to change our thinking, 'seeing' and finally our way of living in terms of our daily choices and modes of consumption. This has to do with living for eternity within time; awareness of our own and everyone else's mortality in the presence of God in such a way that we act with greater mercy and tenderness toward all living beings because we are aware of the fragile gift of our shared vulnerability.

What happens when Christians ask ourselves who in our Church and in the larger culture is invisible and what is my responsibility for this? Who occupies our jails and are homeless in our cities and why?[14] How do Christians get used to rendering some of God's people invisible under the law for centuries at a time? What is my responsibility for having benefited from this, if only indirectly? What happens when the Church has sacrificed its spiritual dialogue and has become a mere echo of political and economic powerbrokers, a form of politico-speak or, on the other hand, has become privatized and 'pietized' to the point that individual spirituality is more separate from the state than the Church itself—becoming a kind of spiritual capitalism in which I seek only my own private religious transformation without regard for what is happening to my community and others in the world?

Alexis de Tocqueville in 1835 suggested that America would eventually produce a new kind of tyranny in the world — a "democratic despotism which would be guilty of genocide against indigenous people ... owing to deep white supremacist practices of the majority."[15] Ironically, Adolph Hitler actually got the idea of concentration camps to eliminate the 'Jewish problem' from his discovery of how the Amer-

---

[14] A third of the homeless in the United States are our forgotten veterans whose suffering caused by protecting American interests is now forgotten by those who have benefited from their sacrifices.

[15] Cornell West, *Democracy Matters* (New York: Penguin Press, 2004), 45.

icans did virtually the same thing with our 'solution' to the Indian 'problem.' Such is only possible where we confuse the love relationship with our Common Creator with ideological religious, cultural or nationalistic appropriations, as in Jesus' day where we fail to see God's mercy and our responsibility extends beyond the confines of our faith and tribe and nation, to all God's children everywhere.

When he was not seen as an outcast Himself, Jesus was repeatedly criticized for His care for extending God's love and care beyond Israel to strangers and outcasts, but He knew a secret: "As you have done unto the least of these, you have done unto Me." The human race is one in Christ. We are saved together. We fall alone. In many ways, it is precisely these angels of otherness in our midst who have the power to awaken conscience in us and invite life-saving philanthropy flowing from the heart, but *only if we can tolerate seeing them.* I used to think of the Gerasene demoniac as a poor deranged person *different than myself.* Now I realize *my name is also Legion for we are many.* I am not merely a two-faced hypocrite, but a multiply divided person who suffers from both spiritual and mental fragmentation. I am blind and deaf to the extent that I think I can see and hear others simply through my own experience instead of taking pains to discover how they experience *themselves.* I remain divided to the extent that I rejoice in feeling physically well and monetarily solvent while failing to observe the paralysis that afflicts my hands when it comes to acts of loving charity and kindness in sharing my assets, both material and spiritual, with the everyday world around me. My life and actions consistently fail to demonstrate that everything belongs to God who freely gives everything to the entire community and invites and hopes for each of us to do the same with what we have received. For this, I need repentance.

As an Orthodox Christian, I am invited to carefully attend to my inner world and conduct spiritual warfare with respect to the *logismoi* or 'thoughts' upon which my attention feeds that shape my reality. But what about the more insidious *logismoi* in the form of public opinions and history that shape opinions in the world? A spiritual battle is ongoing in this arena as well. This too requires vigilance and spiritual discernment to identify and dissolve the dissociation and self-medicating by the passions including cultural idolatries that are part of post-traumatic *spiritual* disorder. One of the more insidious ways we delude ourselves is through the history we write that insulates us from the actual facts that might otherwise move us to take action. This too is a pastoral care issue requiring diagnosis and treatment.

T**HE PROBLEM OF HISTORY.** "Those who do not know history are doomed to repeat it" is one of those shibboleths before which the mind suddenly retreats in docile acceptance as if it were unquestionable. The reality is that history is often written to make sure that people do *not* know what actually happened precisely so that we *will* repeat it. This is why the writing of history cannot be regarded as merely an academic exercise of citing objective facts, but rather as a type of moral and humanitarian enquiry.[16] Does the historian make crimes against humanity visible and support the struggle for justice and community building or does it serve some other purpose? History written by victors rather than the defeated tends to be a kind of 'designer history' serving the interests of the dominant culture by defining normality, depriving certain persons of their voices and rendering crimes and exploitation against them invisible. In democracies, control of the people happens not at the point of a gun, but by *manufactured* consent through manipulation of history and the media[17] and through dependency on and obedience to the increas-

---

[16] "The historian's distortion is more than technical, it is ideological: it is released into a world of contending interests, where any chosen emphasis supports (whether the historian means to or not) some kind of interest, whether economic or political or racial or national or sexual." H. Zinn, *A People's History of the U.S.* (New York: HarperCollins, 2003), 8.

[17] Cf. N. Chomsky, *Necessary Illusions: Thought Control in Democratic Societies* (Boston: South End Press, 1989); N. Chomsky, *Media Control, Second Edition: The Spectacular Achievements of Propaganda* (New York: Open Media Series, 2002); E. Herman & N. Chomsky, *Manufacturing Consent: The Political Economy of the Mass Media* (New York: Pantheon, 2002).

ing efficiency of depersonalizing bureaucracies[18] at the expense of
individual conscience.

The Holy Spirit supports people in tolerating the discomfort of
self-examination, to bear responsibility for wrongdoing, and seeking
to make amends. In the same way, it takes a critical mass within the
community responsive to the Spirit and accountable to one another
in order to 'see' trauma; to be responsible *now* for the history of what
happened *then* so as to learn from it and not repeat the mistakes. This
is spiritual warfare on the communal level and is vitally important
as what goes on in the interior of each person, requiring ongoing
vigilance, continual repentance and sustained dialogue. Without it,
a collective 'false memory' is implanted and cultivated by being repeated and taught to a new generation of students, which influences
and shapes the meaning of their present. To the extent that history
avoids engaging the voices of the oppressed and those who read it fail
to examine it with conscience as God's call to justice now, as did Jesus
and the prophets, such history impedes healing by inducing soul-
numbing denial that blocks communal repentance as a nation just as
it does for perpetrators who remain in denial on the individual level.

What I am calling 'false *history* syndrome' signifies the misrep-
resentation or omission of the historical record for the purpose of
avoiding critical re-examination that promotes justice. This avoidance is symptomatic of the collective psychic numbing of the larger
problem of Post Traumatic Spiritual Disorder that afflicts nations and
the faith communities institutionally most beholding to them. Communal acceptance of historical disinformation in the face of injuries
that go unseen puts everyone at greater risk, including those whose
wealth and power on the surface seems to protect them from it. What
happens on the collective level to deny reality and impede justice very
closely parallels what happens on an individual basis. Healing from
trauma is important for the community as a whole, because, as with

---

[18] R. L. Rubenstein, *The Cunning of History: The Holocaust and the American
Future* (New York: Harper & Row, 1975).

individuals, it makes it less likely that victims will visit similar harm on others. The dissociative elements of not knowing, not seeing and not feeling our history accurately — personally and as a community of nations — and the cost we pay for it, is the theme of my reflections.

G OD'S WORLD OR MINE? Cain and Abel personify a classic spiritual struggle in which one part of humanity sacrifices another because of being unwilling to share living space. In the historical account provided in Genesis, it is the ground who cries out to God with the spilled blood of its voiceless victim and God who calls Cain to account as a result. History is tied to the earth in a way that evokes a response from God. This is often the case with severe brutality. It seems that 'only God sees' what is too great a devastation for human witnesses to bear. Only one out of twelve of Jesus' Apostles could bear the pressures involved in being with Him to the bitter end.

Murder of one's neighbor is a form of self-murder, of suicide, insomuch as the Hebrew underlying Leviticus 19:18, "You must love your neighbor as yourself" means literally your neighbor *as being your own self.* This part of the story provides commentary on the history of tensions between indigenous hunter-gatherer communities who saw themselves as belonging to the earth as given to all by the 'Great Spirit' and those who presumed to *own* and use the earth, justifying this privilege by referencing a *Divine mandate,* even when it entailed the destruction of whole peoples, an ingredient implicit to the history of colonialism such that it is argued "to be in any way an apologist for colonialism is to be an active proponent of genocide."[19]

The history of the destruction of the spiritual descendents of Abel includes all those peoples deliberately and unknowingly sacrificed for colonialist expansion of the gold-seeking spiritual descendents of Cain. Their unheard cries and spilled blood reach God who walks upon the earth, searching out the lost and the oppressed. God

---

[19] W. Churchill, cited in D. Jacobs (ed.), *Unlearning the Language of Conquest* (Austin: University of Texas Press, 2005), 222.

is the Author of history written from the standpoint of victims who are the 'least of these', each of whom is ultimately revealed as being God's own son or daughter. Seen through the history of Judaism and Christianity, these all have a part in the sacrifice of the "Lamb slain from the foundation of the world" (Rev. 13:8), which both reveals and condemns injustice as well as opens the door to reconciling inimical communities at the cost of bearing witness to the Truth in His own blood which, as remembered in the Divine Liturgy, is "on behalf of all and for all."

God, as both King and sacrificial Lamb, is always on the side of the oppressed. Both Mosaic and subsequent Ecclesiastical New Testament history are written from a liberation perspective. When Jesus stands up to read from the Isaiah scroll in His hometown of Nazareth, the people are at first enthralled by His articulate reading of the Scriptures. Religion as 'history' and 'ritual' ensuring the *status quo* is comfortable and familiar. But when the people begin to realize that Jesus is entering history as a threshold over which to pass into God's liberating, community-making activity *now,* as a call to action sharing God's heart, of experiencing the world through God's eyes, and of loving the world with God's love, then as they say in the deep South, he has "gone from preachin' to meddlin.'" Meddlin' can get you lynched.

Why? Because it threatens the power and the privilege of those who use history to avoid being *responsible* for current injustices; to avoid repentance and argue as did Cain after murdering his brother, "Am I my brother's keeper?" (Gen. 4:9). Why does the CIA routinely provide funding and philanthropy for prominent professors to do research and write essays that back U.S. policy?[20] Can the same forces go so far as to bring about the assassination of our own president if he moves too far from American military and corporate 'interests' in support of global interests and self-determination, while creating a

---

[20] Cf. D. Gibbs, "The Question of Whitewashing in American History and Social Science," in D. Jacobs, *Unlearning the Language of Conquest* (Austin: University of Texas Press, 2005).

falsified cover up 'history' in order to mollify an otherwise outraged populace?[21] This is ideological strategic warfare conducted in the public and intellectual arena. History is not neutral. It has a valence and serves either to discover the truth and awaken conscience or to put it to sleep with comforting lies and so reflects the struggle in every human heart on a daily basis. Healing and empowerment on the individual, personal level is connected to healing collectively, and we can learn a great deal from examining this connection closely.

WHEN BELIEVING BECOMES SEEING. A woman who was raped developed PTSD symptoms months after her rape when she learned that her rapist had killed another rape victim. Why? Because she re-interpreted the history (memory) of her rape as having been "a life-threatening attack." "*The critical ingredient that makes an event traumatic is the subjective assessment by victims of how threatened and helpless they feel.*"[22] History is meaning-making. When I believe it, it becomes so, and as the mind goes, so goes the body. PTSD symptoms are always experienced here and now, even though the original events that precipitated them occurred in the past. It is the new meaning evoked by the rewriting and subsequent believing of that history that creates destructive changes for the person in the present. History can create trauma where there was none and can heal it by the mere fact of reworking the *meaning* of the event through a retelling of it and engaging it in the present.

In this way, a man, who was gently and tenderly sexually molested by his mother over a period of years on a weekly basis, found healing 40 years later as his story was told for the first time after he had been mandated to therapy for boundary violations in an otherwise successful military and industrial career. It had come to light unconsciously and destructively through his acting out the untold

---

[21] Cf. J. Douglass, *JFK and the Unspeakable: Why He Died and Why It Matters* (New York: Touchstone, 2008).

[22] Van der Kolk, McFarlane, Weisaeth, *Traumatic Stress* (New York: Guilford Press, 1996), 6.

story in some compulsive behavior. He began to find healing and an emotionally available new life by courageously revisiting the original scenes of the childhood victimization and reworking the meaning of the events that had shaped his beliefs at the time, incarnating the pain and thereby honoring the voiceless cry of the child-victim still alive and mute within his nervous system. Atonement with his dissociated visceral self occurred slowly as the man embraced and incarnated those unheard cries of pain, rage and sadness lying dormant in the ground of his own flesh. God heard his cries in the presence of another human being. It is never too late to redeem the ravages of the past, but this can only be done *now* by facing the truth of what has been denied, not merely intellectually but embodied and witnessed in community through dialogue with others. History is replete with the voices of victims crying out from the ground waiting to be heard.

This is why the telling of the history of God's people, including all crimes against humanity, such as slavery, holocaust and other forms of collective genocide, is so vital and must be retold and witnessed within the community who enter into it afresh as a kind of spiritual plumb line and call to action in the present. Where this does not occur, the seed of the original crime continues to produce the fruits of further destruction wherever it is planted, and God's word remains dormant until activated by personal encounter. 'Doing' history is a form of spiritual warfare on the collective level as much as is mental prayer within the inner being of each person and each involves a relationship of dialogue. They are two dimensions of the same indissoluble link between the Spirit (ontological) and the flesh (existential) given the divine gift of free *choice*: the true coin of the spiritual realm, e.g. "I set before you this day life and death. Blessing and curse, therefore, *choose* life so that you and your descendents may live" (Deut. 30:19). It is only when the body confirms the truth of the words, that feelings appear and people are set free. In the same way, it is only when the body politic is willing to privilege and engage the voices of the oppressed that justice can emerge as the foundation for building authentic community.

There is both a personal and a larger sociopolitical context for 'seeing' trauma. What if, like a person afraid of grief and shame, the culture as a whole is not ready and/or able to 'see' the event and avoids the truth. What then? Sexual abuse of children was well documented during the second half of the 19ᵗʰ century in France. In 1859, French psychiatrist Briquet made the first connection between symptoms of 'hysteria' (somatization and dissociation) and childhood histories of trauma.[23] Interestingly, as soon as this occurred, people like Alfred Fournier objected that the memory was being falsified. At the time, he called this 'pseudologica phantastica,' which meant that the traumatized children were falsely accusing their parents of incest; they were only *imagining* their injuries. Pseudologica phantastica represented societal resistance to seeing the victimization. It was just too painful and would require too much work to bring justice. So the answer was to blame the victim, even if it was France's own children. Collectively, this is the same as avoiding repentance on the personal level. Maintaining the *illusion* of propriety and righteousness of the oppressors is valued over protecting the victims from abuse. This is a theme that repeats itself over and over in history and is no different in the 21ˢᵗ century than it was in first-century Palestine during Jesus' time or 5,000–6,000 years earlier with Cain and Abel. It is a denial and abandonment of Christ wherever and whenever it occurs.

POST-TRAUMATIC *SPIRITUAL* DISORDER. On the individual personal level, the core issue in post-traumatic stress is the inability of the soul to integrate the reality of particular experiences resulting in psychic numbing, hyperarousal and repetitive intrusion of the trauma in the form of unintegrated images, behaviors, feelings, physiological states, and interpersonal relationships. The experience of helplessness at the core is a kind of biochemical fixative that stabilizes traumatic stress in the autonomic nervous system like a photograph that does not change so long as the victims are voiceless and the community re-

---

[23] Ibid., 49.

fuses to *see* any alternative. Shame and the attack on character resulting from helplessness in the face of victimization dismembers a person. Silence of the community in the face of victimization of a person
or a people, in effect demoralizes or discourages them, by attacking at
its root their sense of belovedness, cutting them off from self, others
and God in the depths of the heart which is frozen in mute helplessness. This dismemberment is the spiritual core of the injury evoking
despair, the most dangerous of the so-called seven deadly sins, because it paralyzes freedom of choice; the place of *personhood* from
which the active encouragers of hope, faith and love arise.

The strongest predictor of whether someone will develop PTSD
is whether or not they dissociate during a trauma. Interestingly, the
rate of total amnesia following traumatic experiences is three times
as high for Hispanics and two times as high for African-Americans as
for Caucasians.[24] Could this have anything to do with who has power
and control in society; with who already feels helpless because of systemic cultural circumstances and historical fallout? Like the nurse in
her tent who later discovers news of her near death, victims of aggression are tempted to dissociate in the context of a society for whom
they remain invisible, exploited and constantly under threat.

Racial profiling and equating economic class with divine blessing
and/or failing to consider the impact of arbitrary privilege inherited
by white citizens is a clear signal to people of color that they are more
likely to be injured again; and if they are, that no one will respond because they are not visible. *They do not matter* except as a commodity
for exploitation by the dominant group that has dehumanized them
for the purpose of using them and because they are reminders of how
suspect is some of the foundation upon which the privilege of a few
is built. When there is a clear history of exploitation for centuries that
does not figure prominently into current historical analysis, this in itself constitutes a factor engendering traumatic stress. In the same way

---

[24] Elliot & Briere, "Posttraumatic stress associated with delayed recall of sexual
abuse: A general population study," *Journal of Traumatic Stress* 8 (1995): 629–647.

as the victim of incest is injured again by the denial of her perpetrator when he is confronted, if there is no validation, it is more difficult for the victim to persevere in her recovery from the damage of her past. She may regress and be thrown into doubt about her own experience. *"Did it really happen? Was I at fault?"* This is why public memory of every crime against humanity in any form is so vital to identify. It is invisibility that helps make such crimes possible in the first place, but it is a peculiar kind of invisibility — very public and yet hidden at the same time. Hitler's so-called 'final solution' to the Jewish 'problem' was made possible because first having had their citizenship revoked without any public outcry, the Jews became invisible from a purely bureaucratic standpoint. That is, since the state did not recognize them legally as citizens, they were not protected by law and could be imprisoned and exterminated without having broken any laws and, hence, without remorse of conscience.[25] How do we explain public silence and passive compliance in the face of this and other atrocities?

I see the central dynamic of Christian faith as the overwhelming impact on the human heart of the encounter of the created order with Uncreated Divine love manifesting in and through Jesus Christ on behalf of all creation. This encounter is traumatic for both God and humanity, yet God risks everything in order to create a marriage between heaven and earth. I am using the signifier of post-traumatic spiritual disorder to refer to the range of reactions resulting from this encounter in which we are passive witnesses, victims and perpetrators in the denial, rejection, torment and murder of Christ as well as beneficiaries of the gift of God's eternal love, mercy and forgiveness through which we are invited to become co-creative partners in dialogue with God. More than being about attaining personal well-being and salvation, the revelation of the Christian mystery is that humanity is involved in a struggle along with Christ, as were His first disciples, for the life of the world. Just as Christ fights for the world, for love,

---

[25] Cf. R. L. Rubenstein, *The Cunning of History: The Holocaust and the American Future* (New York: Harper & Row, 1975).

facing the unfathomable abyss of resistance He encountered and faced
in His prayers in Gethsemane and later in His suffering and death, He
in effect faces this repeatedly over and over in the lives of all persons
throughout history, "for as you have done unto the least of these you
have done unto Me."

Our spiritual 'disorder' reflects both developmental (spiritual) im-
maturity and the immense potential for relationship with God that is
ours, as well as the state of fragmentation, dissociation and captivity
to the passions into which we fall in response to the enormity of this
lifelong challenge. The invitation of love, like a moth to a flame, is both
inviting and terrifying, for we sense that the way Christ bids us who
would encounter the world through Him to 'come and see' ultimately
evokes the prescient observation of a monk who said, "Those who
do not love are dead, and those who do love will be put to death." To
know God the Father's heart, one must travel in the direction God
the Son goes. Where love does not reach, life, healing, growth and
redemption do not occur. Recalling St. Gregory the Theologian's observation referring to the dogma of the Theanthropos and salvation,
it remains true that "whatever is not assumed, is not healed." We can
think of this as a theological 'parallel process' with regard to healing
trauma on the psychological level. It is equally true that whatever is
not assumed, whatever is not consciously experienced viscerally and
somatically with mindfulness and brought into the meaning of verbal-
ized form, cannot be integrated. Spiritually, it is the same. If the *nous*
does not descend into the heart, how can the body participate in the
energies of Grace? Flesh and blood on their own cannot reveal Christ.
Neither can desire. Or intellectual reasoning. The organ of the 'inner person of the heart' that experiences the Divine Energies appears
when the mind is in the heart and the heart is in the body. Trying to
encounter God by keeping these separate, we do bad theology, and it
is also bad therapy. Trauma dissociates. Eucharist re-members.

In post-traumatic spiritual disorder, the passions act like spiritual tranquilizers to dampen and disrupt the link between 'hearing'
the word of the Lord and 'doing' it. They swallow our attention like

Leviathans diverting the will through the pleasures of phantasia into alternative realities that separate energies of mind and body, like flint and steel, so that the heart is not sparked to action by the fire of the word landing on good soil. Christ stands knocking at the door of the heart with His word, waiting to be received on the throne, where as Lord and King, He can lead us into the battle of love for the fate of the world. Christ does not call us out of history to abandon the world for some kind of personal salvation that can be had for ourselves while letting the world go to hell, but deeper into the hell of the world with Him in order to help redeem it.[26] The throne of the heart belongs to Christ only when the usurper 'little i's' of personal egotism have found their proper place in the whole as servants, crucified for love so that "it is no longer egotism but Christ who lives in me" (Galatians 2:20), seeking to love the world as Christ loves me. Paradoxically, I become myself only in those moments when I am no longer interested in myself (decrease of characterological defenses), but rather in comprehending and serving the other. In these instances, I am no longer primarily concerned and driven by the need to manage the impressions people have of me, of projecting an image, but of obeying the Spirit who calls me to existential choice confirmed with action.

HEALING AND JUSTICE REQUIRE A COMMUNITY. Image-making and the fear of grief and loss that are connected with preservation of it, along with the reputation and the privilege's afforded by a successful career, can cause us to avoid the truth about ourselves in the effort to 'save face.' Even the late Dr. Sigmund Freud, founder of psychoanalysis, zealously defended a theory that emerged out of his own denial regarding the problem of sexual abuse of women because the Victorian society he lived in at the time was not ready to hear it, and his fear of rejection by his peers outweighed his desire to honor

---

[26] I am grateful to Dr. Jamie Moran, who powerfully articulates this in his passion writings entitled, "The Wound of Existence," which will be forthcoming in a Russian edition.

the truth. This human frailty underscores why, as Judith Herman, MD, in her classic volume *Trauma and Recovery*, has pointed out, a community witness is needed.

> The systematic study of psychological trauma depends on the support of a political movement. Indeed, whether such a study can be pursued or discussed in public is itself a political question. The study of war trauma becomes legitimate only in a context that challenges the sacrifice of young men in war. The study of trauma in sexual and domestic life becomes legitimate only in a context that challenges the subordination of women and children. Advances in the field occur only when they are supported by a political movement powerful enough to legitimate an alliance between investigators and patients and to counteract the ordinary social processes of silencing and denial. In the absence of strong political movements for human rights, the active process of bearing witness inevitably gives way to the active process of forgetting. Repression, dissociation, and denial are phenomena of social as well as individual consciousness."[27]

In Freud's case, under pressure of societal censure and rejection, he retracted his original theory that sexual abuse was the cause of 'hysteria' in his women patients, replacing it with the 'Oedipal' theory that it was the children's longing for the parents that created in their imagination memories of abuse by adults who should have protected them — blaming the victim again. His psychoanalytic work unwittingly compromised his patients' history by seeing it from the perspective of the abuser, and more than a half century later, the leading U.S. textbook on psychiatry (Kaplan, Friedman & Sadock, 1980) still appeared blind to women's reality stating that "incest happens to fewer than 1 in one million women and the impact is not particularly damaging." We now know the enormity of the problem as one out

---

[27] J. Herman, *Trauma and Recovery* (New York: Basic Books, 1992), 9.

of three women report sexual assault in childhood,[28] and the U.S. Justice Department estimates 250,000 children are sexually abused annually[29] while another three million children in the U.S. were reported abused and/or neglected.[30]

What happens on an individual level happens on the collective as well. Denial affects churches and nations, and it is much more difficult to get at because, as Dr. Herman points out, a critical mass of people is needed who are able to *tolerate seeing the problem as a problem*. This is one of the essential points of James Loewen's thesis in his book *Lies My Teacher Told Me* that systematically surveys history books used in American high schools. Ironically, the U.S. spends billions of dollars to ban and police mind-altering drugs, yet we let these mind-altering, character-deadening 'history' books pass without any problem, even though they are soul-dulling patriotic propaganda that do not help our children dig deep enough to find facts that invite wrestling with the ambiguities and moral issues that could help build their character, test their values and inspire in them a thirst for justice and a willingness to make sacrifices for it.

HISTORY AS A FORM OF DENIAL. Instead, in many instances, the same social forces that silenced Sigmund Freud keep our communities naively celebrating as hero's people like Christopher Columbus by ignoring or downplaying certain facts. In Harvard historian Sam Eliot Morison's 1954 book *Christopher Columbus Mariner,* to his credit, he includes the observation: "The cruel policy initiated by Columbus and pursued by his successors resulted in complete genocide." Yet, as contemporary historian Howard Zinn points out, the author's concluding summary provides a different emphasis for his readers, directing them away from critical moral analysis.

---

[28] D. Russell, *The Secret Trauma* (New York: Basic Books, 1986).
[29] McFarlane & van der Kolk, 1996, 38.
[30] National Victim Center Report, *Crime and victimization in America: Statistical Overview* (Arlington, VA, 1993).

> Columbus had his faults and his defects, but they were largely
> the defects of the qualities that made him great — his indomi-
> table will, his superb faith in God and in his own mission as the
> Christ-bearer to lands beyond the seas, his stubborn persistence
> despite neglect, poverty, and discouragement. But there was no
> flaw, no dark side to this most outstanding and essential of all
> his qualities — his seamanship.[31]

What is intended by the misdirection of saying there was "no dark
side" to his *seamanship* while ignoring the litany of glaring blas-
phemies and savage cruelty of his leadership recorded in his own
published journals that evidence the malevolent dark side to him as
a '*Christ-bearer*'? Like a movie director, the angle of the historian's
camera directs the reader's attention. Jewels of truth are then placed
in the setting of a summary that trumpets the glory of seamanship,
effectively denying weight to the enormous atrocities that point to
the dark side of Columbus's character and intentions which surely
reflect the rapacious imperialism of European culture at the time,
having betrayed Christ for Mammon and now, like the Prophet Jonah, finding itself in the belly of a Trojan horse version of Christianity foisted on the natives to their near utter destruction. Cultural genocide is only briefly alluded to with a whisper, thus leading
the reader far afield from conscience and instead toward a cheap
religious-patriotic sentimentality that has no substance and purpose
other than to help readers find pleasure in contemplating an illusion that supports the mythical foundations of American culture. It
is like focusing on a slave's happiness in receiving an extra helping
of potatoes from the kindly slave master who rewards him for his
excellent blacksmith skills, all the while overlooking the great evil
of slavery itself! Such a spin throws water on the coals of conscience
that could have been ignited by critical examination of how these

---

[31] H. Zinn, *A People's History of the U.S.* (New York: HarperCollins Publishers,
2003), 8.

same colonialist policies are at work today keeping Americans blind and numb to our contemporary collective sins, which include continued militarization of the world through second rate arms selling; misrepresenting the *raison d'être* of continuing expansionist wars aimed at control of natural resources; and economic exploitation of labor throughout the third world, all under the overt auspices of democratization and human rights.

FACING INJUSTICE FROM THE GROUND UP. While it is true, as the late Rev. William Sloan Coffin observed, "All nations make decisions based on self-interest and then defend them in the name of morality,"[32] the test of a democracy is its capacity to engage in critical self-examination that supports ongoing justice making. (This is analogous to taking a moral inventory and making amends that is part of every 12 step program of recovery from addiction.) But, as with the cry of sexually abused children in 19th-century France, when self-examination threatens to call to account the larger hidden power structures and entrenched privilege that have been operating outside our own laws without accountability to the people, intense resistance arises.

The fight to arouse conscience and interest of the privileged and comfortable members of a society is almost always brought about from the ground up by the oppressed themselves banding together, rather than by those in power. It took 400 years to find enough critical mass to begin to change the effects of racial discrimination in America and only then, a hundred years after a bloody civil war fought largely over this issue, and the victims themselves began to organize and resist continued oppression at a sacrificial price that won over the 'silent' majority by activating their consciences.

Gaining the right to hold property and to vote in the American democracy, along with putting an end to the crime of woman abuse,

---

[32] Cited in C. West, *Democracy Matters: Winning the Fight against Imperialism* (New York: Penguin Press, 2004), 155.

was begun by women themselves challenging religiously justified, legally protected and socially entrenched male power and privilege permitting economic, political and sexual exploitation of women. The right of a man to beat his wife "as long as the stick was no thicker than his thumb" was protected by American and English law until the beginning of the twentieth century. There were no safehouses for women in the United States until the mid-1970's. Assault was not considered a crime, because it was 'domestic' — a justification not so different from permitting a slave master to punish and dominate the slaves he 'owned' in ways that society would not tolerate being done to a free white man, because they are seen as less than human.

It is our own heartlessness, self-indulgence, complacency and greed that permit us to write and passively accept innocuous, superficial, historical romances that do not stimulate critical examination and questioning for its meaning for us today. This has proved extremely difficult in the Church, which all too easily aligns with worldly power as well. A recent case in point is that until the early 1990's, Americans denied the fact that as many as 10% of our clergy were sexually abusing their own parishioners, violating their professional and faith covenants and the church hierarchy was covering it up. Literature in the clinical arena began to show up coterminous with lawsuits in the public arena, and more and more victims came forward to be heard now that the community was listening and money was at stake.

Like Freud, once having denied the truth our hearts know, having sold ourselves to lesser gods than the Living One who is the Creator of all peoples, it becomes inevitable that we live in various forms of psychological denial and rigidity in order to keep our sins hidden. This means the truth of our hearts is betrayed. Jesus said, "The sheep will not answer to anyone but the Master's voice." Thus, great effort is spent writing history imitating the master's voice, using religious justifications so we have the appearance of righteousness, but without its substance, 'religion without power,' as Timothy writes. The Truth sets us free, but only if it we risk choosing to fight for it and *live* it.

H ONORING VOICES FROM THE WILDERNESS. For those with ears to hear, the voice of God cries out most clearly from the unknown depths and most loudly from the voiceless dispossessed. Jesus of Nazareth was born in a forgotten, despised enclave of Galilee among the 'people of the land,' as they were called by Jerusalem's elite who owned 90% of the wealth of Israel at the time. Israelites were a subjugated people held in contempt by the Roman Empire which saw the Jews as a strange and insignificant people. Jerusalem's elite, in turn, saw the people of Galilee as "not worthy of being butchered."[33] They considered their women 'vermin.' The Apostle Luke was well aware of the irony of these tremendous discrepancies in political power and socioeconomic status when he wrote:

> *In the fifteenth year of the reign of Tiberius Caesar, Pontius Pilate being governor of Judea; and Herod being Tetrarch of Galilee, and his brother Philip tetrarch of the region of Ituraea and Trachonitis, and Lysanais Tetrarch of Abilene, in the high-priesthood of Annas and Caiphas ... the Word of God came to John, son of Zechariah,* **in the wilderness.**

To whom will the word come alive again in our time? And who will risk loss of power and privilege by speaking and fighting for it? There are multiple justice issues related to America's unconscious denial of the class elitism, virulent racism, economic exploitation and violence that continue to funnel people into our judicial and prison systems. America has more people incarcerated than any other country in the world with a disproportionate number of African American, Indians and Hispanic (not to mention mentally ill, whose numbers are increasing dramatically as funding for public mental health treatment dries up), again evidencing the inequities that remain from our legacy of materialism, discrimination and culturally genocidal practices.

Such injustices remain quietly ignored not only in our prisons, but in the backyards of forgotten crossroads in our country, such

---

[33] D. Kraybill, *The Upside-Down Kingdom* (Pennsylvania: Herald Press, 1978).

as in White Clay, Nebraska, where four liquor stores exist in an un-
incorporated 'town' of 18 people just outside the dry Lakota Pine
Ridge Reservation (which former President Bill Clinton described
as a "third world country" in America's heartland).[34] Ten thousand
cans of beer are sold in a single day to the impoverished Lakota people, whose genetic make-up puts them more at risk for alcoholism
than any people in the world. This slow genocide justified by American economic interests protected by law is filling the pockets of a
few people at the expense of the entire Lakota nation. While technically legal, in spirit and according to conscience, it is not unlike the
smallpox-infected blankets deceptively given out by British General
Jeffrey Amherst which decimated the Indian people a couple centuries earlier.[35] The same old story continues of exploitation of the
otherized group whose humanity is disregarded except in terms of
its capacity for consumption in order to provide wealth to the dominant culture. Why does this story get told over and over and not
recognized for what it is? History again. Who is telling the story and
for which purpose?

> (T)he easy acceptance of atrocities as a deplorable but neces-
> sary price to pay for progress (Hiroshima and Vietnam, to save
> Western civilization; Kronstadt and Hungary, to save socialism;
> nuclear proliferation to save us all)— is still with us. One reason
> these atrocities are still with us is that we have learned to bury
> them in a mass of other facts, as radioactive wastes are buried
> in containers in the earth. We have learned to give them exactly
> the same proportion of attention that teachers and writers often

---

[34] Cf. "The Battle For Whiteclay" — awarded "best political documentary" at
the 2009 New York International Independent Film Festival. DVD and study
guide are available at www.battleforwhiteclay.org.

[35] The same tactic was unsuccessfully attempted by the CIA without the president's knowledge, when an attempt was made to offer a deadly fungus-infested
diving suit as a gift to Fidel Castro. Cf. D. Campbell, "638 Ways to Kill Castro,"
The Guardian, August 3, 2006 (http://www.guardian.co.uk/world/2006/aug/03/
cuba.duncancampbell2).

give them in the most respectable of classrooms and textbooks. This learned sense of moral proportion, coming from the apparent objectivity of the scholar, is accepted more easily than when it comes from politicians at press conferences. *It is therefore more deadly.*[36]

In the American context, what is particularly disturbing is that the 'legal' basis for Western civilization's treatment of the indigenous peoples (estimated to have been as many as 100 million in the Americas prior to 1492), including the founding of the city of Columbus, Georgia, where the author lives, which was created by the forced removal of Creek and Cherokee in the Trail of Tears, rests on the spurious and blasphemous religious law of a medieval Pope known as the "Doctrine of Discovery."[37] In practice, this law presumed the inherent superiority of Western European Christian civilization which was entitled to have first rights on any lands their explorers 'discovered.' And this is exactly what happened, even when it meant contradicting Christianity and our own laws and democratic process in order to acquire possession. President Andrew Jackson, for example, used executive privilege and the authority of the presidency, as others before and since him have done, to overrule the will of Congress and throw the Cherokees off the land, even though they had converted to Christianity in large numbers, clearly had 'discovered' the land before the Europeans and even done due diligence to acquire it legally through use of the American system of law and upheld by the Supreme Court — all to no avail. Why? Historian Richard White explains:

---

[36] H. Zinn, 2003, 9 (my italics).

[37] The Doctrine of Discovery remains influential in American Indian law not only in the United States, but in Canada, New Zealand and Australia. (Cf. Robert J. Miller, Jacinta Ruru, Larissa Behrendt and Tracey Lindberg. *Discovering Indigenous Lands: The Doctrine of Discovery in the English Colonies.* Oxford: Oxford University Press, 2010.) Significantly, these four countries were the only ones who voted against the UN Declaration on the Rights of Indigenous Peoples.

The Cherokee are probably the most tragic instance of what could have succeeded in American Indian policy and didn't. All these things that Americans would proudly see as the hallmarks of civilization was done by Indian people. They did everything they were asked except one thing. What the Cherokees ultimately are, they may be Christian, they may be literate, they may have a government like ours, but ultimately they are Indian. And in the end, being Indian is what kills them.[38]

In other words, neither our own law, other nation's law or divine law would be allowed to stop European economic expansion, even if it meant cultural and biological genocide.

BEING **R**ESPONSIBLE FOR THE **P**AINFUL **T**RUTH. Some argue genocide is too strong a word. Nazi Germany's clear intentions in World War II galvanized a horrified public momentarily shaken from complacency by photographs of crematoriums and mass graves of German citizens evidencing clear genocidal intent, but only after the fact. Drawing on the work of Raphael Lemkin, who first coined the term 'genocide' in 1944, Ward Churchill, scholar of the impact of federal schools on the destruction of Indian culture, suggests that "*any* policy undertaken with the intent of bringing about the dissolution and ultimate disappearance of a targeted human group *as such*" is genocide.[39] But it need not be so stark and clear. In fact, the insidious nature of seemingly lesser forms are just as dangerous. Addressing the U.N. committee drafting international law to protect world citizens, Lemkin defined three forms of genocide: *biological, physical* and *cultural.*

Among the acts specified in the original draft are "the forced transfer of children … forced and systematic exile of individuals

[38] Trail of Tears National Historic Trail (Comprehensive Management and Use Plan, U.S. Dept of Interior, National Park Service).
[39] Cited by D. Gabbard, in D. Jacobs, op. cit., 219.

representing the culture of the group ... prohibition of the use of the national language, or religious works, or the prohibition of new publications ... systematic destruction of national or religious monuments or their diversion to alien uses ... destruction or dispersion of objects of historical, artistic, or religious value and of objects used in religious worship."[40]

Significantly, the chair of the U.N. committee was the delegate from the United States who orchestrated the elimination of the entire category of *cultural* genocide from the final document, presumably because it did not serve U.S. interests.

Does it matter that we fail to question the meaning of these actions in our city councils when they decide to declare Columbus Day a holiday or that we do not debate this history in our schools as more than an ancient artifact, but as a vital memory having meaning for all Americans now and a claim upon our future? As Pastor Martin Niemuller observed in Nazi Germany in his time, we are all affected by the slowly creeping injustices that go unchallenged among us wherever we are. If we do not challenge genocidal activity as a community, then we are inviting it to continue until one day the monster eats us all, as is the case for every addiction, which is always a symptom of some degree of denial and evasion of the truth that is part of the moral sickness of post traumatic spiritual disorder.

> In Germany, they first came for the Communists,
> and I didn't speak up because I wasn't a Communist;
> Then they came for the Jews,
> and I didn't speak up because I wasn't a Jew.
> Then they came for the Trade Unionists,
> and I didn't speak up because I wasn't a Trade Unionist.
> Then they came for the Catholics,
> and I didn't speak up because I was a Protestant ...

---

[40] Ibid., 220.

In a terrible twist on an old biblical maxim, "The first shall be last," perhaps the most 'forgotten' of all Americans are the original inhabitants of the United States. They are part of America's greatest blind spot because we, like Freud, are in denial about the real price they paid and continue to pay, for our profit. The truth is that Americans live on land we stole from the indigenous peoples, breaking the word of our own laws again and again, as in the 1868 Treaty of Laramie, practicing cultural genocide and sending out a plethora of sentimental, one-sided propaganda in our children's history books and from Hollywood over our television screens to continue falsifying the historical record. Such illusions served the myth of American rugged individualism to preserve and grow the so-called 'American Dream' — itself a fantasy invented in the 1930's after the Great Depression, probably as a kind of dangling carrot for people coping with the depression of the times. Pursuing the 'American Dream' is a sloganizing metaphor meant to encourage hard work in the hope of advancement, when in fact the large majority never will be able to succeed in this, and it only helps fuel the coffers of the very elite rich who become even wealthier and more powerful at the expense of the rest. This is particularly appalling when it is observed how the disparity between rich and poor continues to increase:

> Between 1983 and 1998, the net worth of the top 1 percent grew by 42.2 percent, while the net worth of the bottom 40 percent dropped by 76.3 percent. In other words, the bottom 40 percent of the United States population lost three-fourths of their family wealth over the past twenty years. As of 1998, the top 1 percent of Americans owned 95 percent of the country's assets, and the top 60 percent own 99.8 percent of the nation's wealth.[41]

---

[41] R. Inchausti, *Subversive Orthodoxy: Outlaws, Revolutionaries, and Other Christians in Disguise* (Michigan: Brazos Press, 2005), 85.

To the extent that these few actually enjoy such a 'dream' while most are striving to attain it without questioning what it continues to cost the world, we, like Sigmund Freud, are likely to remain defensive about sustained self-examination, e.g. of our commitment to promote justice and human rights in the world, even while proclaiming to the world how we are experts in it.

According to my friend, Psychologist Jamie Moran, a.k.a. Poorwolf, sub-chief of the Lakota Cante Tinze 'Strong Heart' society, in the Iroquois tongue, the 'warrior' is one who accepts responsibility for 'protecting the Sacred Origins.' From this perspective, he emphasizes how important it is to understand that Jesus was executed in accordance with religious and political law, not because He was a miracle worker, healer and sage, but because as King, He threatened the entrenched religious, political and economic power-possessing beings seeking to preserve the status quo. Ultimately, Jesus was fighting for truth in the heart and justice in the community regarding the Sacred Origins that gives life to all cultures and races. He did this at the price of His own life and predicted the same might be expected of those who followed him. This is always the sacrificial stance of every great prophet, priest and king who stakes their life to the meaning of their word spoken on behalf of all the people, not out of being beholden to any person or group, but in obedience to God. "Unless a seed is planted in the ground and dies, it dwells alone." If we cannot see that protecting the Sacred Origins is exactly what is at stake in how we write and disseminate history, then we are missing a critical hermeneutic that separates history as artifact and curio from history as the trail of blood, sweat and tears of such warriors who became martyrs (witnesses) in their efforts to secure freedom, not for the few, but for all human beings.

A CALL TO CHRISTIAN CONSCIENCE AND AWAY FROM FALSE RELIGION. If it is only back then in the first century that Christ was betrayed, what is there to do now? If I have never owned slaves, am I responsible for my ancestors' actions? Does a painting or an archeological 'artifact' belong to a museum because it has possessed it since it was first stolen or was illegally removed by desecrating an ancient burial ground a half century earlier or two or three? Am I free of responsibility to others for my inheritance of the power and privileges handed on to me as an English-American, middle class, heterosexual male? What if, as in the Divine Liturgy of the Orthodox Church, the Gospel is a kind of 'icon of eternity'? In other words, the betrayal of Christ is something that is happening *now*, just as when Jesus was reading the scroll of Isaiah, He realized it was being fulfilled *at that moment*. The powers and principalities that threaten to devour us cannot be defeated by slogans or eliminated by rituals alone. These may help us suffer the disease or tolerate it, but the cure of the infection lies much deeper. Perhaps Christ saw it in the difference between what motivated the widow to offer her 'penny' and the philanthropists whose large sums surely took the front page of the *Jerusalem Times* away from her not to make the same kind of sacrifice. Jesus saw the spiritual poverty and injustice involved in uncommitted, heart-numbing complacency: "Worldliness … is essentially the capacity to look past the unfair distribution of the world's wealth in order to affirm one's right to its spoils."[42]

But worldliness is not only America's problem. Nicholas Berdiaev diagnosed it as a spiritual disease affecting Russia a century earlier, weakening it to the point that a terrible anti-Christian revolution took place that was far worse than the feckless Christian theocracy it replaced.[43] Unfortunately, this spiritual virus is spreading fast around the globe. The same forces at work tempting Jesus 2,000 years ago are at our doorsteps today, inviting us to choose where we stand.

> On a global scale the shift of capital in to fewer and fewer hands has been even more pronounced. According to the 1999 United

---

[42] Ibid., 92.

[43] N. Berdiaev, in M. Plekon (ed.), *Tradition Alive: On the Church and the Christian Life in Our Time, Readings from the Eastern Church* (Maryland: Rowman & Littlefield Publishers, 2003).

Nations Development Report, eighty countries have per capita incomes lower than they were a decade ago, and the assets of the world's two hundred richest people total more than the combined assets of 41 percent of the world's population — that's more than the combined wealth of two billion people.[44]

What does it cost the world for so few people to enjoy such control? Not to recognize this and to continue with the illusion that the majority can 'have it all' perpetuates the false-history syndrome.

Religious affluence easily suffers this same fate as well. When the Romans sacked Jerusalem in 70 AD, they flooded the empire with so much gold recovered from the Temple that the gold market in Syria dropped by half its value. Ironically, it was the wealth taken from the Temple of Jerusalem which was later used to build the Coliseum where Christians were tortured and ripped to shreds by lions in front of spectators for their enjoyment. Such enjoyment is surely part of the collective psychic numbing and hyperarousal of the Roman populace, sick with post-traumatic spiritual disorder. More than likely, they also suffered from false memory syndrome perpetrated by historians weaving myths about *Pax Romana*, Roman superiority and the inferiority of the nations that the Romans colonized. "The stigmatization of poverty is closely connected with the psycho-social dynamics of stigmatization in general ... since those who are stigmatized are imputed to be impoverished, that is, fundamentally defective as persons."[45]

According to Jesus, the Kingdom of God is revealed not in great fanfare and notoriety of the powerful, but invisibly and in unheralded actions of sacrificial love like the poor widow. Viewing the world through the heart of the divine historian, this woman's penny revealed her infinite riches in the Kingdom of God. She who had

---

[44] Op. cit., 86.

[45] J. Jones, "Confronting Poverty and Stigmatization: An Eastern Orthodox Perspective. (http://www.incommunion.org/articles/resources/confronting-poverty-and-stigmatization, 2006), 2.

no worldly income and, therefore, little worldly value, in recognizing that everything belongs to God whose good pleasure is to give it
away, she revealed herself as a spiritual child of Abel, beloved to God.
Blessed are they whose love renders them empty of vainglory (*kenodoxia*) as our Lord was empty, for they shall be filled with the God
glory (*orthodoxia*) of the Lord's table. She had not acquired the fear
that so easily accrues to a heart so sated with unexamined privilege
and possession that it leads to excusing oneself from the Divine invitation to the wedding feast of Grace. Wherever the 'business' of making a profit is placed ahead of love for humankind and stewarding the
Creation as belonging to God who gives it to the *whole* community,
and not just for the welfare of a few, it serves as an excuse to betray
the call to "love kindness and to do justice and to walk humbly with
God" (Micah 6:8) by sharing communion with all others. Surely this
is a destructive course.[46]

REPENTANCE AND LOVE FOR ENEMIES INCLUDES ALL. Having raised up and acknowledged these things, I must also admit
that, like the first century individualists Annanias and Sapphira (Acts
5:1ff), I hold back a portion from the community for myself and my
family out of fear justified as common sense and reason. I struggle
with the fact that I do not trust the heart of humanity or God enough
to risk putting everything at God's disposal in order to follow Christ.
To the extent that I work the fields of my vocation in this life, not to
contribute to the family of humankind, but to overeat at the trough
of the bottom line of "profits for the few at the expense of the many,"
securing my own comfort, I will doubtless be hungry in the Kingdom
of God. Why? Because I have learned to nourish my soul on food
fit only for pigs, course nourishment indigestible by the soul which
lives "not by bread alone, but by every Word that proceeds from the

[46] If you are interested in exploring this further in your own life, I invite the
reader to look in Appendix I and answer the questions found in the *Pastoral
Counseling and Economic Justice Questionnaire: A Pastoral Theological Tool for
Examining Christian Vocation from the Standpoint of Economic Justice* issues.

mouth of God" giving life to all the world.

I, who have inherited the spoils my ancestors, received by systematically cheating and killing the original inhabitants and exploiting millions from other continents, will suffer the fire of conscience of being forgiven by those same forgotten victims who have been robbed, lied to, enslaved and murdered. God will show me Grace only through their mercy in order to heal my heart of stone and give me a heart of flesh. I, who have often lacked the will and desire to pay the price of entering into the Wedding Feast prepared by the Lord and the Widow and all others like her, shall be last. Nevertheless, I have hope that, by the mercy and economy of God, even the likes of me shall receive a portion of the distribution made to the starving masses of us who in living, failed to realize that God *is* Love and it is not possible to enter the joy of paradise by betraying any part of earth and anyone on earth. In the end, I will approach God and my ignored and despised 'lesser' brothers and sisters as a beggar, crying out, "Lord Jesus Christ have mercy on me a sinner!" believing and hoping not only in the Lord's mercy and goodness, but asking forgiveness from Abel and all his descendents as well.

What are the implications of this hope and prayer now while I am yet alive? Metropolitan Anthony of Sourozh I am told, used to say that the only possible stance for an Orthodox Christian in the Church is one of repentance. Approaches to pastoral care and counseling that fail to address the impact of the spiritual struggle with powers and principalities of culture and society, realizing the need for both internal and systemic spiritual diagnosis and spiritual warfare in the course of the call and response to suffering people, fails to be faithful to Christ. The sword of the Spirit has one edge of limitless love and mercy that cuts away all condemnation and another edge of truth so sharp it wounds whomever seeks to wield it apart from giving their all in return for the full life of God which Christ offers the world. As we Orthodox Christians chant near the end of every Divine Liturgy, "We have found the true faith," it is not cause for feeling superior in any way, but rather for entering still more deeply on the path where even Jesus Himself feared to go, into the world's Gethsemane, crying out to the Holy Spirit for strength to continue when our own human strength fails. It cannot be otherwise, for unless God builds the person, the temple, the community or the country, those who build it build in vain. Yet, dare we say it, God cannot build a love relationship with humanity alone for God is love, an eternal διά-Λογος.

Pastoral Counseling and Economic Justice Questionnaire: A Pastoral Theological Tool for Examining Christian Vocation from the Standpoint of Economic Justice Issues

1) How do you know what is your calling in life? (Your duty toward something greater than yourself.)

2) How does what you do in your work and *how* you do it contribute to the well-being of all people and the world as a whole in contrast to benefiting only a few at the expense of rendering others invisible?

3) What criteria do you use to assess the value and effectiveness of your work?

4) How does your socio-economic position affect your goals and methods in the way you exercise power and influence in your profession?

5) How are you accountable in your work for how you use the power you have?

6) In your life and work, how do you experience the tension between God's ownership and gift of the world intended for the welfare of all and human ownership which tends toward privilege and power for a few at the expense of the many?

7) As a Christian, in terms of providing for the welfare of all people, what are the three greatest challenges to you and your work presented by American culture at this time?

8) What has your relationship to money been like over your life-time? Has it changed at all over time? How does this influence how you see and value people with more or less assets than you?

9) How did compensation impact your decision to enter your field, and do you hold any different views about its importance now?

10) What has been the biggest conflict between your Christian faith and the values inherent to your life in the workplace?

11) When citizens living 100 years from now look back on our time period, what issue(s) facing us today will be judged and found lacking in the manner we have addressed them or failed to address them? How are you responding to this in your life now?

12) How can a global free-market capitalism, which is inherently a movement of self-interest devoted to profit for select stakehold-ers, be compatible with a servant leadership approach which is inherently about empowering the growth and well-being of *all* persons, particularly those without power, voice and a place at the table due to inequities in capital?

13) In what ways have you consciously tried to align your work to include serving those you see as the most in need?

14) How do you feel after conversation around all these questions?

15) How do you think you will be different in the way you work with people in therapy or as a priest if you fail to examine closely these kinds of questions in your life?

Four Realms of Human Need[1]

BASIC PHYSICAL NEEDS:
(food, water, shelter, clothing, air, impressions)

EMOTIONAL NEEDS:
Touch
Empathy
Confirmation of our humanity and inner world
Guidance & support
Understanding
Affection
Friendship and belonging
Contributing to community
Freedom to identify and express full range of feelings
Trust
Enjoyment
Play
Safety

INTELLECTUAL NEEDS:
Intellectual challenge: creative exploration and discovery
Meaning and purpose in life
Being understood

---

[1] Adapted from Maslow, 1962; Miller, 1981; Weil, 1973; Glasser, 1985; Whitfield, 1989; Farrington, 2000

Work
Awareness of Self & Others
Fresh impressions without distortion by passions
Education

SPIRITUAL NEEDS:
Worship
Repentance
Mindfulness
Prayer
Almsgiving
Loving kindness
Freedom of choice
Hope
Faith
Belovedness
Grace
Confession & Forgiveness
Spiritual Communion with God and others
Hospitality
Silence

Bibliography

Agassi, J. B. (ed.). *Martin Buber on Psychology and Psychotherapy.* Syracuse, NY: Syracuse University Press, 1999.

Begley, S. *Train Your Mind Change Your Brain.* New York: Ballantine Books, 2007.

Bellah, R. et al. *Habits of the Heart.* Berkeley, CA: University of California Press, 1985.

Benjamin, L. S. *Interpersonal Diagnosis and Treatment of Personality Disorders, 2nd edition.* New York: Guilford Press, 1996.

Bloom, A. *Beginning To Pray.* New York: Paulist Press, 1970.

Bonhoeffer, D. *Life Together.* London: SCM Press, 1954.

Borders, L. D. and Leddick, G. R. *Handbook of Counseling Supervision.* Alexandria, VA: Association for Counselor Education and Supervision, 1987.

Bowen, M. *Family Theory in Clinical Practice.* New York: Jason Aronson, 1978.

Bremmer, J. *Does Stress Damage the Brain?* New York: W. W. Norton & Co., 2002.

Browning, D. *The Moral Context of Pastoral Care.* Philadelphia: Westminster Press, 1976.

Buber, M. *I and Thou.* New York: Charles Scribners & Sons, 1970.

_____, trans. M. Friedman, et al. *The Eclipse of God; Studies in the Relation Between Religion and Philosophy.* New York: Harper Torchbooks, 1952.

_____. *Between Man and Man.* New York: Routledge and Kegan Paul, 1993.

_____. *The Way of Man According to the Teaching of Hasidism*. New York: Kensington Publishing Corp., 1994.

_____. (2002) *Meetings: Autobiographical Fragments.*, 3rd edition. London & New York: Routledge, 2002.

Cannon, K. "Racism and Economics: The Perspective of Oliver C. Cox" in *The Public Vocation of Christian Ethics*. New York: Pilgrim Press, 1986.

Capsanis, G. *The Eros of Repentance*. Newbury, MA: Praxis Institute Press, 1993.

Cardenal, E. *Abide in Love*. New York: Maryknoll, 1995.

Cashdon, S. *Object Relations Therapy*. New York: Norton & Co., 1988.

Chirban, J. *Clergy Sexual Misconduct*. Brookline, MA: Holy Cross Orthodox Press, 1994.

_____ (ed.). *Personhood: Orthodox Christianity and the Connection between Body, Mind and Soul*. London: Bergin & Garvey, 1995.

_____ (ed.). *Sickness or Sin: Spiritual Discernment and Differential Diagnosis*. Brookline, MA: Holy Cross Orthodox Press, 2001.

Chomsky, N. *Media Control, Second Edition: The Spectacular Achievements of Propaganda*. New York: Open Media Series, 2002.

_____. *Necessary Illusions: Thought Control in Democratic Societies*. Boston: South End Press, 1989.

Chrysostomos, Archbishop of Etna. *Orthodoxy and Psychology*. Etna, CA: Center for Traditionalist Orthodox Studies, 2004.

_____. *A Guide to Orthodox Psychotherapy: The Science, Theology, and Spiritual Practice Behind It and Its Clinical Application*. Lanham, MD: University Press of America, 2006.

_____. *Themes in Orthodox Patristic Psychology: Humility, Obedience, Repentance, and Love*. Etna, CA: Center for Traditionalist Orthodox Studies, 2010.

Clawson, J. *Everyday Justice: The Global Impact of Our Daily Choices*. Downers Grove: IVP Books, 2009.

Clement, O. *On Human Being: A Spiritual Anthropology*. London: New City Press, 2000.

Colliander, Tito. *Way of the Ascetics: The Ancient Tradition of Disci-

pline and Inner Growth. New York: St. Vladimir's Press, 1985.

Cooper-White, P. *Shared Wisdom: Use of the Self in Pastoral Care and Counseling*. Minneapolis: Fortress Press, 2003.

Crichton, M. *Travels*. New York: Alfred Knopf, 1988.

Cushing, R. C. *Opening to Empathy: The Experience of Opening to Understanding What Has Been Preventing or Blocking a Supervisee from Opening to Empathy with a Client*. Ph.D. dissertation. California Institute of Integral Studies, 1989. UMI order number 8926006.

Damasio, A. *The Feeling of What Happens: Body and Brain in the Making of Emotion*. New York: Mariner Books, 2000.

de Unamuno, M. *Tragic Sense of Life*. J. E. Crawford Flitch, Trans. New York: Cosimo Inc., 2005.

Doehring, C. *The Practice of Pastoral Care: A Postmodern Approach*. Louisville, Kentucky: Westminster John Knox, 2006.

Dossey, L. *Healing Words*. New York: Harper Collins, 1997.

_____. *Reinventing Medicine: Beyond Mind-Body to a New Era of Healing*. New York: HarperCollins, 2000.

Douglass, J. *JFK and the Unspeakable: Why He Died and Why It Matters*. New York: Touchstone Books, 2008.

Dowd, E. T. & Nielsen, S. L. (eds.). *The Psychologies in Religion: Working with the Religious Client*. New York: Springer Publishing Company, 2006.

Dunlop. J. *Staretz Amvrosy*. Europe: Buchervertriebsanstalt; Belmont, MA: Distributed by Notable & Academic Books, 1988.

Durckheim, K. *Hara: The Vital Centre of Man*. England: Unwin Paperbacks, 1988.

Dyche, L. & Zayas, L. H. "The value of curiosity and naivete for the cross-cultural psychotherapist," *Family Process* 34 (1995) 389–399.

Estadt, B., Compton, J., Blanchette M. *Pastoral Counseling*. New Jersey:Prentice Hall, 1983.

_____. *The Art of Clinical Supervision: A Pastoral Counseling Perspective*. New York: Integration Books, 1987.

Eusebius, *The History of the Church*. London: Penguin Books, 1989.

Figley, C (ed.). *Compassion Fatigue: Coping with Secondary Traumatic Stress Disorder in Those Who Treat the Traumatized*. New York: Routledge, Taylor & Francis, 1995.

————. *Treating Compassion Fatigue*. New York: Routledge, Taylor & Francis, 2002.

Fowler, J. W. *Stages of faith*. San Francisco: Harper & Row, Publishers, 1981.

Frankl, V. *Man's Search for Meaning*. New York: Pocket Books, 1963.

Friedman, M. *Martin Buber: The Life of Dialogue, 4ᵗʰ Edition*. New York: Routledge, Kegan Paul, 2002.

Gaist, B. *Creative Suffering and the Wounded Healer: Analytical Psychology and Orthodox Christian Theology*. Rollinsford, NH: Orthodox Research Institute, 2010.

Gherkin, C. *The Living Human Document: Revisioning Pastoral Counseling in a Hermeneutical Mode*. Nashville, TN: Abingdon Press, 1984.

Gibbs, D. "The Question of Whitewashing in American History and Social Science" in Jacobs, D. *Unlearning the Language of Conquest*. Austin: University of Texas Press, 2005.

Grant, B. (2001) *A Theology for Pastoral Psychotherapy*. Binghamton, NY: The Haworth Pastoral Press, 2001.

Guest, P. D. & Beutler, L. E. (1988). "Impact of psychotherapy supervision on therapist orientation and values," *Journal of Consulting and Clinical Psychology* 56 (1988): 653–658.

Haddad, D. & Fialcov, C. *Creating a Context for Talking about Supervision*. Cantor Institute, 1997. [Video.]

Hardy, V. K. & Laszloffy, T. A. "The cultural genogram: Key to training culturally competent family therapists," *Journal of Marital and Family Therapy* 21(3) (1995): 227–237.

Heppner, P. P. and Roehlke, H. J. "Differences among supervisees at different levels of training: Implications for a developmental model of supervision," *Journal of Counseling Psychology* 31 (1984) 76–90.

Herman, E. & Chomsky, N. *Manufacturing Consent: The Political Economy of the Mass Media*. New York: Pantheon, 2002.

Herman, J. *Trauma and Recovery.* New York: BasicBooks, 1992.

Herrigel, E. *Zen and the Art of Archery.* New York: Vintage, 1999.

Hess, A. K. "Training models and the nature of psychotherapy supervision," A. K. Hess (ed.). *Psychotherapy Supervision: Theory, Research and Practice.* (pp. 15–28). New York: John Wiley & Sons, 1980.

Hoge, D. & Wenger, J. *Pastors in Transition: Why Clergy Leave Local Church Ministry.* Michigan/UK: Eerdmans Publishing Co., 2005.

Hopko, T. *Christian Faith and Same Sex Attraction: Eastern Orthodox Reflections.* Ben Lomond, CA: Conciliar Press, 2006.

Inchausti, R. *Subversive Orthodoxy: Outlaws, Revolutionaries, and Other Christians in Disguise.* Michigan: Brazos Press, 2005.

Ioannidis, K. *Elder Porphyrios: Testimonies and Experiences.* Athens: Holy Convent of the Transfiguration of the Savior, 1997.

Jacobs, D. (ed.). *Unlearning the Language of Conquest.* Austin: University of Texas Press, 2005.

Jenkins, M. *The Ancient Laugh of God.* Kentucky: Westminster/John Knox Press, 1994.

John of Kronstadt, St. *My Life in Christ.* Russia: Holy Trinity Monastery, 1911.

Joseph of Vatopaidi. *Elder Joseph the Hesychast: Struggles, Experiences, Teachings (1898–1959).* Greece: Vatopaidi Monastery, 1999.

Jung, C. G. *Modern Man in Search of a Soul.* New York: Harcourt, 1934.

Kadloubovsky, E. & Palmer, G. E. H. (eds.). *Writings from the Philokalia on Prayer of the Heart.* London: Faber & Faber, 1966.

Kaldor P. & Bullpitt R. *Burnout in Church Leaders.* Australia: Openbook Publishers, 2001.

Kaplan, H.; Freedman, A.; & Sadock, B. (eds.) *Comprehensive Textbook on Psychiatry.* Baltimore: Williams & Wilkins, 1980.

Koenig, H. *The Healing Power of Faith: How Belief and Prayer Can Help You Triumph Over Disease.* New York: Simon & Schuster, 2001.

_____. *Medicine, Religion, and Health: Where Science and Spirituality Meet Templeton Science and Religion Series).* Philadelphia: Templeton Press, 2008.

Kontzevitch, I. M. *The Acquisition of the Holy Spirit in Ancient Russia.*

Platina, CA: St. Herman of Alaska Brotherhood, 1988.

Kornarakis, I. *Pastoral Psychology and Inner Conflict.* Brookline, MA: Holy Cross Orthdoox Press, 1990.

Kramer, P. *Martin Buber's I and Thou: Practicing Living Dialogue.* New York: Paulist Press, 2003.

Kramer, T. & Reitz, M. "Using video playback to train family therapists," *Family Process* 19(2) (1980): 145–150.

Kraybill, D. *The Upside-Down Kingdom.* Pennsylvania: Herald Press, 1978.

Kuhn, T. *The Structure of Scientific Revolutions* Chicago: University of Chicago Press, 1962.

Larchet, Jean-Claude. *The Theology of Illness.* Creswood, NY: St. Vladimir's Seminary Press, 2002.

_____. *Mental Disorders & Spiritual Healing: Teachings from the Early Christian East.* Indiana: Sophia Perennis, 2005.

Lartey, E. (2003) *In Living Color: An Intercultural Approach to Pastoral Care and Counseling.* London: Jessica Kingsley Publishers, 2003.

_____. *Pastoral Theology in an Intercultural World.* New York: Guilford Press, 2006.

Lawrence, B.; Blaiklock, E. M. (trans.). *The Practice of the Presence of God.* Nashville: Thomas Nelson Publishers, 1981.

LeDoux, J. *The Emotional Brain: The Mysterious Underpinnings of Emotional Life.* New York: Touchstone, 1996.

Liddle, H. A.; Breunlin, D. C.; and Schwartz, R. C. (eds.). *Handbook of Family Therapy Training and Supervision.* New York: Guilford Press, 1988.

MacDonald, J. *Thieves in the Temple: The Christian Church and the Selling of the American Soul.* New York: Basic Books, 2010.

Markides, K. *The Mountain of Silence: A Search for Orthodox Spirituality.* New York: Doubleday, 2001.

Marushchak, V. *The Blessed Surgeon: The Life of Saint Luke of Simferopol.* Point Reyes Station, CA: Divine Ascent Press, 2002.

May, G. *Will and Spirit: A Contemplative Psychology.* New York: HarperOne, 1987.

_____. *Addiction and Grace: Love and Spirituality in the Healing of Addictions.* New York: HarperOne, 2007.

McGoldrick, M. & Gerson, R. *Genograms in Family Assessment.* New York: W. W. Norton & Company, 1985.

Mead, D. E. (ed.). *Readings in Marriage and Family Therapy Supervision.* Provo, UT: Department of Independent Study, Division of Continuing Education, Brigham Young University, 1990.

Middleton, H. *Precious Vessels of the Holy Spirit.* Thessaloniki, Greece: Protecting Veil Press, 2003.

Millar, L. *Grand Duchess Elizabeth of Russia: New Martyr of the Communist Yoke.* California: Nikodemos Orthodox Publication Society, 1988.

Minuchin, S. *Families & Family Therapy.* Cambridge, MA: Harvard University Press, 1974.

Moore, A. *An Extraordinary Peace: St. Seraphim Flame of Sarov.* Washington: Anaphora Press, 2009.

Muse, S. (ed.). *Beside Still Waters: Resources for Shepherds in the Marketplace.* Macon, GA: Smyth & Helwys, 2000.

_____ (ed.). *Raising Lazarus: Integral healing in Orthodox Christianity.* Brookline, MA: Holy Cross Orthodox Press, 2004.

Needleman, J. *Lost Christianity.* New York: Doubleday, 1988.

Nesteruk A. V. *Light for the East: Theology, Science, and the Eastern Orthodox Tradition.* Minneapolis: Fortress Press, 2003.

Neuger, C. *Counseling Women.* Minneapolis: Fortress Press, 2001.

Ornish, D. *Dr. Dean Ornish's Program for Reversing Heart Disease.* New York: Random House, 1990.

Paisios, Elder. *Epistles.* Thessaloniki, Greece: Holy Monastery of Evangelist John the Theologian, Souriti.

Paisios. *Spiritual Awakening. Vol. II of Elder Paisios of Mount Athos Spiritual Counsels.* Thessaloniki, Greece: Holy Monastery of Evangelist John the Theologian, Souriti, 2008.

Palmer, G. E. H.; Sherrard, P.; & Ware, K. (eds.). *The Philokalia: The Complete Text.* 4 vols. London: Faber & Faber, 1995.

Palmer, P. *Let Your Life Speak: Listening to the Voice of Vocation.* California: Jossey-Bass, 2000.

Pargament, K. I., in *Spiritually Integrated Psychotherapy: Understanding and Addressing the Sacred.* New York: Guilford Press, 2007.

Papero, D. V. "Training in Bowen theory," in H. A. Liddle; D. C. Breunlin; and R. C. Schwartz (eds.). *Handbook of family therapy training and supervision.* (pp. 62–77) New York: Guilford Press, 1988.

Peck, M. S. *The Road Less Traveled: A New Psychology of Love, Traditional Values and Spiritual Growth.* New York: Simon & Schuster, 1978.

Pert, C. *The Molecules of Emotion.* New York: Simon & Schuster, 1997.

Plekon, M. *Tradition Alive: On the Church and the Christian Life in Our Time, Readings from the Eastern Church.* Maryland: Rowman & Littlefield Publishers, 2003.

Poling, J. *Deliver Us From Evil: Resisting Racial and Gender Oppression.* Minneapolis: Fortress Press, 1996.

_____. *Render Unto God: Economic Vulnerability, Family Violence and Pastoral Theology.* St. Louis, MO: Chalice Press, 2002.

Rizzuto, A. *The Birth of the Living God.* Chicago: University of Chicago Press, 1981.

Rothschild, B. *Help for the Helper: The Psychophysiology of Compassion Fatigue and Vicarious Trauma.* New York: W. W. Norton & Co., 2006.

Rubenstein, R. L. *The Cunning of History: The Holocaust and the American Future.* New York: Harper & Row, 1975.

Ruden, R. *The Craving Brain.* New York: HarperCollins, 1997.

Russell, D. *The Secret Trauma.* New York: Basic Books, 1986.

Scharff, J. S. *Projective and Introjective Identification and the Use of the Therapist's Self.* New Jersey: Jason Aronson, Inc., 1992.

Schnarch, D. *Constructing the Sexual Crucible: An Integration of Sexual and Marital Therapy.* London: W. W. Norton & Co., 1991.

_____. *Passionate Marriage.* London: W. W. Norton & Co., 1997.

Schwartz, R. C., et al. (eds.). *Handbook of Family Therapy Training and Supervision.* New York: Guilford Press, 1988.

Siegel, Daniel. *The Mindful Brain: Reflections and Attunement in the Cultivation of Well-Being.* New York: W. W. Norton & Co., 2007.

Skobtsova, M. *Essential Writings*. New York: Orbis Books, 2003.

Shapiro, F. (1995) *Eye Movement Desensitization and Reprocessing*. New York: Guilford, 1995, Vol. 14, 142–160.

Sophrony, A. *His Life is Mine*. Crestwood, NY: St. Valdimir's Seminary Press, 1977.

_____. (1988) *We Shall See Him As He Is*. Essex, England: Stavropegic Monastery of St. John the Baptist, 1988.

_____. (1991) *St. Silouan the Athonite*. Essex, England: Stavropegic Monatery of St. John the Baptist, 1991.

Sopko, A. *For a Culture of Co-Suffering Love: The Theology of Archbishop Lazar Puhalo*. Californnia: Archive Publications, 2004.

Stoltenberg, C. D. and Delworth, U. *Supervising Counselors and Therapists: A Developmental Approach*. San Francisco: Jossey-Bass Publishers, 1987.

Theophan the Recluse. *Turning the Heart Toward God*. California: Conciliar Press, 2001.

Thermos, V. *In Search of the Person: True and False Self According to Donald Winnicott and St. Gregory Palamas*. Montreal: Alexander Press, 2002.

_____. *Thirst For Love and Truth: Encounters of Orthodox Theology and Psychological Science*. Montreal: Alexander Press, 2010.

Van der Kolk, B.; McFarlane, C.; & Weisaeth, L. *Traumatic Stress*. New York: Guilford Press, 1996.

Van Deusen, D. *Theology and Pastoral Counseling: A New Interdisciplinary Approach*. New York: Eerdmans Publishing Company, 1995.

Vlachos, H. *The Illness and Cure of the Soul in Orthodox Tradition*. Levadia, Greece: Birth of the Theotokos Monastery, 1993.

_____. *Orthodox Psychotherapy*. Levadia, Greece: Birth of the Theotokos Monastery, 1994.

Wallin, D. *Attachment in Psychotherapy*. New York: Guilford Press, 2007.

Walsh, F. (ed.). *Normal Family Processes*. 3rd edition. New York: Guilford Press, 2002.

Wampold, B. *The Great Psychotherapy Debate: Models, Methods and*

Findings. London: Lawrence Erlbaum Associates, Publishers, 2001.

Watzlawick, P. *How real is real?: Confusion, disinformation, communication*. New York: Vintage Books, 1977.

Weber, M. *Steps of Transformation: An Orthodox Priest Explores the Twelve Steps*. Ben Lomond, CA: Conciliar Press: California, 2003.

Welwood, J. *Awakening the Heart: East/West approaches to psychotherapy and the healing relationship*. Boston: New Science Library, 1985.

West, C. *Democracy Matters*. New York: Penguin Press, 2004.

Wicks, R. *Overcoming Secondary Stress in Medical and Nursing Practice: A Guide to Professional Resilience and Personal Well-being*. New York: Oxford University Press, 2006.

_____. *The Resilient Clinician*. New York: Oxford University Press, 2008.

_____. *Bounce: Living the Resilient Life*. New York: Oxford University Press, 2010.

Wittgenstein, L. *Tractatus Logico-Philosophicus*. United States: Seven Treasures Publications, 2010.

Worthington, E. L. Jr., and Roehlke, H. J. "Effective supervision as perceived by beginning counselors-in-training," *Journal of Counseling Psychology* 26 (1979): 64–73.

Yalom, I. *The Theory and Practice of Group Psychotherapy*. New York: Basic Books, 1985.

_____. *Love's executioner*. New York: HarperCollins Publishers, 1989.

Yannaras, C. (1984) *The Freedom of Morality*. (E. Briere, trans.) Crestwood, NY: St. Vladimir's Seminary Press, 1984.

_____. *Person and Eros (To prosopo kai o eros)*. Athens 1987, translation by Holy Cross Orthodox Press, 2007.

Yiannitsiotis, C. *With Elder Porphyrios: A Spiritual Child Remembers*. (Marina Robb, trans.) Athens: Holy Convent of the Transfiguration of the Savior, 2001.

Zinn, H. *A People's History of the U.S.* New York: HarperCollins Publishers, 2003.

About the Author

Stephen Muse, Ph.D., LMFT, LPC, B.C.E.T.S is Director responsible for the Pastoral Counselor Training program and Clinical Services for the D. A. & Elizabeth Turner Ministry Resource Center of the Pastoral Institute, Inc. in Columbus, Georgia.

He is author of chapters in seven books and numerous articles, book reviews and poetry for professional journals and trade magazines, including national award-winning research in the area of religious integration and clinical empathy of therapists. He served as Managing Editor of the *Pastoral Forum* from 1993 to 2002. Previous books include *Beside Still Waters: Restoring the Souls of Shepherds in the Market Place* (2000) and *Raising Lazarus: Integral Healing in Orthodox Christianity* (2004).

Dr. Muse has served as PT instructor with Columbus State University graduate counseling education program and as adjunct faculty with Garrett Evangelical Theological Seminary, McAfee School of Theology D.Min program and Union Graduate Institute. He serves as a training supervisor for the U.S. Army family life military chaplains and in field education for the Counseling Psychology doctoral program of Auburn University. He has taught and led professional workshops internationally and throughout the U.S. in the civilian sector as well as for the U.S. Army Chaplains in the areas of his specialties, which include post-traumatic stress, clergy wellness, marriage and family issues, Christian formation, and stress and burnout.

Dr. Muse holds a bachelors degree in philosophy from Davidson College, an M.Div. from Princeton Theological Seminary emphasizing Greek New Testament exegesis and early church spirituality, M.S. and Ph.D. degrees from Loyola University of Maryland in Pastoral Counseling and post graduate work in marriage and family studies through the University of Georgia. He holds Diplomate certification in the American Association of Pastoral Counselors; in Professional Psychotherapy with the International Academy of Behavioral Medicine, Counseling and Psychotherapy, is a Diplomate Board Certified Expert in Traumatic stress, an AAMFT Approved supervisor, and national board certified in clinical hypnotherapy. He is licensed in the state of Georgia as a Professional Counselor and a Marriage and Family Therapist.

Prior to his reception into the Greek Orthodox Church, where he is ordained as a Subdeacon and set apart for ministry as a pastoral counselor, Dr. Muse pastored a Presbyterian congregation for 11 years and helped begin an out-patient psychiatric clinic in Delta, PA. He is past president of the Orthodox Christian Association of Medicine, Psychology and Religion and a founder and first parish council President of Holy Transfiguration Greek Orthodox Mission Church in Columbus. He and his wife Claudia have four children: a daughter killed in 1982, a daughter 32, a son 29, a daughter 26 and a granddaughter, 3. He can be contacted at smuse@pilink.org and through the website of the Pastoral Institute, Inc., in Columbus, Georgia, at www.pilink.org, which contains a page listing workshops and presentations offered by the author.

CPSIA information can be obtained at www.ICGtesting.com
Printed in the USA
LVOW041821130412

277551LV00009B/16/P